*Yanmar*

# YANMAR MARINE DIESEL ENGINE

*2TM, 3TM, 4TM*

*Yanmar*

**YANMAR MARINE DIESEL ENGINE**

2TM, 3TM, 4TM

ISBN/EAN: 9783954272778
Erscheinungsjahr: 2013
Erscheinungsort: Bremen, Deutschland

© maritimepress in Europäischer Hochschulverlag GmbH & Co. KG, Fahrenheitstr. 1, 28359 Bremen. Alle Rechte beim Verlag und bei den jeweiligen Lizenzgebern.
www.maritimepress.de | office@maritimepress.de

Bei diesem Titel handelt es sich um den Nachdruck eines historischen, lange vergriffenen Buches. Da elektronische Druckvorlagen für diese Titel nicht existieren, musste auf alte Vorlagen zurückgegriffen werden. Hieraus zwangsläufig resultierende Qualitätsverluste bitten wir zu entschuldigen.

# YANMAR
# SERVICE MANUAL

**MARINE DIESEL ENGINE**

MODEL
**2TM**
**3TM**
**4TM**

# FOREWORD

YANMAR's TM series engine is a vertical in-line type marine propulsion diesel engine with 2, 3 or 4 cylinders and overhead valves. It has been developed with a completely new design in the 1980's and is suited for heavy duty use in all kinds of boats. It is similar to the YANMAR T-series engines which have been popular for commercial boats of every type for the last twenty years.

In compliance with keen demand from our customers many features of the existing engines have been retained. These include the independent provision of cylinder heads and fuel injection pumps to each cylinder, the reciprocating type cooling water pump and the mechanical big disc plate type marine gear. These offer easy maintenance and high durability.

But besides these the new series also employs the most advanced technologies such as YANMAR's uniquely developed direct fuel injection system, high-grade heat treatment of the major parts and qualitative improvement of the materials used. These will be of primary importance in minimizing operational costs, (fuel and maintenance), for the boat owner.

# Models 2TM·3TM·4TM

## CHAPTER 1 GENERAL
1. External View .................................................. 1-1
2. Specifications ................................................. 1-4
3. Performance Curve ......................................... 1-5
4. Engine Cross-section ...................................... 1-9
5. Piping Diagram ............................................... 1-11
6. Disassembly and Reassembly Tools .............. 1-14

## CHAPTER 2 BASIC ENGINE
1. Cylinder Block ................................................ 2-1
2. Cylinder Liner ................................................. 2-4
3. Cylinder Head ................................................. 2-7
4. Piston ............................................................. 2-18
5. Connecting Rod ............................................. 2-23
6. Crankshaft ..................................................... 2-26
7. Camshaft ....................................................... 2-31
8. Timing Gears ................................................. 2-35
9. Flywheel and Housing ................................... 2-37

## CHAPTER 3 FUEL SYSTEM
1. Fuel Supply System ....................................... 3-1
2. Injection Pump ............................................... 3-3
3. Governor and Linkage ................................... 3-9
4. Fuel Injection Nozzle ..................................... 3-13
5. Fuel Feed Pump ............................................ 3-17
6. Fuel Filter ....................................................... 3-18
7. Water Separator ............................................ 3-21
8. Fuel Tank (Option) ......................................... 3-22

## CHAPTER 4 INTAKE AND EXHAUST SYSTEM
1. Intake and Exhaust System ........................... 4-1

## CHAPTER 5 LUBRICATION SYSTEM
1. Lubrication System ........................................ 5-1
2. Oil Pump ........................................................ 5-5
3. Oil Filter ......................................................... 5-8
4. Oil Cooler ....................................................... 5-9

## CHAPTER 6 COOLING SYSTYEM
1. Cooking System ............................................ 6-1
2. Water Pump .................................................. 6-4
3. Kingston Cock ............................................... 6-7
4. Sea Water Filter (Option) .............................. 6-8

## CHAPTER 7 CHAIN OVERDRIVE HAND-OPERATED SYSTEM
1. Chain Overdrive Hand-operated System ...... 7-1

## CHAPTER 8 REDUCTION AND REVERSING GEAR
[A] FOR MODEL 2TM AND 3TM
1. Construction .................................................. 8-1
2. Disassembly .................................................. 8-6
3. Inspection and servicing ............................... 8-10
4. Reassembly .................................................. 8-12
5. Adjustment ................................................... 8-13

[B] FOR MODEL 4TM
1. Construction .................................................. 8-15
2. Disassembly .................................................. 8-20
3. Inspection and servicing ............................... 8-23
4. Reassembly .................................................. 8-24
5. Adjustment ................................................... 8-25

## CHAPTER 9 ELECTRICAL SYSTEM
1. Composition .................................................. 9-1
2. Battery .......................................................... 9-2
3. Starter Motor ................................................. 9-5
4. Alternator, Option ......................................... 9-16

## CHAPTER 10 STERN EQUIPMENT
1. Stern Arrangement (Yanmar Standard) ....... 10-1
2. Stern Bearings ............................................. 10-2

## CHAPTER 11 TROUBLESHOOTING
1. Troubleshooting ............................................ 11-1

## CHAPTER 12 INSPECTION AND SERVICING
1. Periodic Inspections and Servicing .............. 12-1
2. Specifications .............................................. 12-2
3. Tightening Torque ........................................ 12-3

# CHAPTER 1
# GENERAL

1. External View .................................................................................................1-1
2. Specifications ................................................................................................1-4
3. Performance Curve ......................................................................................1-5
4. Engine Cross-section ...................................................................................1-9
5. Piping Diagram ...........................................................................................1-11
6. Disassembly and Reassembly Tools .........................................................1-14

*Chapter 1 General*
*1. External View*                                                                                              *TM*

# 1. External View

**1-1  4TM**

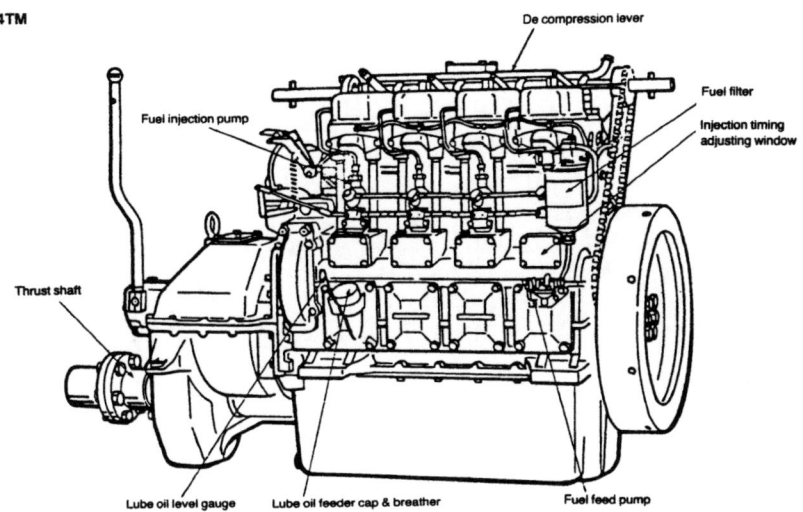

Operation side of 4TM  (Chain starting)

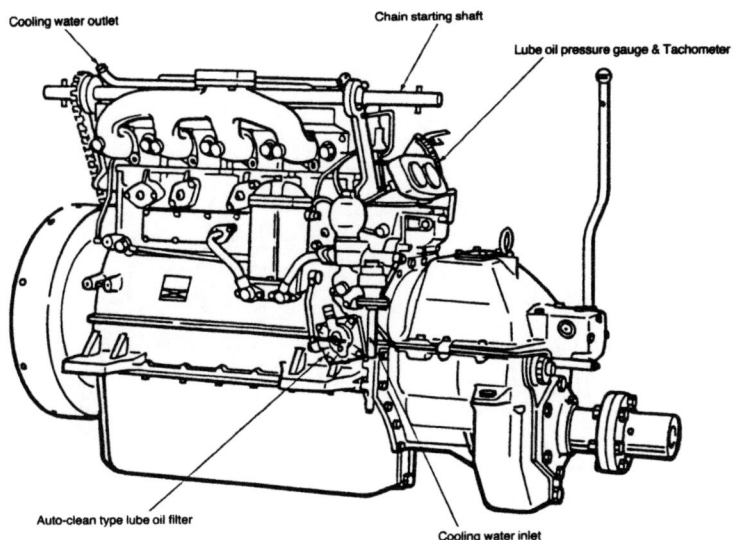

Exhaust side of 4TM  (Chain starting)

*Chapter 1 General*
*1. External View*
TM

**1-2 3TM**

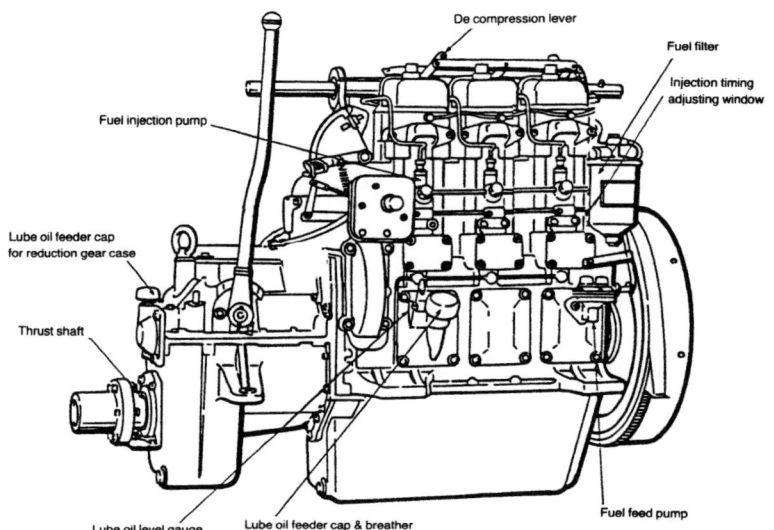

Operation side of 3TM (Electric and Chain Starting)

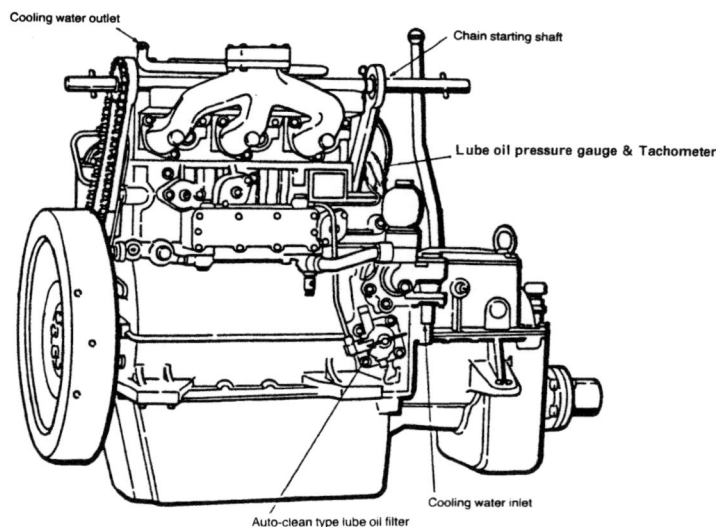

Exhaust side of 3TM (Electric and Chain starting)

*Chapter 1 General*
*1. External View* _____ *TM*

**1-3  2TM**

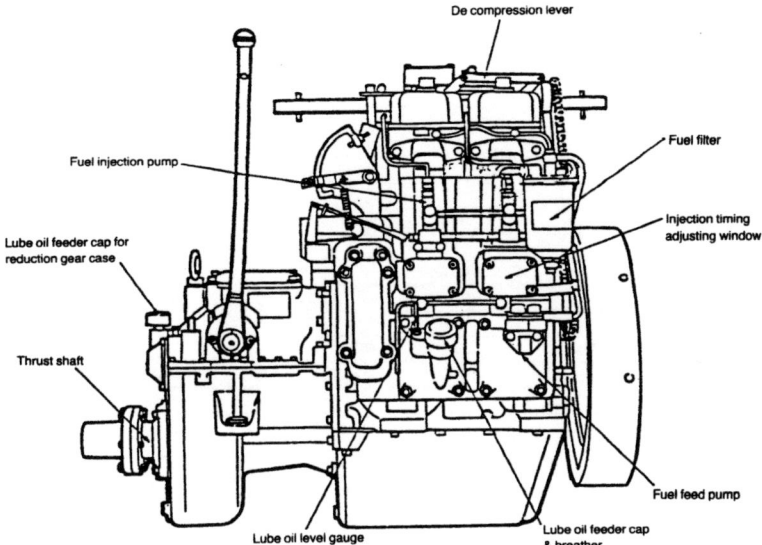

**Operation side of 2TM  (Chain Starting)**

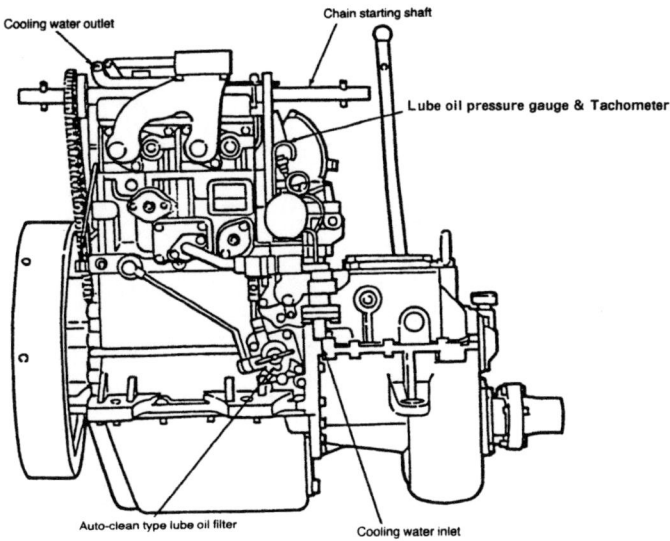

**Exhaust side of 2TM  (Chain Starting)**

## Chapter 1 General
## 2. Specifications

# 2. Specifications

### 2-1 Engine

| Model name | | | 2TM (G,GG) | 3TM (G,GG) | 4TM (G,GG,GGG) |
|---|---|---|---|---|---|
| Type | | | 4-cycle, vertical, natural aspirated diesel engine | | |
| Combustion system | | | Direct injection | | |
| No. of cylinders | | | 2 | 3 | 4 |
| Piston bore × stroke | | mm | φ100 × 115 | | |
| Displacement | | ℓ | 1.806 | 2.710 | 3.613 |
| Continuous rating output | | HP/rpm | 26/2100 | 39/2100 | 52/2100 |
| Max. output | | HP/rpm | 29/2200 | 43/2200 | 57/2200 |
| Idling speed | High | rpm | 2400 ~ 2450 | | |
| | Low | rpm | 450 | | |
| Starting system | | | Manual chain (Electric, Electric with manual available as optional) | | |
| Firing order | | | 1-2-1 | 1-2-3-1 | 1-2-4-3-1 |
| Operation side | | | Starboard of engine | | |
| Direction of rotation | Crankshaft | | Counterclockwise viewed from stern | | |
| | Propeller shaft | | Clockwise viewed from stern | | |
| Engine lube oil sump | Total | ℓ | 8 | 12 | 18 |
| | Effective | ℓ | 4 | 5.5 | 9 |
| Fuel injection pump type | | | Bosch type, each cylinder individual | | |
| Fuel injection timing | | b.T.D.C | 18 ~ 20deg. (19±1deg.) | | |
| Fuel injection valve | | | Hole valve (5-0.27 φ -140°) | | |
| Fuel injection pressre | | kg/cm² | 200 ~ 210 | | |
| Lubrication system | | | Forced lubrication with trochoid pump | | |
| Lube oil pressure | | kg/cm² | 3 ~ 4 at 2200rpm | | |
| Cooling system | | | Raw water cooling with reciprocating type pump | | |
| Cooling water capacity at 2,100rpm point | | ℓ/Hr | 1,350 | | 1,700 |
| Dry weight (approx.) | Manual start | kg. | 330 | 400 | 510 |
| | Electric start | kg. | 345 | 415 | 525 |
| Dimension manual st. (electric st.) | Lenght | mm | 874 ( 936 ) | 1,010 ( 1,072 ) | 1,236 ( 1,298 ) |
| | Breadts | mm | 530(606) | 530(606) | 547(606) |
| | Height | mm | 805 ( 805 ) | 825 ( 825 ) | 855(855) |

### 2-2 Marine Gear

| Engine model | | | 2TM | 2TMG | 2TMGG | 3TM | 3TMG | 3TMGG | 4TM | 4TMG | 4TMGG | 4TMGGG |
|---|---|---|---|---|---|---|---|---|---|---|---|---|
| Type | | | Wet, single friction plate (ahead) | | | | | | Wet, friction plates(V-lever type) | | | |
| Reduction ratio | Ahead | | 2.14 | 2.50 | 3.14 | 2.14 | 2.50 | 3.14 | 2.13 | 2.59 | 3.22 | 3.80 |
| | Astem | | 2.53 | 2.95 | 3.71 | 2.53 | 2.95 | 3.71 | 2.20 | 2.68 | 3.33 | 3.93 |
| Propeller shaft speed at engine 2,100rpm | Ahead rpm | | 982 | 840 | 670 | 982 | 840 | 670 | 986 | 810 | 653 | 553 |
| | Astem rpm | | 831 | 711 | 567 | 831 | 711 | 567 | 953 | 783 | 631 | 534 |
| Lubrication system | | | Forced lubrication | | | | | | | | | |
| Reduction gear case lube oil sump | Total | ℓ | 1.5 | | | | | | Common oil with engine oil sump | | | |
| | Effective | ℓ | 0.5 | | | | | | | | | |

# 3. Performance Curves

## 3-1  4TM

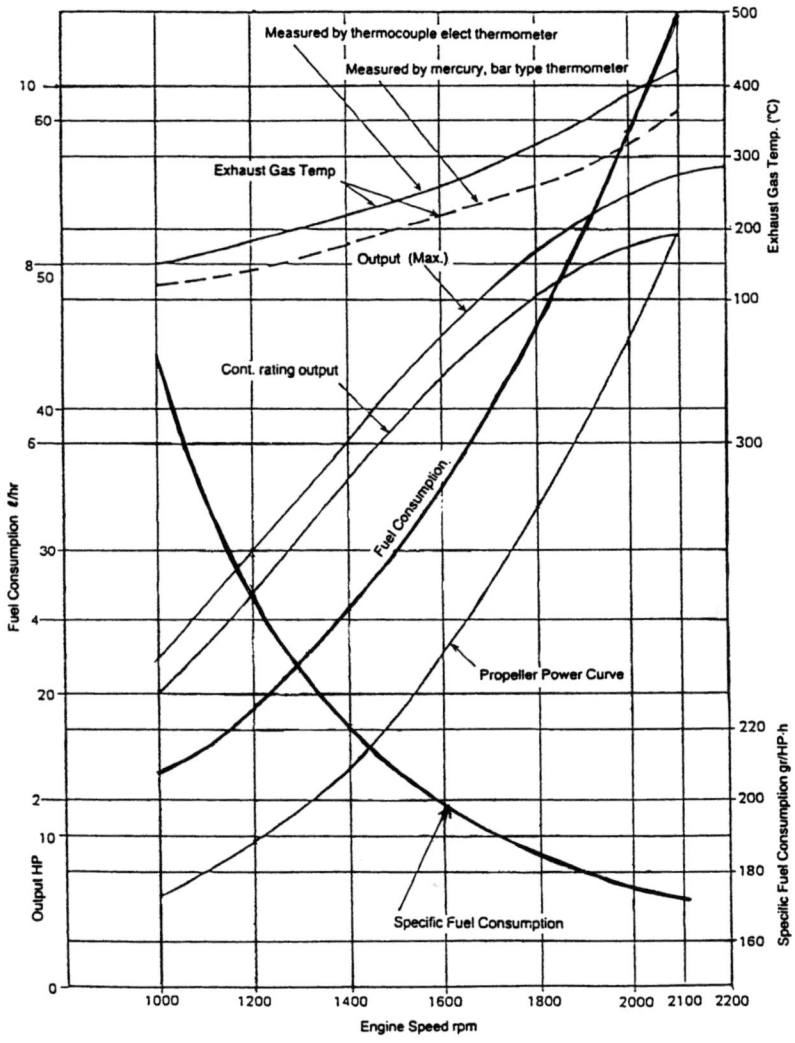

4TM Performance curves

Chapter 1 General
3. Performance Curve  _TM_

### 3-2  3TM

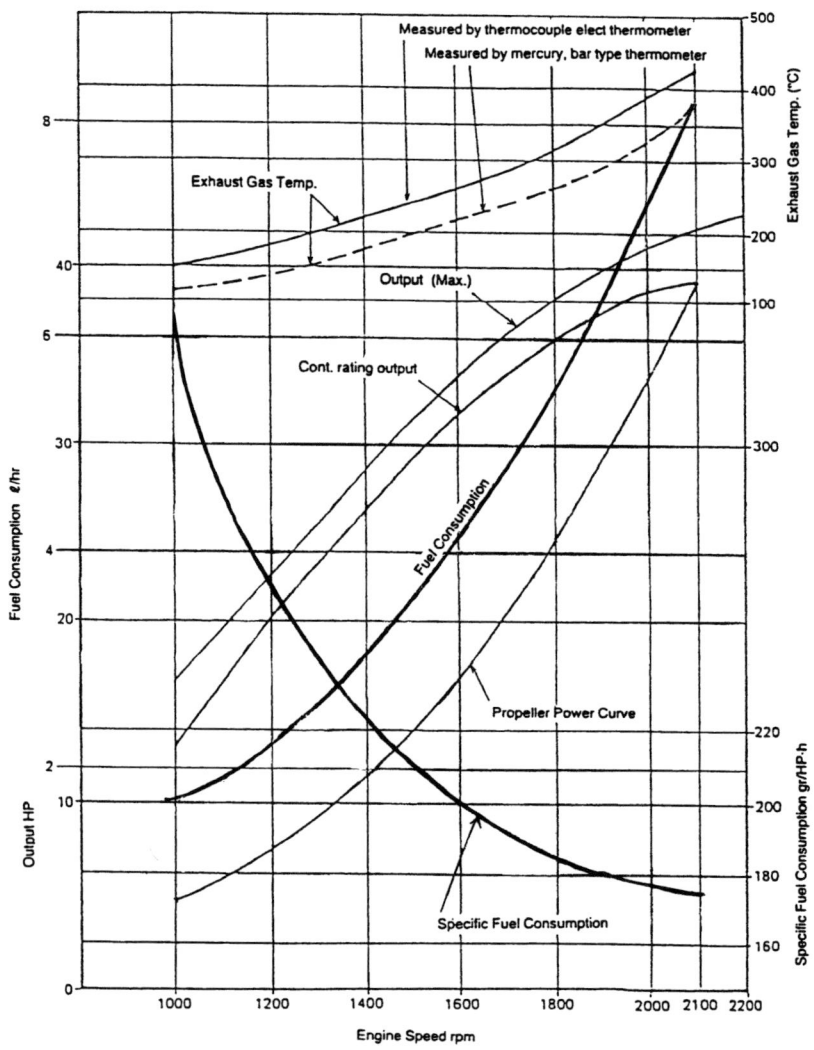

3TM Performance curves

*Chapter 1 General*
*3. Performance curve* _____*TM*

## 3-3  2TM

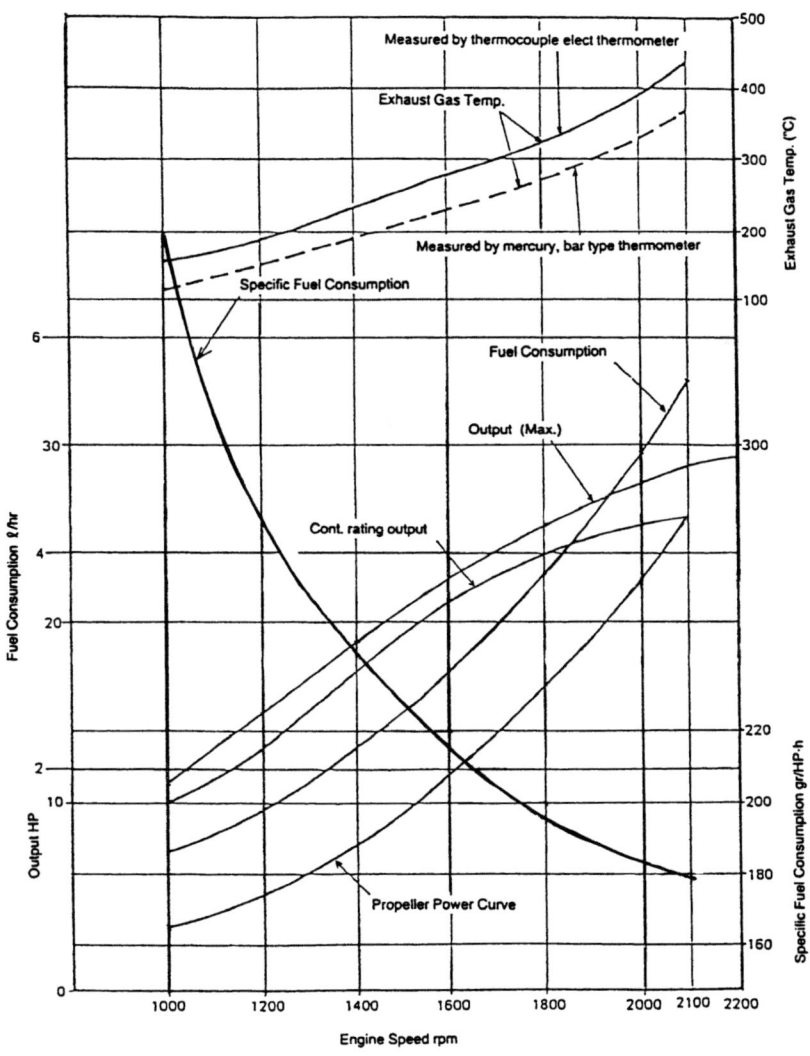

2TM **Performance curves**

*Chapter 1 General*
*4. Engine Cross-section*

# 4. Engine Cross-section

4-1 4TM

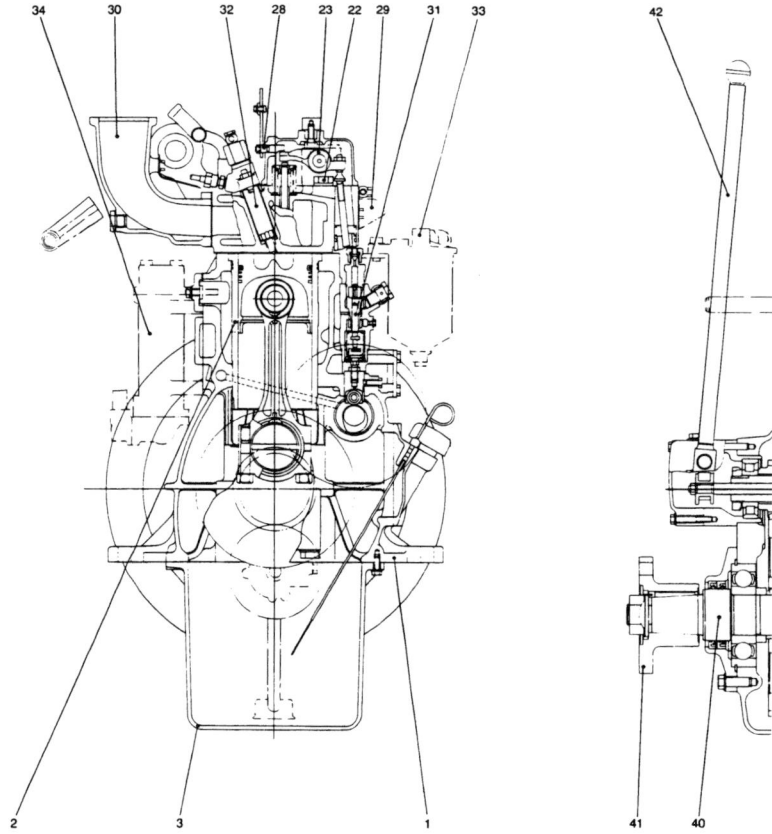

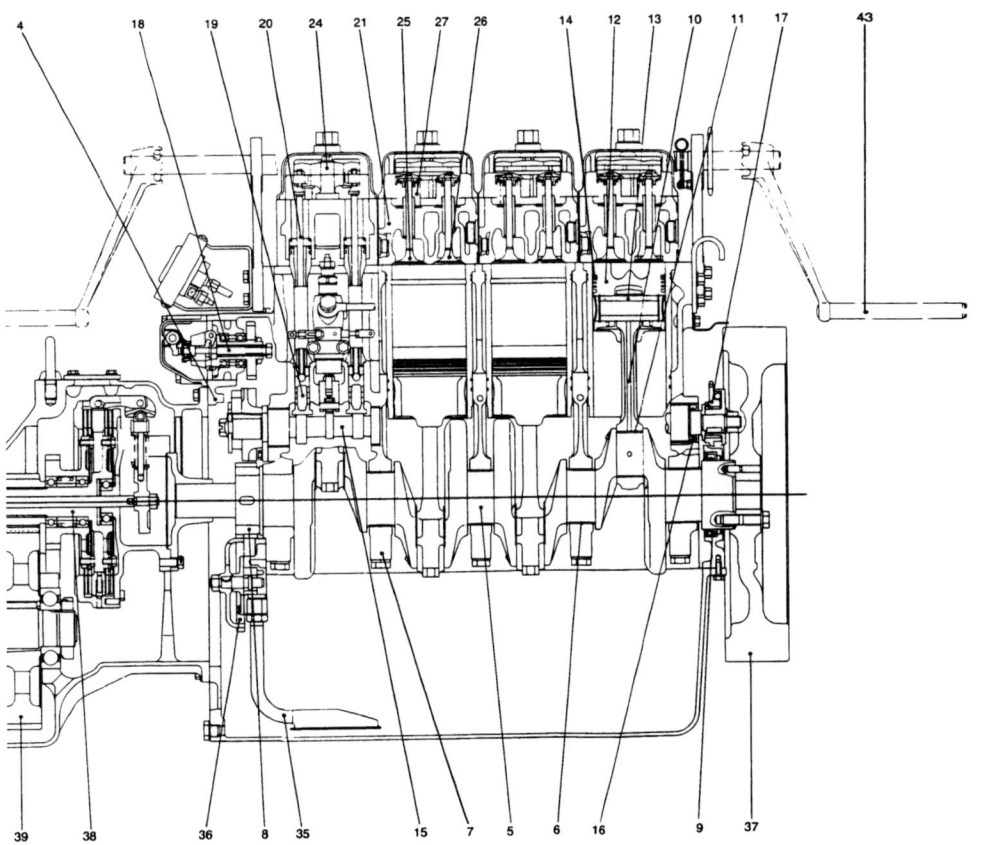

| | | |
|---|---|---|
| 1. Cylinder block | 11. Crank pin bushing | 21. Cylinder head | 31. Fuel injection pump | 41. Output coupling |
| 2. Cylinder liner | 12. Piston | 22. Cylinder head bolt | 32. Fuel injection nozzle | 42. Clutch lever |
| 3. Oil pan | 13. Piston pin | 23. Valve rocker arm | 33. Fuel filter | 43. Start handle |
| 4. Timing gear case | 14. Piston ring | 24. Rocker arm support | 34. Lub. oil cooler | |
| 5. Camshaft | 15. Camshaft | 25. Suction valve | 35. Lub. oil suction tube | |
| 6. Main bearing bushing | 16. Camshaft oil seal | 26. Exhaust valve | 36. Lub. oil pump | |
| 7. Main bearing cap | 17. Free wheel | 27. Valve spring | 37. Flywheel | |
| 8. Crankshaft gear | 18. Governor assembly | 28. Decompression shaft | 38. Forward shaft | |
| 9. Crankshaft oil seal | 19. Tappet | 29. Intake port | 39. Thrust gear | |
| 10. Connecting rod | 20. Push rod | 30. Exhaust manifold | 40. Thrust shaft | |

1-9

*Chapter 1 General*
*4. Engine Cross-section*

*Chapter 1 General*
*5. Piping Diagram*

# 5. Piping Diagram

5-1 4TM
3TM
2TM

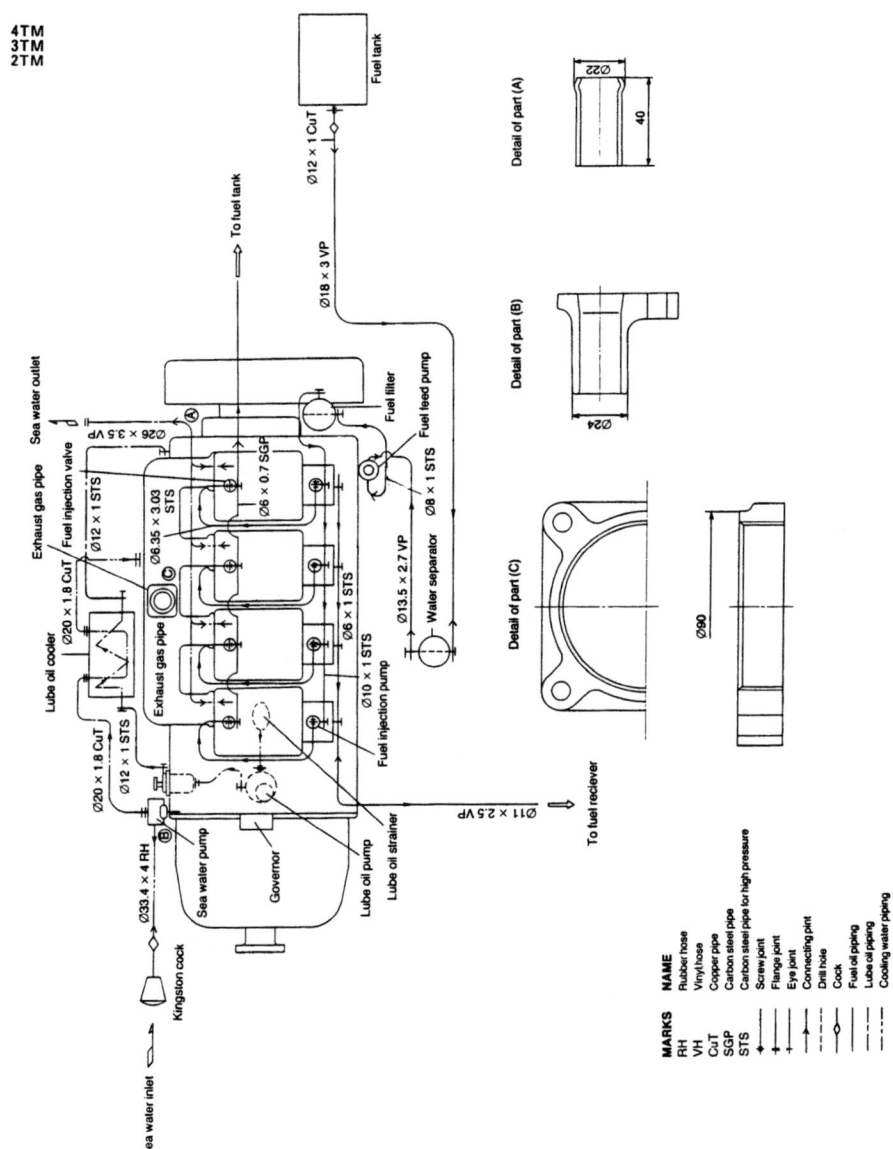

# Chapter 1 General
## 5. Piping Diagram

### 5-2 3TM

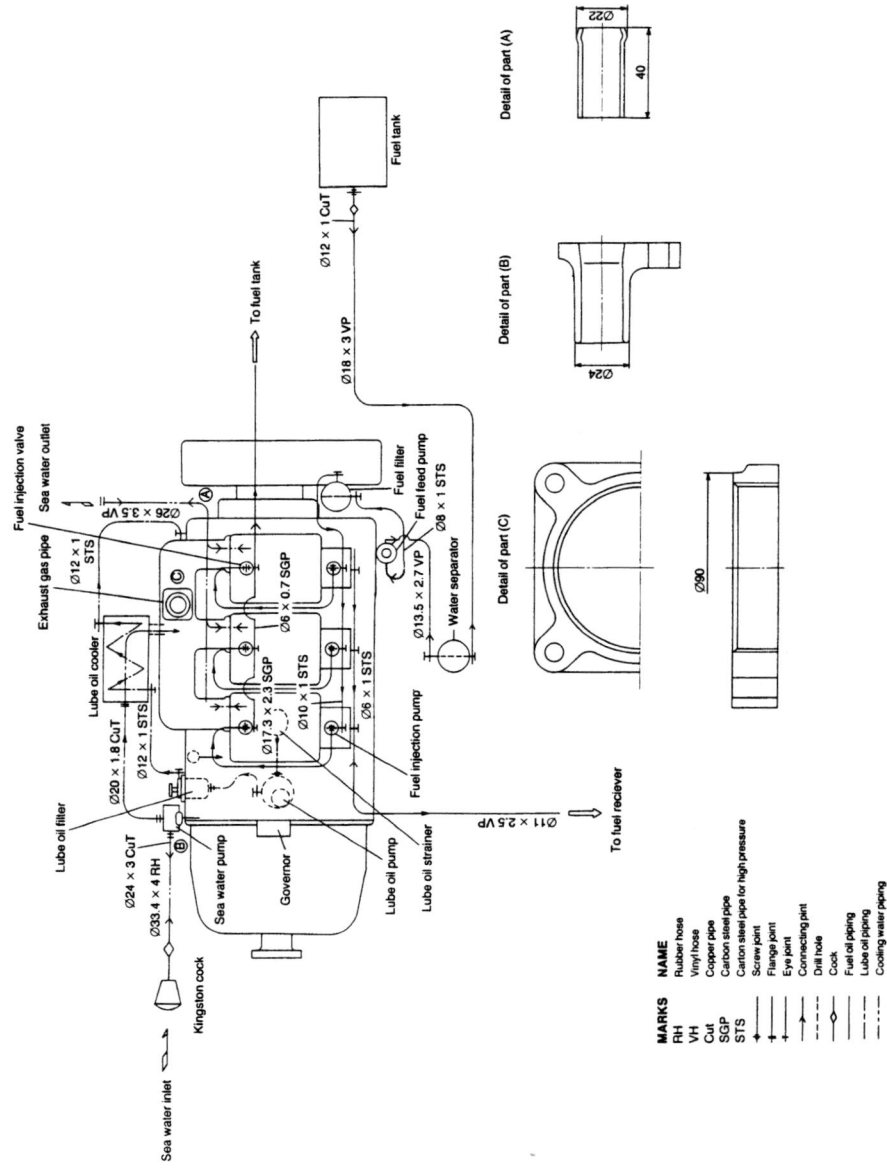

*Chapter 1 General*
*5. Piping Diagram*                                                                                       *TM*

**5-3 2TM**

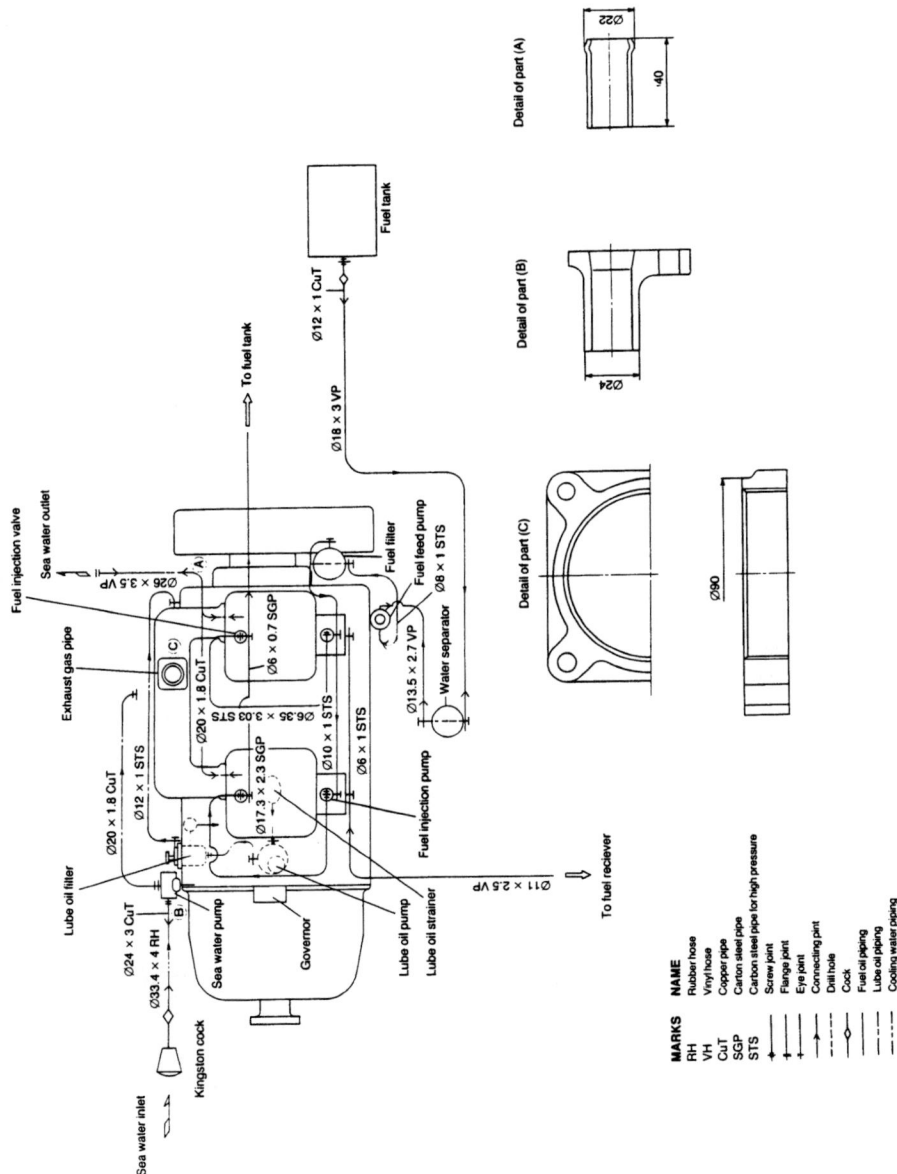

Chapter I General
6. Disassembly and Reassembly Tools

# 6. Disassembly and Reassembly Tools

### 6-1 Standard Tools
Daily maintenance tools
YANMAR's TM-series models contain, as a standard accessory, a complete tool kit for daily maintenance work.
These tools are arranged so as to enable the owner or operator of the boat to do daily maintenance in the engine room by himself.

Advise your customers to take anticorrosive measures and store the tools carefully in the boat. Otherwise, they may become rusted and unusable when needed.

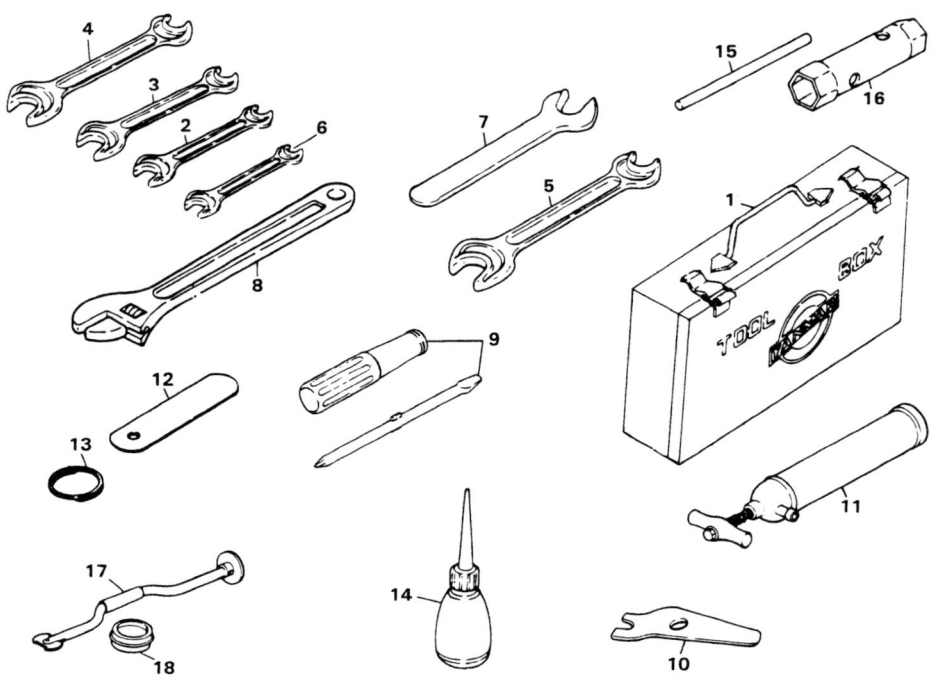

**STANDARD TOOLS LIST**

| No. | Part Name | 2TM | 3TM | 4TM | No. | Part Name | 2TM | 3TM | 4TM |
|---|---|---|---|---|---|---|---|---|---|
| 1 | Tool box | 1 | 1 | 1 | 10 | Valve Pull-out device | 1 | 1 | 1 |
| 2 | Wrench 12 × 14 | 1 | 1 | 1 | 11 | Manual pump (w/pipe) | 1 | 1 | 1 |
| 3 | Wrench 17 × 19 | 1 | 1 | 1 | 12 | Thickness gauge 0.25 | 1 | 1 | 1 |
| 4 | Wrench 22 × 24 | 1 | 1 | 1 | 13 | Ring (gauge) | 1 | 1 | 1 |
| 5 | Wrench 26 × 32 | 1 | 1 | 1 | 14 | Oiler | 1 | 1 | 1 |
| 6 | Wrench 10 × 13 | 1 | 1 | 1 | 15 | Turning bar | 1 | 1 | 1 |
| 7 | Wrench 27 | 1 | 1 | 1 | 16 | Box wrench 12 × 300 | 1 | 1 | 1 |
| 8 | Monkey wrench 250 | 1 | 1 | 1 | 17 | Valve lapping tool | 1 | 1 | 1 |
| 9 | Screwdriver (replaceable) | 1 | 1 | 1 | 18 | Lapping powder | 1 | 1 | 1 |

*Chapter 1 General*
*6. Disassembly and Reassembly Tools*                                                                                       *TM*

### 6-2 Workshop Tools

For more important overhaul work, use the tools specified by YANMAR or the equivalent. YANMAR engines are designed so that even untrained local mechanics can usually check and maintain them with tools for general use, without using any special disassembly tools. However, workshops which undertake major overhauling work for TM-series engines should be furnished with at least the following tools.

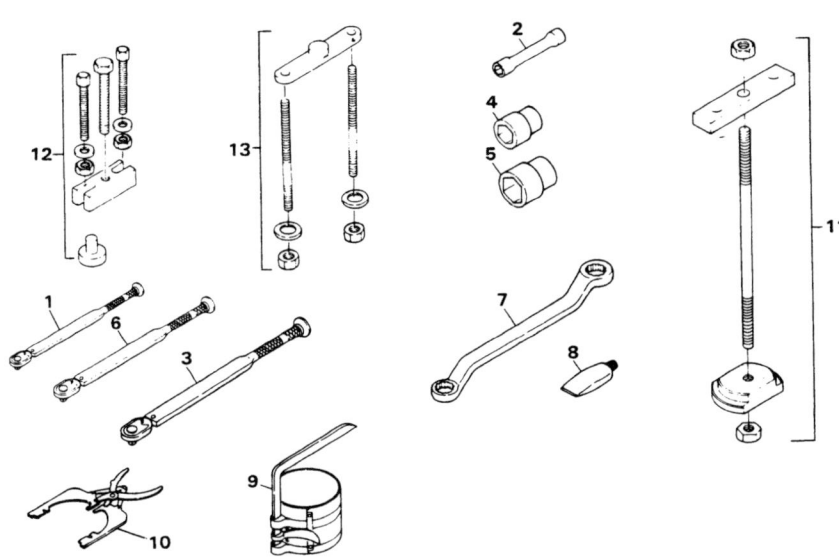

### WORKSHOP TOOLS LIST

| No. | Yanmar Part No. | Description | No. | Yanmar Part No. | Description |
|---|---|---|---|---|---|
| 1 | 123340-92600 | Torque wrench 230 QLK 0.7 ~ 2.3 kg-m for F.O. injectionvalve | 7 | 28160-190220 | Eye wrench 19 × 22 for F.O. injection |
| 2 | 123340-92620 | Socket B = 12 for F.O. inj. valve torque wrench | 8 | 97775-500050 | Paste type lubricant containing $MOS_2$ ($MOS_2$ = Molibdenum disulfide) for injection valve etc. 50 gr. |
| 3 | 123340-92630 | Torque wrench 2,800 QLK 6 ~ 28 Kg-m for bearing cap bolt. | 9 | 95550-002476 | Piston with ring insert tool 2476N |
| 4 | 12330-92640 | Socket B = 19 VS4190 for con-rod bolt | 10 | 95550-002468 | Piston ring removal & insertion tool 2467C |
| 5 | 123340-92650 | Socket B = 22 VS6620 for head nut, bearing cap bolt | 11 | 723340-93590 | Cylinder liner remover assy. |
| 6 | 123340-92670 | Torque wrench 1,800 QLK Max. 18 Kg-m for head, con-rod bolt | *12 | 723210-92530 | Clutch spline metal puller assy. |
|  |  |  | *13 | 723210-92540 | Reverse gear box puller assy. |

Note: * Reverse gear box puller and clutch spline metal puller are only used for 2 & 3TM series.

## Chapter 1 General
### 6. Disassembly and Reassembly Tools

#### 6-2.1 Puller application

(1) Cylinder liner remover

(3) Reverse gear box puller

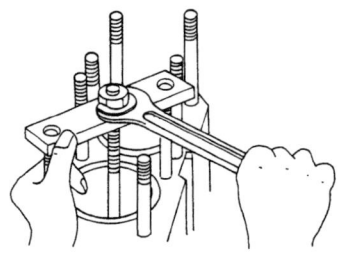

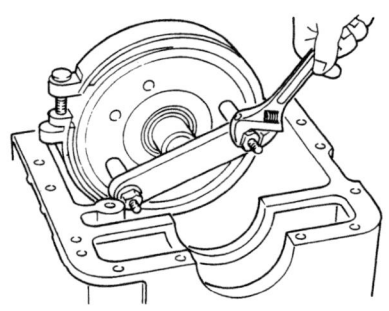

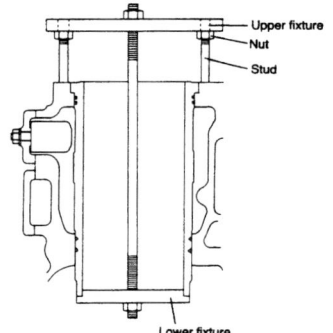

Upper fixture
Nut
Stud

Lower fixture

(2) Spline metal puller

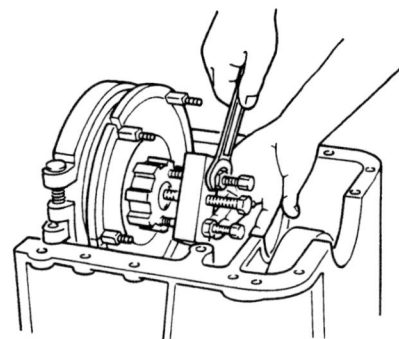

*Chapter I General*
*6. Disassembly and Reassembly Tools* _____ *TM*

## 6-3 Measuring Instruments

| Name of tool | Shape and size | Application |
|---|---|---|
| Vernier Calipers | | 0.05mm (0.0020 in.), 0 ~ 150mm (0 ~ 5.9055 in.) |
| Micrometer | | 0.01mm (0.0004 in.), 0 ~ 25mm (0 ~ 0.9843 in.), 25 ~ 50mm (0.9843 ~ 1.9685 in.), 50 ~ 75mm (1.9685 ~ 2.9528 in.), 75 ~ 100mm (2.9528 ~ 3.9370 in.), 100 ~ 125mm (3.9730 ~ 4.9213 in.), 125 ~ 150mm (4.9213 ~ 5.9055 in.). |
| Cylinder gauge | | 0.01mm (0.0004 in.), 18 ~ 35mm (0.7087 ~ 1.3780 in.), 35 ~ 60mm (1.3780 ~ 2.3622 in.), 50 ~ 100mm (1.9685 ~ 3.9370 in.). |
| Thickness gauge | | Adjusting cylinder head valve clearance<br><br>0.05 ~ 2mm (0.0020 ~ 0.0787 in.). |
| Hand tachometer electric, reflect type | | Checking engine RPM<br>Flywheel<br>Reflection sticker.<br>Engine<br>Engine bed |
| Exhaust gas thermometer bar type, mercury 28573-500050 | | |

1-17

## Chapter 1 General
### 6. Disassembly and Reassembly Tools

_____TM

| Name of tool | Shape and size | Application |
|---|---|---|
| Dial Gauge | | Measuring cylinder liner projection and gear backlash<br>0 ~ 1.0mm (0 ~ 0.4 in.). |
| Nozzle tester | | 0 ~ 500kg/cm$^2$  (0 ~ 7111.7 lb/in.$^2$). |

1-18

## Chapter 1 General
### 6. Disassembly and Reassembly Tools

#### 6-4 Others

(1) Supplementary packing agent

The surface to be coated must be thoroughly cleaned with thinner or benzene and completely dry. The coating must be thin and uniform.

The packing used in this engine is asbestos sheet sealed at both mating faces.

Be sure to use the correct supplement in accordance with the table below.

| Location | Packing (coated) | Packing agent and adhesive |
|---|---|---|
| Cylinder head | Both sides of cylinder head side cover packing<br>Cylinder head top and bottom casting sand hole plug<br>Rocker arm chamber packing (rocker arm chamber side)<br>Both sides of cylinder head gasket packing | "Three Bond No.4"<br><br><br>"Three Bond No.50" |
| Timing gear | Both sides of timing gear case packing | "Three Bond 3B8-005" |
| Cylinder block | Both sides of oil pan packing<br>Outside surface of cylinder liner<br>Cooling water pipe joint threads<br>Lubricating oil suction pipe threads<br>Lubricating oil intake pipe blind plug threads<br>Oil pressure regulator valve threads<br>Oil pressure switch threads<br>Cylinder head bolt stud | "Three Bond 3B8-005"<br>White paint<br>"Three Bond No.20"<br>"Screw Lock Super 203M"<br><br><br><br>"Three Bond 3B8-005" |
| Cooling system | Water drain joint (cylinder, exhaust pipe) | "Three Bond No.4" |

(2) Paint

Color spray

Only Metallic Ecole Silver is used on this engine.

Wipe the surface to be painted with thinner or benzene, shake the spray can well, push the button at the top of the can and spray the paint onto the surface from a distance of 30 ~ 40 cm.

| Type | Use |
|---|---|
| White paint<br>(Mixed oil paint) | Paint parts that contact with the cylinder body when inserting the cylinder liner to prevent rusting and water leakage. |

(3) Yanmar cleaner (Ref.)

Cooling passage cleaner is mixed by adding one part "Unicon 146" to about 16 parts water (specific gravity ratio). To use, drain the water from the cooling system, fill the system with cleaner, allowing it to stand overnight (10 ~ 15 hours). Then drain out the cleaner, refill the system with water, and operate the engine for at least one hour.

(4) NEJI LOCK SUPER  203M: a locking agent for screws  (Ref.)

For coating on screws and bolts to prevent loosening, rusting, and leaking. To use, wipe off all oil and water on the threads of the studs, coat the threads with screw lock, tighten the stud bolt, and allow them to stand until the screw lock hardens. Use screw lock on the oil intake pipe threads, oil pressure switch threads, fuel injection timing shim faces, and front axle bracket mounting bolts.

CHAPTER 2
# BASIC ENGINE

1. Cylinder Block .................................................................... 2-1
2. Cylinder Liner .................................................................... 2-4
3. Cylinder Head .................................................................... 2-7
4. Piston ............................................................................... 2-18
5. Connecting Rod ................................................................ 2-23
6. Crankshaft ........................................................................ 2-26
7. Camshaft .......................................................................... 2-31
8. Timing Gears .................................................................... 2-35
9. Flywheel and Housing ...................................................... 2-37

# 1. Cylinder Block

The cylinder block is thin-skinned, (low-weight), short skirt type with rationally placed ribs. The side walls are wave shaped to maximize ridigity for strength and low noise.

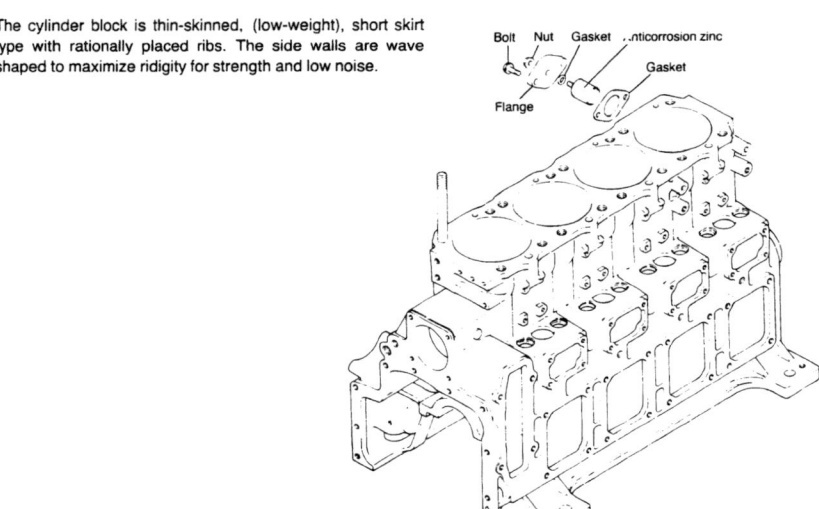

## 1-1 Inspection

### 1-1.1 Inspection of parts

Make a visual inspection to check for cracks on engines that have frozen up, overturned or otherwise been subjected to undue stress. Perform a color check on any portions that appear to be cracked, and replace the cylinder block if the crack is not repairable.

### 1-1.2 Cleaning of oil holes

Clean all oil holes, making sure that none are clogged up and the blind plugs do not come off.

Color check kit
Part code No.97550-004560

|  | Quantity |
|---|---|
| Penetrant | 1 |
| Developer | 2 |
| Cleaner | 3 |

### 1-1.3 Color check procedure

(1) Clean the area to be inspected.
(2) Color check kit
The color check test kit consists of an aerosol cleaner, penetrant and developer.
(3) Clean the area to be inspected with the cleaner.
Either spray the cleaner on directly and wipe, or wipe the area with a cloth moistened with cleaner.
(4) Spray on red penetrant
After cleaning, spray on the red penetrant and allow 5 ~ 10 minutes for penetration. Spray on more red penetrant if it dries before it has been able to penetrate.
(5) Spray on developer.
Remove any residual penetrant on the surface after the penetrant has penetrated, and spray on the developer.
If there are any cracks in the surface, red dots or a red line will appear several minutes after the developer dries.
Hold the developer 300 ~ 400mm (11.8110 ~ 15.7480 in.) away from the area being inspected when spraying, making sure to coat the surface uniformly.
(6) Clean the surface with the cleaner.

NOTE: Without fail, read the instructions for the color check kit before use.

## Chapter 2 Basic Engine
## 1. Cylinder Block

### 1-1.4 Cylinder head bolts

Check for loose cylinder head bolts and for cracking caused by abnormal tightening, either by visual inspection or by a color check.
Replace the cylinder block if cracked.

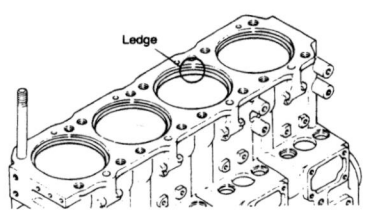

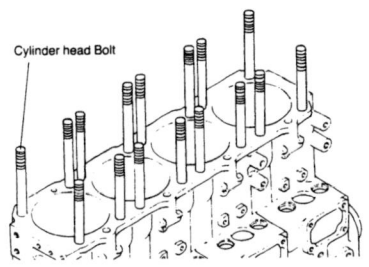

### 1-1.7 Cylinder bore measurement

Measure the inside diameter of the part which contacts the cylinder liner, and repair or replace if it is severely distorted.

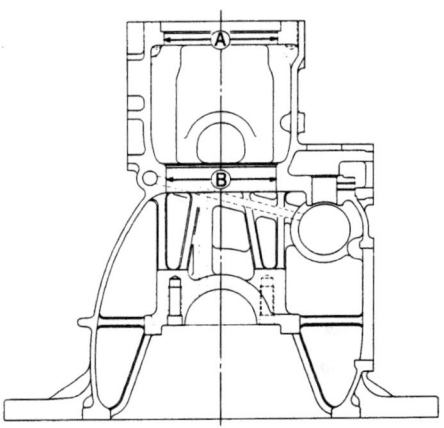

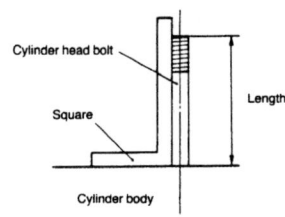

| Tightening torque | 13.5 ~ 14.5 |
|---|---|

kg-m

| Model | Cylinder Head Bolt Parts No. | Length mm (in.) | Quantity |
|---|---|---|---|
| 2TM | | About 125 (4,921) | 8 |
| 3TM | 120445-01230 | | 12 |
| 4TM | | | 16 |

### 1-1.5 Oil and water passages

Check the oil and water passages for clogging and build-up of foreign matter.

### 1-1.6 Cylinder bore and ledge

Perform a color check on the ledge at the top of the cylinder bore, and replace the cylinder block if any cracks are detected.

mm (in.)

| | Maintenance standard | Roundness |
|---|---|---|
| Top A | Ø118+0.035 (4.6457~4.6470) | 0.02 (0.0008) |
| Bottom B | Ø115+0.035 (4.5276~4.5289) | 0.02 (0.0008) |

## 1-2 Anticorrosion Zinc

### 1-2.1 Principles

Anticorrosion zinc is installed to prevent electrolytic corrosion by sea water.

When different metals, i.e., iron and copper, are placed in a highly conductive liquid, such as sea water, the iron gradually rusts. The anticorrosion zinc provides protection against corrosion by being corroded in place of the sea water pump, fresh water tank and other iron parts. The anticorrosion zinc for fresh water cooling systems is attached on the cover of the sea water inlet port.

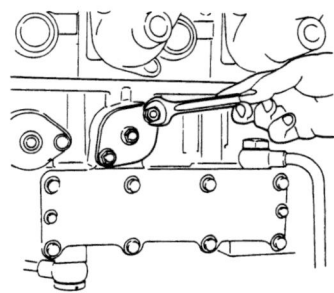

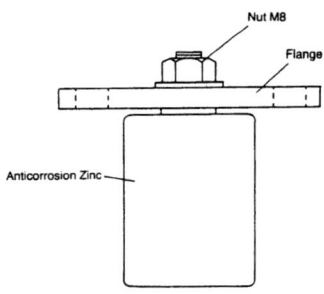

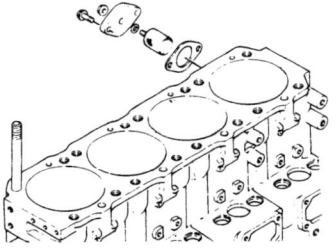

### 1-2.2 Inspection

Generally, replace the anticorrosion zinc every 500 hours of operation. However, since this period depends on the properties of the sea water and operating conditions, periodically inspect the anticorrosion zinc and remove the oxidized film on its surface, using a steel brush.

Volumetric ratio with new zinc = 1/2

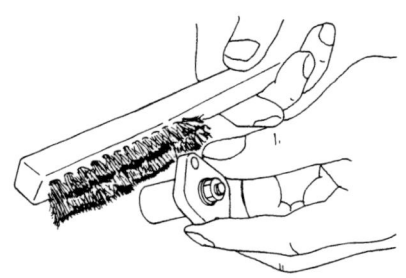

### 1-2.3 Replacement

Replace the anticorrosion zinc by pulling the old zinc from the zinc mounting plug and screwing in the new zinc.

# 2. Cylinder Liner

### 2-1 Construction

High-quality special high-phosphorous cast iron wet type cylinder liners are used. The outside of the cylinder liner is machined to a uniform thickness to prevent local heat expansion and improve durability. Four O-rings (rubber packing) are installed at the cylinder liner neck and skirt to prevent cylinder liner deformation and distortion, and to keep cooling water from leaking into the crankcase.

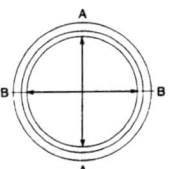

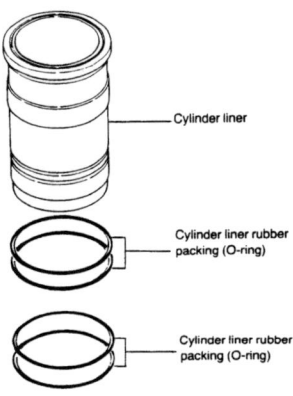

Cylinder liner

Cylinder liner rubber packing (O-ring)

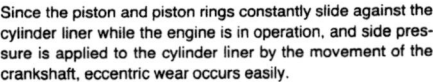

Cylinder liner rubber packing (O-ring)

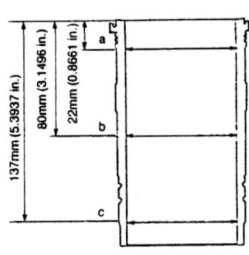

mm (in.)

| | Standard | Wear limit |
|---|---|---|
| Cylinder liner | Ø100.00~100.03 (Ø3.9370~3.9382) | Ø99.8 (Ø3.9291) |

NOTE: Be sure to measure A-A, B-B and a, b and c.

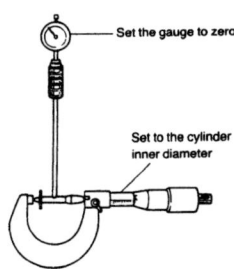

Set the gauge to zero

Set to the cylinder inner diameter

Since the piston and piston rings constantly slide against the cylinder liner while the engine is in operation, and side pressure is applied to the cylinder liner by the movement of the crankshaft, eccentric wear occurs easily.
Also, if lubrication and cooling are insufficient, the inner surface will be damaged or rusted. Inspect the inner surface and replace the cylinder liner if the surface is noticeably damaged or rusted.

#### 2-2.1 Cylinder liner bore diameter measurement

Measure the bore diameter of the cylinder liner with a cylinder gauge at the positions shown in the figure.
Replace the cylinder liner when the measured value exceeds the wear limit.

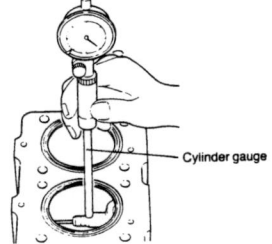

Cylinder gauge

Chapter 2 Basic Engine
2. Cylinder Liner
TM

### 2-3 Cylinder liner replacement

(1) Pull the cylinder liner to the top of the cylinder block as shown in the figure, using the special cylinder liner puller tool.

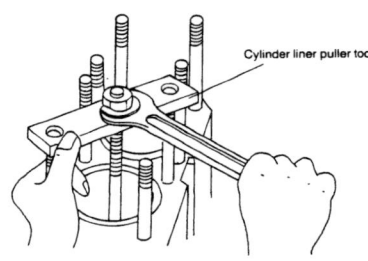
Cylinder liner puller tool

(5) Coat the outside of the liner with oil, and insert lightly by hand. Do not tap it with a wooden hammer as this may deform the liner.

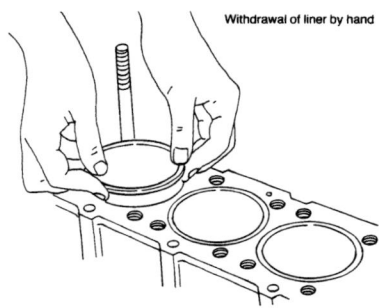
Withdrawal of liner by hand

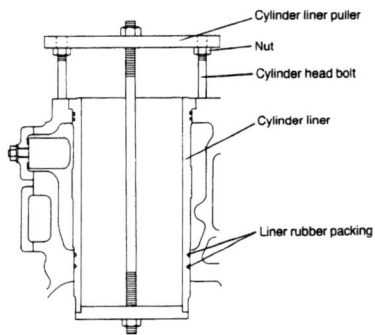
Cylinder liner puller
Nut
Cylinder head bolt
Cylinder liner
Liner rubber packing

(6) After inserting the liner, measure its bore diameter.
(7) Measure the amount of liner projection.

(2) Remove the rust from the area where the cylinder liner contacts the cylinder block.
(3) Insert the rubber packing, taking care not to twist it.
(4) Coat the O-rings and the outside of the cylinder liner with waterproof paint or grease.

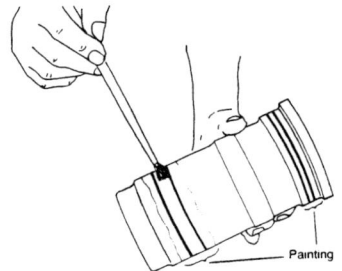
Painting

2-5

Chapter 2 Basic Engine
2. Cylinder Liner

## 2-4 Measuring cylinder liner projection

If replacing or removing the cylinder liner, measure the cylinder liner projection using a dial gauge and magnetic stand.

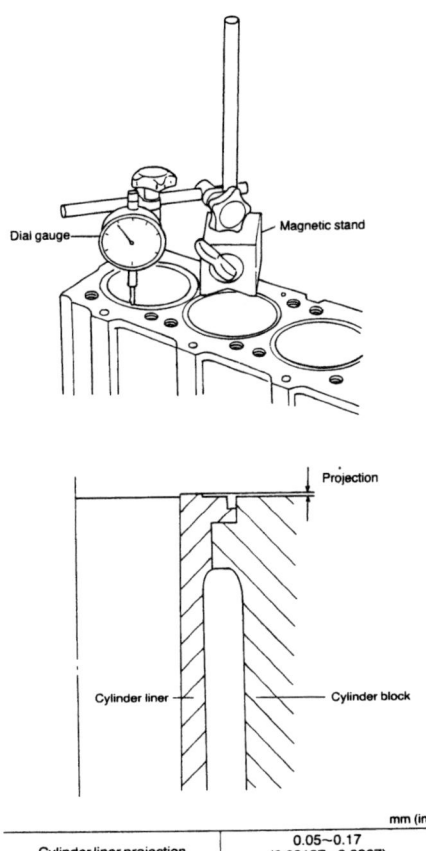

| Cylinder liner projection | mm (in.)<br>0.05~0.17<br>(0.00197~0.0067) |
|---|---|

If the cylinder liner projects too far from the block, the torque reactance will increase, causing the compression ratio to drop and the gasket packing to be damaged.

NOTE: *Excessive cylinder liner projection is frequently caused by incomplete removal of the rust on the edge of the cylinder block.*

# 3. Cylinder Head

## 3-1 Construction

The cylinder head is monoblock type. Models 2TM, 3TM and 4TM have two, three, and four cylinder heads respectively. Each cylinder head is tightened to the head bolt on the cylinder block by a washer and nut.

The exhaust valve seat is made from a chilled, specially sintered alloy which is superior in heat- and wear-resisting characteristics. The large diameter intake valve has a superior air-intake capacity and results in better combustion performance. The most distinctive feature of the engine is the uniform cooling of the combustion chamber by the continuous flow of cooling water. Anti-corrosion zinc is incorporated in the cylinder head to prevent the water jacket from electrolytic corrosion.

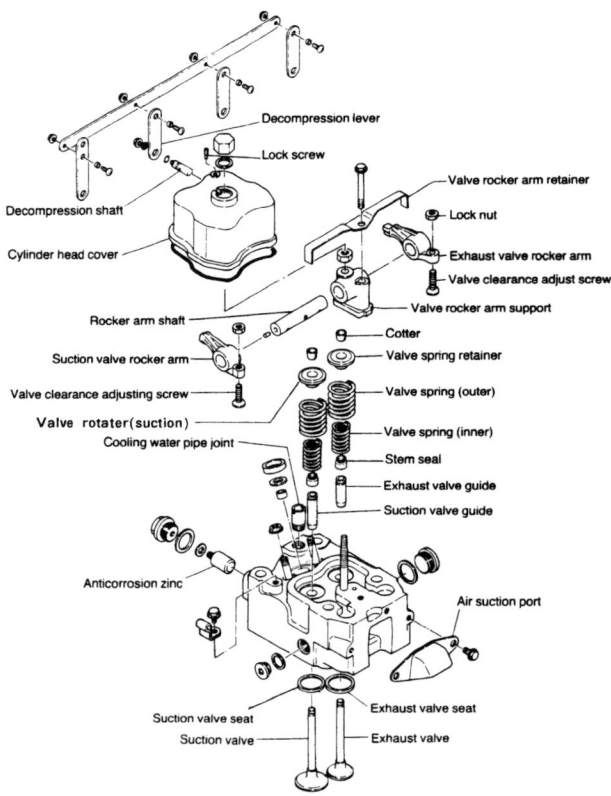

## 3.2 Cylinder head inspection

### 3-2.1 Measurement of carbon build-up at combustion surface and intake and exhaust ports

Visually check for carbon build-up around the combustion surface and the port near the intake and exhaust valve seats, and remove any build-up.
When a large amount of carbon has built up, check the top of the combustion chamber for oil flow at the intake and exhaust valve guides, and take suitable corrective action.

### 3-2.2 Deposit build-up at water passages

Check for build-up of deposit at the water passages, and remove any deposit with a deposit remover. When a large amount of deposit has built up, check each part of the cooling system.

### 3-2.3 Corrosion at water passages and anticorrosion zinc

Inspect the state of corrosion of the water passages, and replace the cylinder head when corrosion is severe.
  Corrosion pitting limit: 2mm (0.0787 in.)
Inspect the anticorrosion zinc on the cylinder head, and replace the zinc when it is worn beyond the wear limit.

Anticorrosion zinc wear limit: Volumetric ratio with new zinc = 1/2

### 3-2.4 Cracking of combustion surface

The combustion surface is exposed to high temperature, high pressure gas and low temperature air, and is repeatedly flexed during operation. It is thus used under extremely severe conditions, such as the high temperature difference between the combustion surface and cooling water passages. Inspect the combustion surface for cracking by the color check, and replace the cylinder head if any cracking is detected. At the same time, check for signs of overloading and check the cooling water flow.

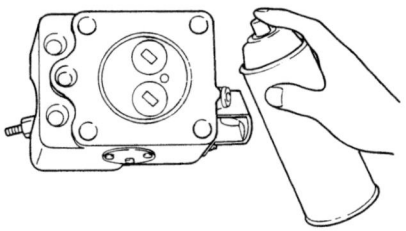

### 3-2.5 Cylinder head distortion

Distortion of the cylinder head causes gasket packing damage, compression leakage, change in compression, etc. Measure the distortion as described below, and replace the cylinder head when the wear limit is exceeded. Since distortion of the cylinder head is caused by irregular tightening forces, faulty repair of the mounting face, and gasket packing damage, these must also be checked.

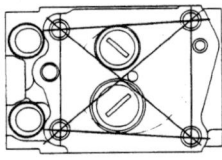

mm (in.)

| | Maintenance standard | Wear limit |
|---|---|---|
| Cylinder head distortion | 0.03 (0.00118) | 0.05 (0.0020) |

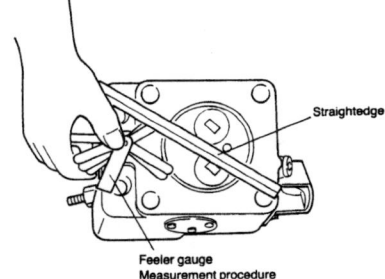

Straightedge
Feeler gauge
Measurement procedure

(1) Clean the cylinder head tightening surface.
(2) Place a straightedge across two symmetrical points at the four sides of the cylinder head, as shown in the figure.
(3) Insert feeler gauges between the straightedge and the cylinder head combustion face.
(4) The thickness of the largest feeler gauge that can be inserted is the amount of distortion.

## Chapter 2 Basic Engine
## 3. Cylinder Head

### 3-2.6 Cylinder head valve seat

The valve seats become wider with use. If the seats become wider than the maintenance standard, carbon build-up at the seats will cause compression leakage. On the other hand, if the seats are too narrow, they will wear quickly and heat transmission efficiency will deteriorate. Clean the carbon and other foreign matter from the valve seats, and check that the seats are not scored or dented.

Measure the seat width with vernier calipers, and repair or replace the seat when the wear limit is exceeded.
When the valves have been lapped and/or ground, measure the amount of valve recess, and replace the valve when the wear limit is exceeded.

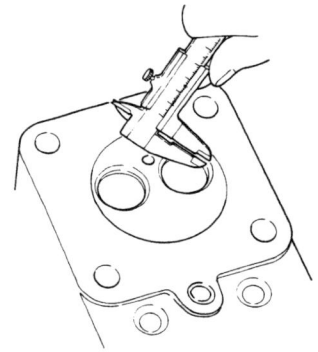

| | | Maintenance standard | Wear limit |
|---|---|---|---|
| Seat width | intake | 1.10 (0.0433) | 2.5 |
| | exhaust | 2.12 (0.0835) | (0.0984) |
| Seat angle | intake | 120° | — |
| | exhaust | 90° | — |

mm (in.)

(1) Lapping the valve seat.
When scoring and pitting of the valve seat is slight, coat the seat with valve compound mixed with oil and lap the seat with a lapping tool.
At this time, be sure that the compound does not flow into the valve stem and valve guide.

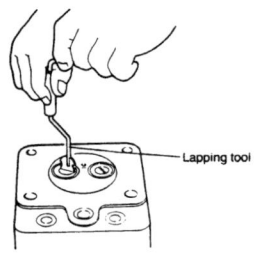

(2) Correcting valve seat width.
When the valve seat is heavily pitted and the seat width must be corrected, repair with a seat grinder.
1) Repair pitting of the seat face with a 45° grinder.
2) Since the valve seat is larger than the initial value, correct the seat width to the maintenance standard by grinding the inside face of the seat with a 70° grinder.
3) Grind the outside face of the valve seat with a 15° grinder, and finish the seat width to the standard value.

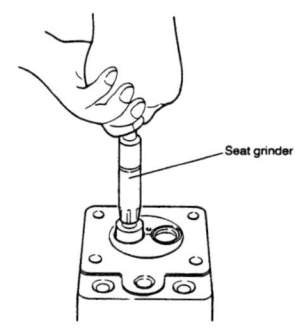

4) Mix the compound with oil, and lap the valve.
5) Finally, lap with oil

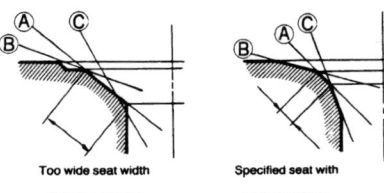

Too wide seat width     Specified seat with
Before correction     After correction

TD5186

(A) Grind with a 45° grinder (exhaust) 60° grinder (intake)
(B) Grind with a 15° grinder
(C) Grind with 65° ~ 75° grinder

NOTE: *When the valve seat has been corrected with the seat grinder, insert an adjusting shim between the valve spring and cylinder head.*

(3) Replacement of exhaust valve seat.
The exhaust valve seat is replaceable. If necessary, replace the exhaust valve seat using the valve seat removing tool.

## Chapter 2 Basic Engine
### 3. Cylinder Head

#### 3-2.7 Measuring valve recess

When the valve has been lapped many times, the valve will become recessed and adversely affect combustion performance. Therefore, measure the valve recess, and replace the valve and cylinder head or exhaust valve seat when the wear limit is exceeded.

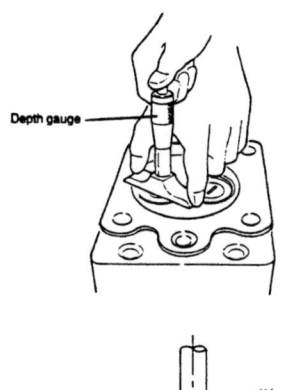

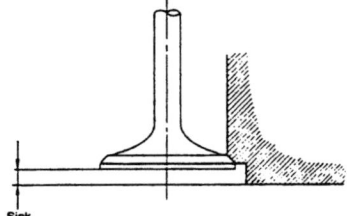

Sink

| | | Standard | Wear limit |
|---|---|---|---|
| Valve sink | Suction | 0.02 ~ 0.38 (0.0008~0.0015) | 1.1 (0.043) |
| | Exhaust | 0.3 ~ 0.7 (0.012~0.0275) | 1.4 (0.055) |

mm (in.)

### 3-3 Dismounting and remounting the cylinder head

When dismounting and remounting the cylinder head, the mounting bolts must be removed and installed gradually and in the prescribed sequence to prevent damaging the gasket packing and distortion of the cylinder head. Since the tightening torque and tightening sequence of the mounting bolts when remounting the cylinder head are especially important from the standpoint of engine performance, the following items must be strictly observed.

#### 3-3.1 Cylinder head stud bolt assembly sequence

(1) Check for loose cylinder head stud bolts, lock any loose bolts with four nuts and then tighten to the prescribed torque.
Cylinder head stud bolt tightening torque: 9.0 ~ 9.5kg-m (65.10 ~ 68.71ft-lb)

(2) Installing the cylinder head ass'y.
Position the cylinder head ass'y parallel to the top of the cylinder block and install the ass'y and block, being careful that the cylinder head ass'y does not touch the threads of the cylinder head bolts.

#### 3-3.2 Tightening the cylinder head

Cyl. Head Tightening Procedures for 2,3,4TM Engines.
If the cylinder head is not tightened uniformly, gas leakage and other troubles will result.
Tighten the cylinder head correctly according to the following procedures during engine disassembly and reassembly:

(1) Tighten the head bolts with the torque wrench 5 times starting from a tightening torque of 2kg-m (14.47 lb-ft):

```
  2   —   4   —   7   —   11   —   14   kg-m
(14.47) (28.93) (50.63) (79.56) (101.2) lb-ft
└ Insert shims ┘        └── Remove shims ──┘
```

(2) Install the cylinder head to the cylinder. Before tightening the cylinder head, insert the shim 0.4mm (0.0157 in) to the bottom its face. First tighten the head bolts with a tightening torque of 2kg-m (14.47lb-ft) then 4kg-m (28.93lb-ft), and remove the shims.

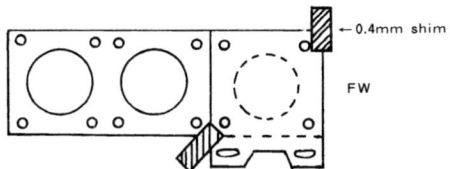

← 0.4mm shim

FW

(3) Head Bolt Tightening Order
Insert the shims in order as shown below:

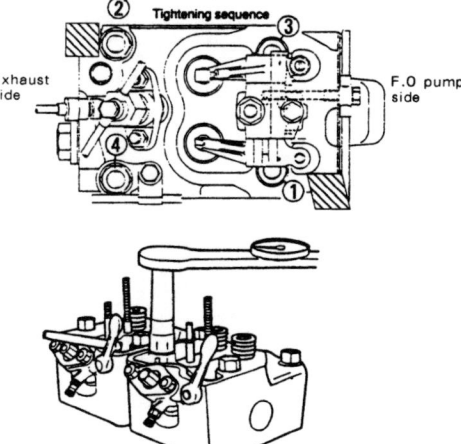

Exhaust side     Tightening sequence     F.O pump side

## Chapter 2 Basic Engine
## 3. Cylinder Head

### 3-3.3 Cylinder head nut loosening sequence
When loosening the cylinder head nuts, reverse the tightening sequence. The cylinder head nut loosening sequence is shown in the figure.

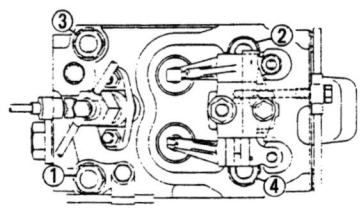

### 3-4. Intake and exhaust valves, valve guide and valve spring

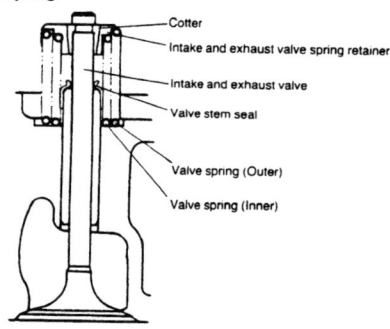

### 3-4.1 Inspecting and measuring the intake and exhaust valves

(1) Valve seat wear and contact width.
Inspect valve seats for carbon build-up and heavy wear. Also check if each valve seat contact width is suitable. If the valve seat contact width is narrower than the valve seat width, the seat angle must be checked and corrected.

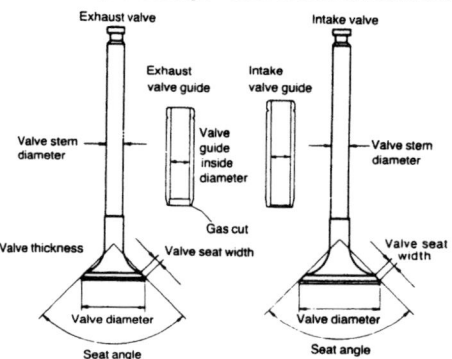

mm (in.)

| | |
|---|---|
| Intake valve diameter | ⌀43.5 (1.7126) |
| Exhaust valve diameter | ⌀36.0 (1.4173) |
| Intake valve seat width | 1.44 (0.0567) |
| Exhaust valve seat width | 2.12 (0.0835) |
| Intake valve seat angle | 120° |
| Exhaust valve seat angle | 90° |

NOTE: Note that the intake valve and exhaust valve have a different diameter.

(2) Valve stem bending and wear.
Check for valve stem wear and staining, and repair when such damage is light. Measure the outside diameter and bend, and replace the valve when the wear limit is exceeded.

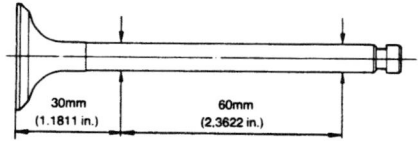

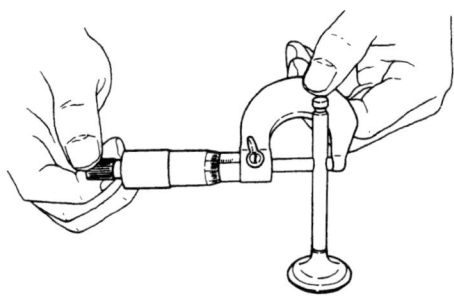

mm (in.)

| Valve stem outside dia. | Standard | Wear limit |
|---|---|---|
| Intake | ⌀8.960~8.975 (⌀0.3528~0.3533) | ⌀8.95 (0.3524) |
| Exhaust | ⌀8.940~8.955 (⌀0.3520~0.3526) | ⌀8.93 (0.3516) |

(3) Valve seat hairline cracks.
Inspect the valve seat by the color check, and replace the seat if cracked.

*Chapter 2 Basic Engine*
*3. Cylinder Head*

### 3-4.2 Inspecting and measuring valve guides

Note that the shape and dimension of the intake and exhaust valve guides are not identical.

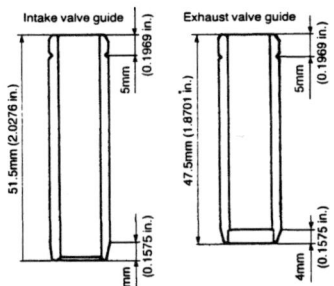

(1) Floating of the intake and exhaust valve guides.
    Check for intake and exhaust valve guide looseness and floating with a test hammer, and replace loose or floating guides with guides with an oversize outside diameter.

(2) Valve guide projection
    Both intake and exhaust valve guides should project 12.8±0.1mm from the top of the cylinder head.

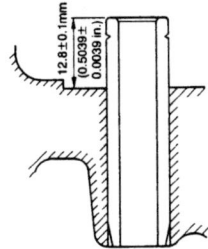

Chapter 2 Basic Engine
3. Cylinder Head

(3) Measuring the valve guide inside diameter.
Measure the valve guide inside diameter and clearance, and replace the guide when wear exceeds the wear limit.

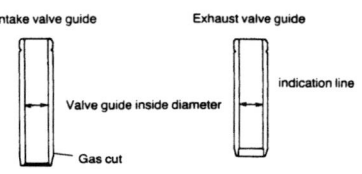

Intake valve guide    Exhaust valve guide
Valve guide inside diameter
indication line
Gas cut

mm (in.)

|  |  | Maintenance standard | Clearance at assembly | Maximum allowable clearance | Wear limit |
|---|---|---|---|---|---|
| Intake | Valve guide inside diameter (after assembly) | Ø9 (0.3543) | 0.025~0.055 (0.0010~0.0022) | 0.07 (0.0028) | Ø8.08 (0.3181) |
|  | Valve stem outside diameter | Ø9 (0.3543) |  |  | Ø7.90 (0.3110) |
| Exhaust | Valve guide inside diameter (after assembly) | Ø9 (0.1543) | 0.045~0.075 (0.0018~0.0030) | 0.09 (0.0035) | Ø8.08 (0.3181) |
|  | Valve stem outside diameter | Ø9 (0.3543) |  |  | Ø7.90 (0.3110) |

### 3-4.3 Valve spring

Note that there are two types of valve spring, i.e., the inner and outer springs. These differ in their outer diametrers and winding directions.

|  | Inner | Outer |
|---|---|---|
| Outer dia. | 24.4mm | 33.6mm |
| Winding direction | Counter-clockwise | Clockwise |

(1) Valve spring inclination.
Since inclination of the valve spring is a direct cause of eccentric contact of the valve stem, always check it at disassembly.
Stand the valve upright on a stool, and check if the entire spring contacts the gauge when a square gauge is placed against the outside diameter of the valve spring.
If there is a gap between the gauge and spring, measure the gap with a feeler gauge.
When the valve spring inclination exceeds the wear limit, replace the spring.

(2) Valve spring free length.
Measure the free length of the valve spring, and replace the spring when the wear limit is exceeded.

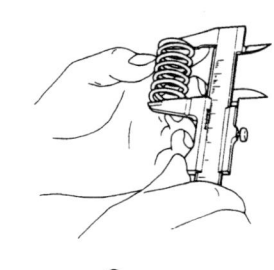

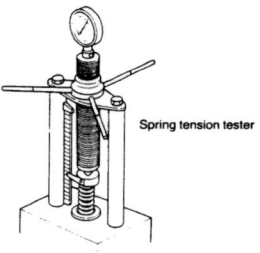

Spring tension tester

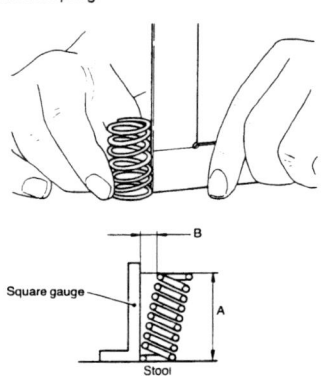

Square gauge
B
A
Stool

|  |  | Maintenance standard | Wear limit |
|---|---|---|---|
| Valve spring free length(A) | inner | 39.7mm(intake) | 39.3mm |
|  |  | 40.4mm(exhast) | 40mm |
|  | outer | 45.15mm | 44.7mm |
| Valve spring inclination(B) | inner | 0~0.7mm | 1.0mm |
|  | outer | 0~0.8mm | 1.0mm |
| Mounted valve spring load | inner | 5.24~5.84kg | 5.0kg |
|  | outer | 17.86~13.86kg | 17.0kg |
| Spring length | inner | 35mm(intake) | – |
|  |  | 35.75mm(exhast) |  |
|  | outer | 35.75mm | – |

※ Remark intake inner spring marked white

## Chapter 2 Basic Engine
### 3. Cylinder Head

#### 3-4.4 Valve stem seal

A valve stem seal is assembled at the top of the valve guide. The valve stem chamber oil is sucked into the combustion chamber through the valve guide (oil down) to prevent an increase in oil consumption.
The valve stem seal must always be replaced whenever it has been removed.
When assembling, coat the valve stem with engine oil before inserting.

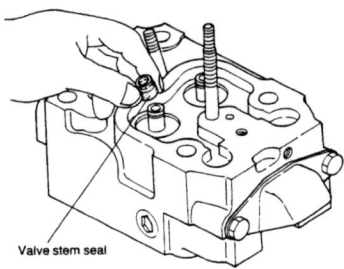

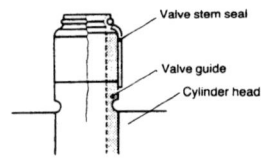

#### 3-4.5 Spring retainer and spring cotter pin

Inspect the inside face of the spring retainer, the outside surface of the spring cotter pin, the contact area of the spring cotter pin inside surface and the notch in the head of the valve stem. Replace the spring retainer and spring cotter pin when the contact area is less than 70% or when the spring cotter pin has been recessed because of wear.

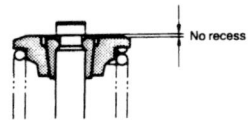

### 3-5 Top clearance

Top clearance is the size of the gap between the cylinder head combustion surface and the top of the piston at top dead center.
Since top clearance has considerable effect on the combustion performance and the starting characteristic of the engine, it must be checked periodically.

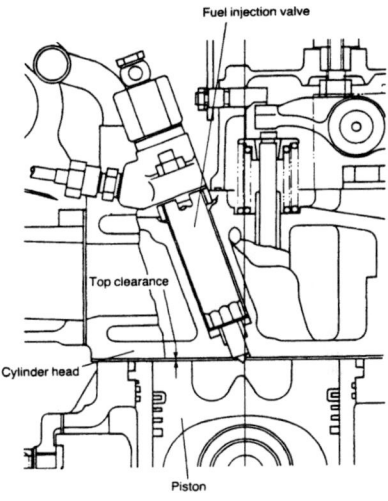

#### 3-5.1 Measuring top clearance

(1) Place a high quality fuse (⌀1.5mm (0.0591 in.), 10mm (0.3937 in.) long) in three positions on the flat part of the piston head.
(2) Assemble the cylinder head gasket and the cylinder block and tighten the bolts in the specified order to the specified torque.
(3) Turn the crank, (in the direction of engine revolution), and press the fuse against the piston until it breaks.
(4) Remove the head and take out the broken fuse.
(5) Measure the three positions where each fuse is broken and calculate the average.
(0.72 ~ 0.94mm (0.0283 ~ 0.0370 in.))

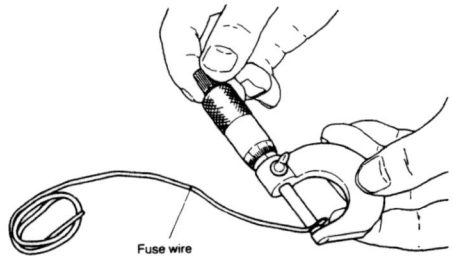

| | mm (in.) |
|---|---|
| Top clearance | 0.8 ~ 1.0 (0.031 ~ 0.039) |

When the top clearance value is not within the above range, check for damaged gasket packing, distortion of the cylinder head combustion surface. or other abnormal conditions.

## Chapter 2 Basic Engine
## 3. Cylinder Head

### 3-6 Intake and exhaust valve rocker arm

Since the intake and exhaust valve rocker arm shaft clearance and valve head and push rod contact wear are directly related to the valve timing, and have an effect on engine performance, they must be carefully serviced.

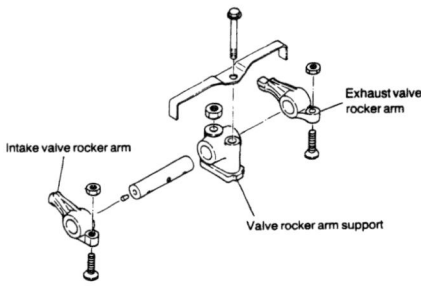

#### 3-6.1 Measuring the valve rocker arm shaft and bushing clearance

Measure the outside diameter of the valve rocker arm shaft and the inside diameter of the bushing, and replace the rocker arm or bushing if the measured value exceeds the wear limit.

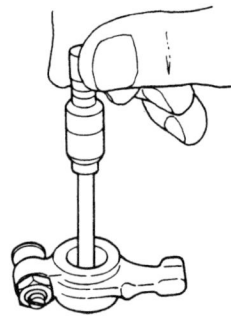

mm (in.)

| | | Standard | Wear limit |
|---|---|---|---|
| Intake and exhaust valve rocker arm shaft outside dia. | A | 17.963 ~ 17.980 (0.7072 ~ 0.7079) | 17.950 (0.7067) |
| Intake and exhaust valve rocker arm inside dia. (assembled) | B | 18.034 ~ 18.016 (0.7100 ~ 0.7093) | 18.106 (0.7128) |
| Valve rocker arm shaft and valve rocker arm clearance at assembly | | 0.053 ~ 0.054 (0.00209~0.00213) | 0.157 (0.0062) |

#### 3-6.2 Valve rocker arm and valve top retainer contact and wear

Check the valve rocker arm and valve top retainer contact, and replace when there is any abnormal wear or peeling.

#### 3-6.3 Valve clearance adjusting screw

Inspect the valve clearance adjusting screw and push rod contact, and replace when there is any abnormal wear or peeling.

#### 3-6.4 Classification of the intake and exhaust valve rocker arms

Since the intake and exhaust valve rocker arms have different shapes, care must be exercised in service and assembly.

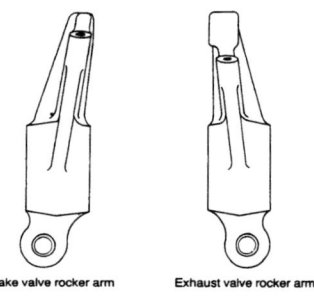

### 3-7 Valve clearance adjustment

Make this adjustment when the engine is cold.
(1) Remove the valve rocker arm cover.
(2) Crank the engine and set the No.1 (flywheel side) piston to top dead center (TDC = 1T) on the compression stroke.

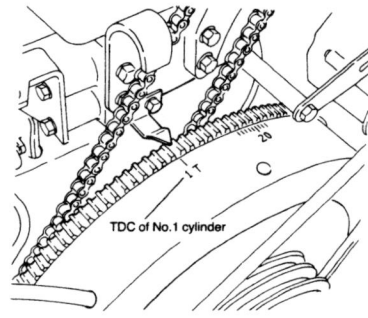

NOTE: Set to the position at which the valve rocker arm shaft does not move even when the crankshaft is turned to the left and right, centered around the TM mark.

## Capter 2 Basic Engine
### 3. Cylinder Head

(3) Check and adjust the intake and exhaust valve head clearances of the No.1 piston.
Loosen the valve clearance adjusting screw lock nut, adjust the clearance to the maintenance standard with a feeler gauge, and retighten the lock nut.

| Intake and exhaust head clearance | mm (in.) |
|---|---|
|  | 0.25 (0.010) |

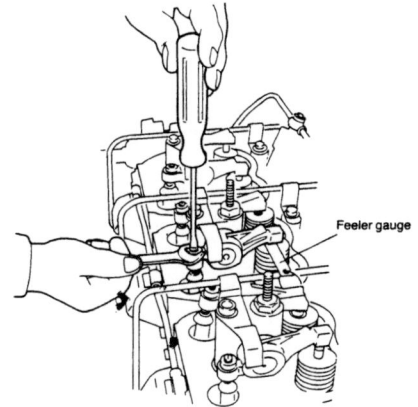

(4) Adjust the valve clearance of remaining pistons, (see below).

|  | No.1 | No.2 | No.3 | No.4 |
|---|---|---|---|---|
| 4TM | 1T mark | 2·3T (180° turn) | | 4T(180°turn) |
| 3TM | 1T mark | 2T (120° turn counterclockwise viewed from stern) | 3T (120° turn counterclockwise) | |
| 2TM | 1T mark | 2T (180° turn) | | |

### 3-8 Decompression mechanism

The decompression mechanism is used when the starter motor fails to rotate sufficiently because the battery is weak, and to facilitate starting in cold weather.
When the decompression lever is operated, the valve is pushed down, the engine decompressed, the engine turns over easily and the flywheel inertia increases, thus making starting easy.

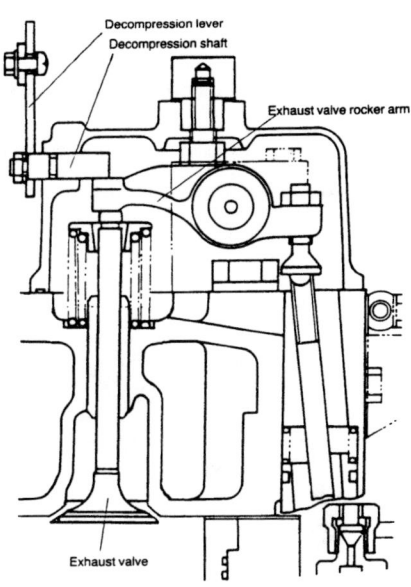

## 3-9 Disassembling and reassembling the cylinder head

### 3-9.1 Disassembling the cylinder head

When disassembling the cylinder head, group the parts separately according to cylinder, intake or exhaust to avoid confusion.

(1) Disassembling the rocker arm ass'y
  1) Remove the rocker arm ass'y mounting nuts.
  2) Remove the rocker arm ass'y
  3) Remove the rocker arm retainer, and pull the rocker from the rocker arm support.

(2) Disassembly of intake and exhaust valves
  1) Push down the valve spring with the valve spring compressor.
  2) Remove the cotter.
  3) Remove the valve spring retainer, and the valve spring.
  4) Pull out the valve from the cylinder head.
  5) Remove the stem seal.
  6) Remove the valve guide.

### 3-9.2 Reassembling the cylinder head

Before reassembling the cylinder head, wash all the parts, inspect and measure the dimensions of each part, and repair or replace any that are abnormal. Be careful not to confuse the parts grouped by cylinder number and intake or exhaust.

(1) Assembling the intake and exhaust valves
  1) Press the valve guide into the cylinder head.
  2) Install the valve stem seal. (Always replace the valve stem seal with a new seal.)
  3) Install the valve in the cylinder head.
  4) Install the valve spring and valve spring seat.
  5) Install the cotter with the valve springs compressed.

(2) Installing the rocker arm ass'y
  1) Install the intake and exhaust rocker arms on the rocker arm support.
  2) Install both the rocker arm supports and rocker arm retainers on the cylinder head, then tighten them with nuts.

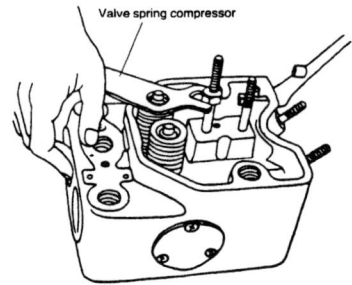

Valve spring compressor

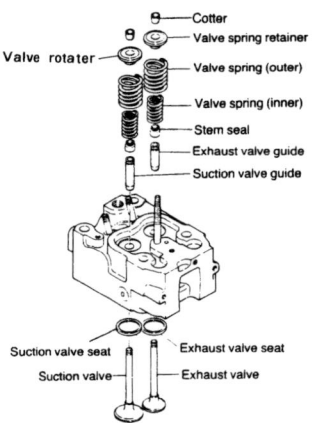

# 4. Piston

### 4-1 Piston ass'y construction

The pistons are made of LO-EX (AC8A-T5) for lightness and are designed for reduced vibration. The outside of the piston is machined to a special oval shape. During operation, thermal expansion is small, the optimum clearance between the piston and cylinder liner is maintained, and a stable supply of lubricating oil is assured.
A swirl type toroidal shaped combustion chamber is fitted on the piston crown.

### 4-2 Piston

#### 4-2.1 Inspecion

(1) Measuring important dimensions
    Measure each important dimension, and replace the piston when the wear limit is exceeded.

**Old type (with 4-rings)**

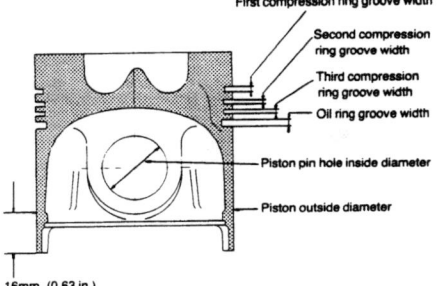

16mm (0.63 in.)

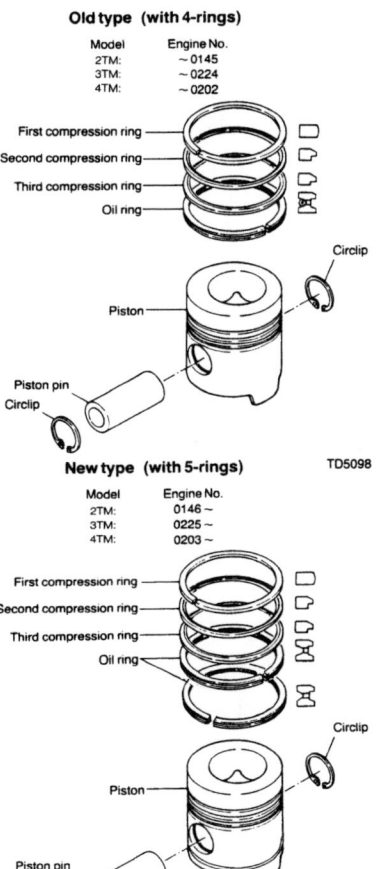

**New type (with 5-rings)**

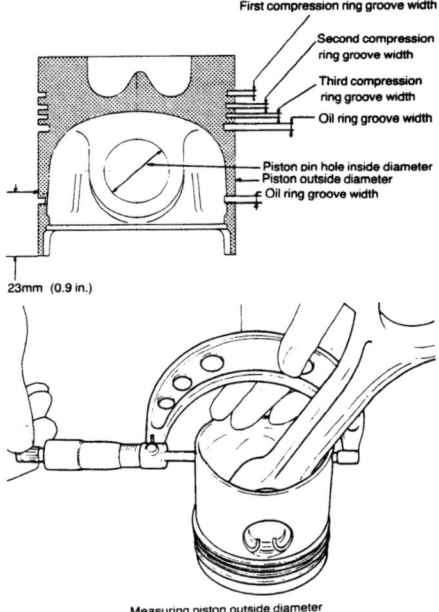

23mm (0.9 in.)

Measuring piston outside diameter

## Chapter 2 Basic Engine
### 4. Piston

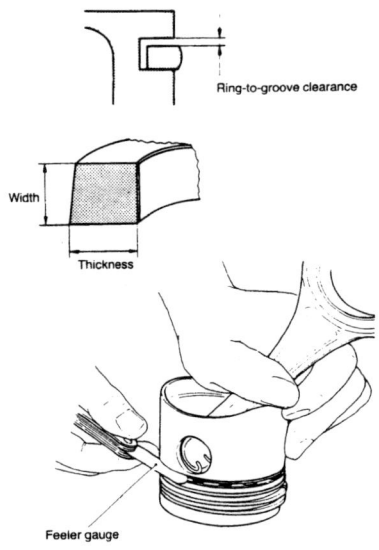

Feeler gauge

(2) Piston pin outside contact and ring groove carbon build-up.
Check if the piston ring grooves are clogged with carbon, whether the rings move freely, and for abnormal contact around the outside of the piston. Repair or replace the piston it faulty.

#### 4-2.2 Replacing a piston

If the dimension of any part is worn past the wear limit or the outside of the piston is scored, replace the piston.
The piston is coupled to the connecting rod through the piston pin.
A floating type piston pin is used in this engine. The piston pin can be pressed into the piston pin hole at room temperature (coat with oil to make it slide in easily).

#### Old type (with 4-rings)

mm (in.)

|  | Maintenance standard | Wear limit |
|---|---|---|
| Piston outside diameter (axial direction) | ⌀99.87 (3.9319) | ⌀99.865 (3.9317) |
| Piston pin hole inside diameter | ⌀35 (1.3780) | ⌀34.95 (1.3760) |
| First compression piston ring-to-groove clearance | 0.055 ~ 0.090 (0.0022 ~ 0.0035) | 0.15 (0.0059) |
| Second and third compression piston ring-to-groove clearance | 0.035 ~ 0.075 (0.0014 ~ 0.0030) | 0.12 (0.0047) |
| Oil ring-to-groove clearance | 0.03 ~ 0.065 (0.0012 ~ 0.00256) | 0.15 (0.0059) |

#### 4-3 Piston pin and piston pin bushing
#### 4-3.1 Piston pin inspection

Measure the dimensions of the piston pin, and replace the pin if it is worn past the wear limit or severely scored.

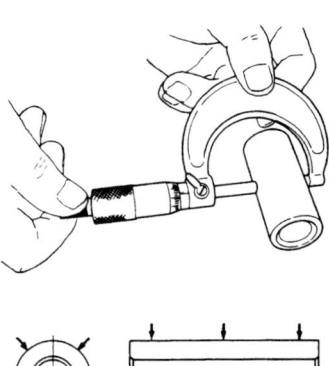

#### New type (with 5-rings)

mm (in.)

|  | Maintenance standard | Wear limit |
|---|---|---|
| Piston outside diameter (axial direction) | ⌀99.89 (3.9327) | ⌀99.886 (3.9325) |
| Piston pin hole inside diameter | ⌀35 (1.3780) | ⌀34.95 (1.3760) |
| First compression piston ring-to-groove clearance | 0.055 ~ 0.090 (0.0022 ~ 0.0035) | 0.15 (0.0059) |
| Second and third compression piston ring-to-groove clearance | 0.025 ~ 0.060 (0.0010 ~ 0.0024) | 0.11 (0.0043) |
| Oil ring-to-groove clearance | 0.025 ~ 0.060 (0.0010 ~ 0.0024) | 0.15 (0.0059) |

## Chapter 2 Basic Engine
## 4. Piston

mm (in.)

|  | Standard | Wear limit |
|---|---|---|
| Piston pin outside dia. | ⌀34.985~35.000 (⌀1.3773~1.3780) | −0.025 (0.0009) |
| Standard clearance | 0 ~ 0.026 (0 ~ 0.0010) | 0.045 (0.0018) |

### 4-3.2 Piston pin bushing inspection

(1) Measuring piston pin clearance
Excessive piston pin bushing wear may result in damage to the piston pin or the piston itself.

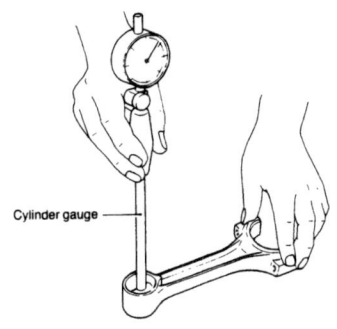

mm (in.)

|  | Standard | Wear limit |
|---|---|---|
| Piston pin bushing inside dia. | ⌀35.030~35.050 (⌀1.3791~1.3799) | ⌀35.12(1.3827) |
| oil clearance | 0.030~0.065 (0.0181~0.0256) | 0.16 (0.0063) |

(2) Replacing piston pin bushing
1) When the bushing for the connecting rod piston pin is either worn out or damaged, replace it by using the "piston pin extracting tool" installed on a press.

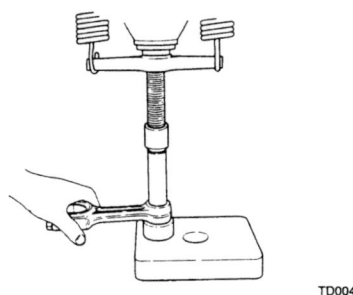

TD0047

NOTE: Force the piston pin bushing into position so that its oil hole coincides with the hole on the small end of the connecting rod.

2) After forcing the piston pin bushing into position, finish the inner surface of the bushing by using a pin honing machine or reamer so that it fits the piston pin to be used.

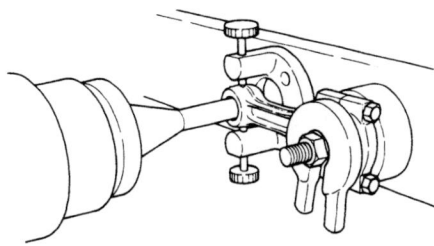

NOTE: Attach the bushing to the piston pin so that a pin coated with engine oil can be pushed into position with your thumb.

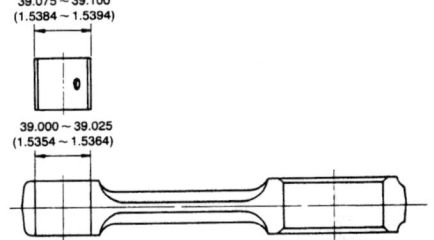

39.075 ~ 39.100 (1.5384 ~ 1.5394)

39.000 ~ 39.025 (1.5354 ~ 1.5364)

### 4-4 Piston rings
#### 4-4.1 Piston ring configuration
(1) The first compression ring is a barrel face ring that effectively prevents abnormal wear caused by engine loading and combustion gas blowby at the initial run-in.

**Old type (with 4-rings)**

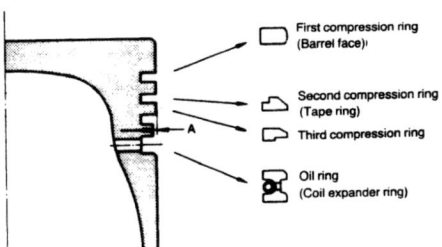

- First compression ring (Barrel face)
- Second compression ring (Tape ring)
- Third compression ring
- Oil ring (Coil expander ring)

## Chapter 2 Basic Engine
## 4. Piston

**New type (with 5-rings)**

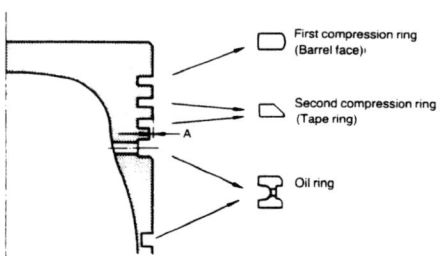

- First compression ring (Barrel face)
- Second compression ring (Tape ring)
- Oil ring

| | Maintenance standard | Wear limit |
|---|---|---|
| | | mm (in.) |
| Piston ring gap (1,2,3) | 0.25 ~ 0.45 (0.0098 ~ 0.0177) | 1.6 (0.063) |
| Oil ring gap (1 used) | 0.2 ~ 0.4 (0.0079 ~ 0.0157) | 1.5 (0.059) |
| Oil ring gap (2 used) | 0.2 ~ 0.4 (0.0079 ~ 0.0157) | 1.2 (0.047) |

(2) The second and third compression rings are taper rings with a sliding face taper of 1° ~ 1°30′. Since the cylinder liner is straight, and the contact area at initial operation is small, they are easily seated on the cylinder liner. Moreover, the bottom of their sliding face is sharp, oil splash is excellent and air-tightness superb.
The rim (A in figure) between the third compression ring and the oil ring has a small 1.0mm outside diameter that effectively improves oil collection and reduces oil consumption.

(3) The oil ring is a chrome-plated coil expander with a small contacting face, and exerts high pressure against the cylinder liner wall. Oil splash at the bottom of the sliding face is excellent, and its oil control is high.

#### 4-4.2 Inspection

(1) Piston ring contact
Inspect the piston ring contact, and replace the ring when contact is faulty. Since the oil ring side contact is closely related to oil consumption, it must be checked with particular care.

(2) Measuring the piston ring gap
Insert the piston into the cylinder liner by pushing the piston ring at the head of the piston as shown in the figure, and measure the piston ring gap with a feeler gauge. Measure the gap at a point about 150mm from the top of the cylinder liner.

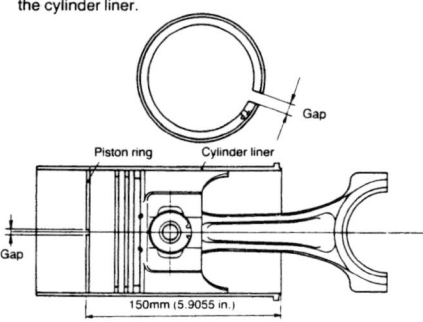

(3) Piston ring replacement precautions
1) Clean the ring grooves carefully when replacing the rings.
2) When installing the rings, assemble the rings so that the manufacturer's mark near the gap is facing the top of the piston.

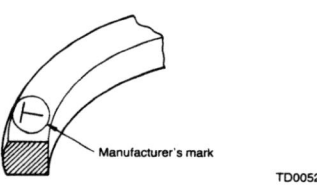

Manufacturer's mark

TD0052

3) After assembly, check that the rings move freely in the grooves.
4) The rings must be installed so that the gaps are 180° apart. Be careful that the ring gap is not lined up with the piston side pressure part.

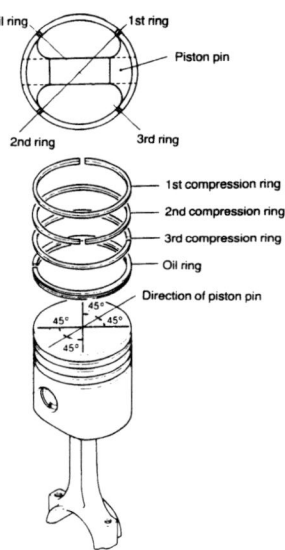

## Chapter 2 Basic Engine
## 4. Piston

5) The oil ring is provided with a coil expander. The coil expander joint should be opposite (staggered 180°) the oil ring gap. (For old type with 4-rings).

(5) Be sure that the size mark on top of piston faces the tappet side.

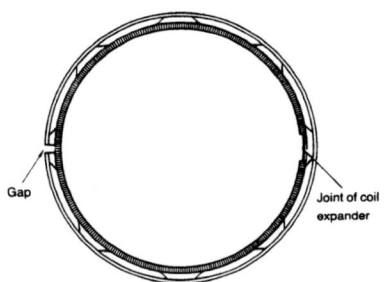

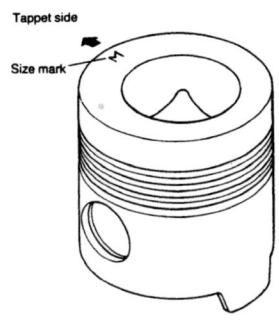

### 4-5 Piston ass'y installation precautions

(1) Clearly distinguish the first cylinder from the other cylinders.
(2) Be sure the number marked on the large end of connecting rod faces the injection pump side.

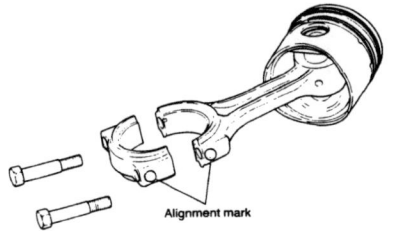

(3) Coat the pistons, liners and inside of the ring compressor with clean engine oil.
(4) Use the ring compressor to carefully install the piston into the liner.

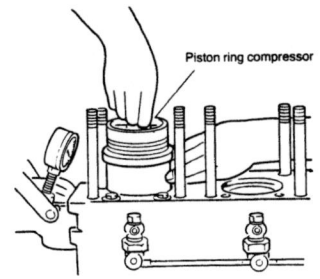

# 5. Connecting Rod

## 5-1 Connecting rod ass'y construction

The connecting rod connects the piston pin and crank pin and transmits the explosive force of the piston to the crankshaft. It is stamp forged for extreme lightness and ample strength against bending. A kelmet bushing split at right angles is installed at the large end of the rod, and a round copper alloy is pressed onto the small end.

Pass a test bar through the large end and small end holes of the connecting rod, place the bars on a V-block on a stool and center the large end test bar. Then set the sensor of a dial indicator against the small end test bar and measure twist and parallelism. When the measured value exceeds the wear limit, replace the connecting rod. Twisting and poor parallelism will cause uneven contact of the piston and bushing and shifting of the piston rings, resulting in compression leakage.

Connecting rod twist and parallelism                              mm (in.)

| | |
|---|---|
| Maintenance standard | 0.03/100 or less (0.00118/3.937) |
| Wear limit | 0.08/100 (0.00315/3.937) |

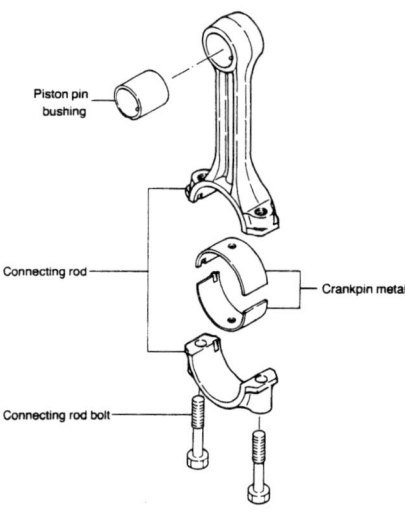

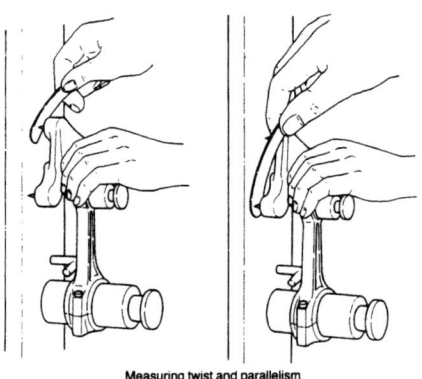

Measuring twist and parallelism

## 5-2 Inspection

### 5-2.1 Large and small end twist and parallelism

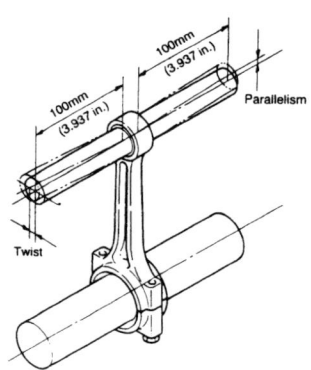

## 5.3 Crank pin bushing

Since the crank pin bushing slides when it receives load from the piston, an easy-to-replace kelmet bushing with a wear-resistant overlay is used.

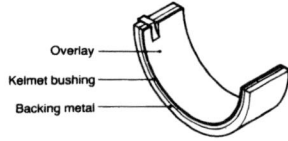

## Chapter 2 Basic Engine
## 5. Connecting Rod

### 5-3.1 Crank pin bushing inside diameter

Tighten the large end of the connecting rod to the prescribed torque with the connecting rod bolts, and measure the inside diameter of the crank pin bushing. Replace the bushing if the inside diameter or the clearance at the crank pin part exceed the wear limit.

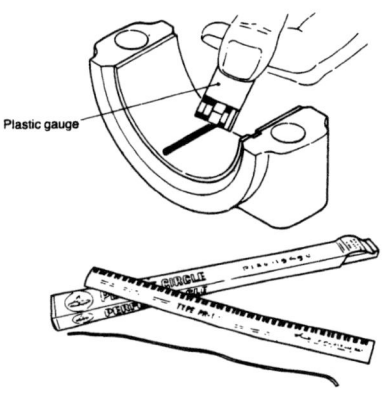
Plastic gauge

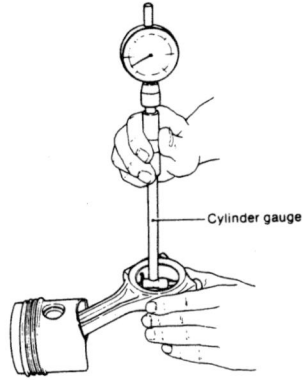
Cylinder gauge

mm (in.)

|  | Maintenance standard | Wear limit |
|---|---|---|
| Crank pin bushing inside diameter | Ø62.00 ~ 62.045 (Ø2.4409 ~ 2.4427) | Ø62.12 (Ø2.4457) |
| Crank pin and bushing oil clearance | 0.036 ~ 0.095 (0.00142~0.00374) | 0.2 (0.0079) |
| Connecting rod bolt tightening torque | 10 kg-m (72.41 ft-lb) ||

NOTE: The crank pin bushing inside diameter must always be measured with the connecting rod bolts tightened to the prescribed torque.

### 5-3.2 Crank pin and bushing clearance (oil clearance)

Since the oil clearance affects both the durability of the bushing and lubricating oil pressure, it must always be the prescribed value. Replace the bushing when the oil clearance exceeds the wear limit.

(1) Measurement
1) Thoroughly clean the inside surface and crank pin section of the crank pin bushing.
2) Install the connecting rod on the crank pin section of the crankshaft and simultaneously fit a plastic gauge on the inside surface of the crank pin bearing.
3) Tighten the connecting rod bolt to the prescribed tightening torque.
   Connecting rod tightening torque: 10.0kg-m (72.41 lb-ft)
4) Loosen the connecting rod bolt and slowly remove the connecting rod big end cap, then measure the crushed plastic gauge with a gauge.
5) The crank pin and bushing clearance (oil clearance) may also be measured with a micrometer, in addition to measurement with a plastic gauge. This method is used to measure the outside diameter of the crankshaft crank pin section and the inside diameter of the connecting rod's big end bushing, when the connecting rod bolt has been tightened to the prescribed torque and the difference between the large end bushing inside diameter and crank pin outside diameter is set as the oil clearance.
6) Under size bushing

(2) Measurement precautions
1) Be careful that the plastic gauge does not enter the crank pin oil hole.
2) Be sure that the crankshaft does not turn when tightening the connecting rod bolt.

2-24

Chapter 2 Basic Engine
5. Connecting Rod
_____ TM

**5-3.3 Crank pin bushing replacement precautions**

(1) Thoroughly clean the crank pin bushing and the rear of the crank pin bushing.
(2) Also clean the big end cap, install the crank pin bushing and check that the bushing contacts the big end cap snugly.
(3) When assembling the connecting rod, match the numbers of the big end section and the big end cap, coat the bolts with engine oil, and alternately tighten the bolts gradually to the prescribed tightening torque. If a torque wrench is not available, put matching marks (torque indication lines) on the bolt head and big end cap before disassembly and tighten the bolts until the two are aligned.

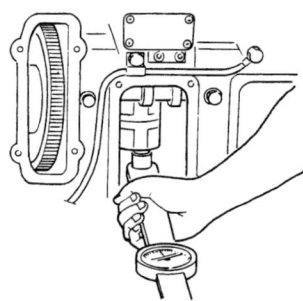

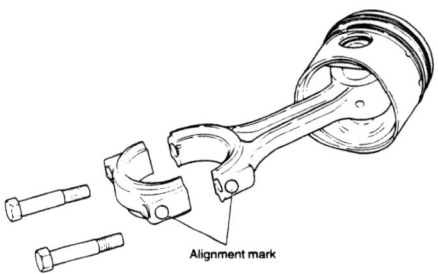

Alignment mark

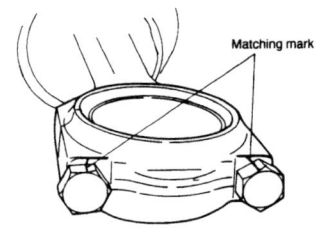

Matching mark

(4) Check that there are no sand or metal particles in the lubricating oil and that the crankshaft is not pitted. Clean the oil holes with particular care.

**5-4 Tightening the connecting rod bolts**

When tightening the connecting rod bolts, coat the threads of the bolts with engine oil.
Gradually tighten the two bolts alternately to the prescribed tightening torque. If a torque wrench is not available, make matching marks (torque indication lines) on the head of the bolt and the big end cap and tighten the bolts until these two marks are aligned.
Connecting rod tightening torque: 10.0 kg-m (72.41 lb-ft)

**5-5 Connecting rod side clearance**

After installing the connecting rod on the crankshaft, push the rod to one side and measure the side clearance by inserting a feeler gauge into the gap produced at the other side.
In this case, the connecting rod bolts must also be tightened to the prescribed tightening torque.

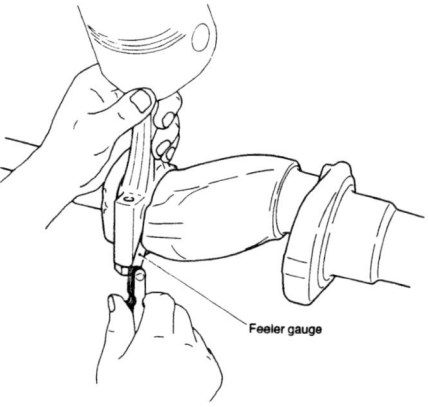

Feeler gauge

mm (in.)

| | Maintenance standard | Wear limit |
|---|---|---|
| Connecting rod side clearance | 0.15 ~ 0.35 (0.0059 ~ 0.0138) | 0.5 (0.0197) |

# 6. Crankshaft

### 6-1 Crankshaft ass'y and bearing construction

The crankshaft is stamp-forged, and the crank pin and journal sections are high-frequency induction hardened and ground and polished to a high precision finish.
The contact surface with the bushing is excellent and durability is superb.
The crankshaft is a balance weight integral type. Engine imbalance, which causes vibration, has been minimized by balancing the V-pulley, flywheel, and crankshaft.

The crankshaft main bearing is of the hanger type, with the upper metal (cylinder block side) provided with an oil groove, and no oil groove on the lower metal (bearing cap side). The bearing cap (location cap) of the flywheel side has a thrust metal which supports the thrust load.

Model: 4TM

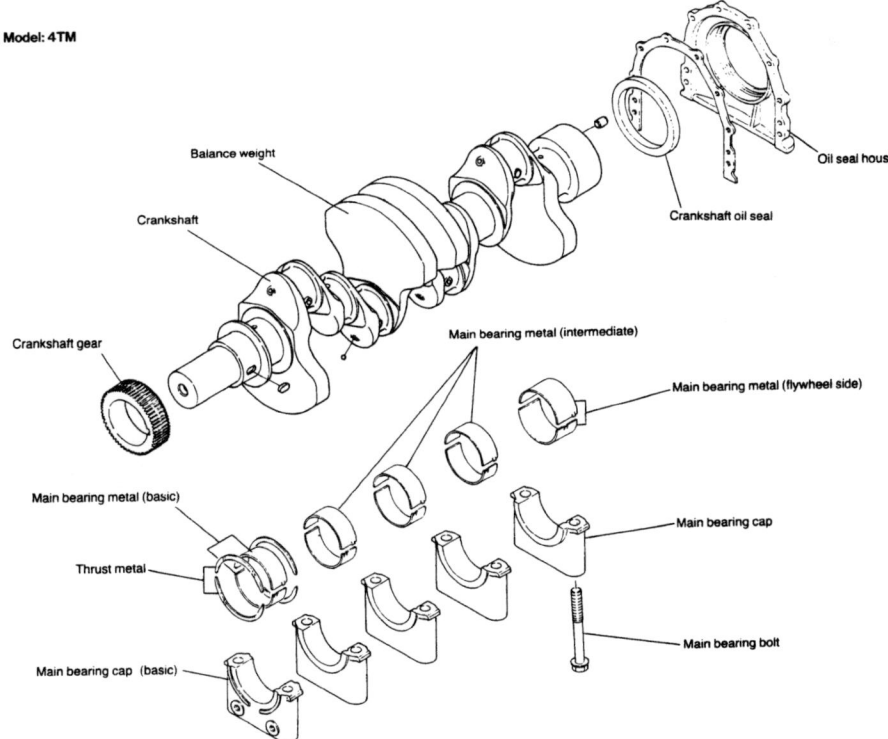

## Chapter 2 Basic Engine
## 6. Crankshaft

### 6-2 Inspection
#### 6-2.1 Crank journal and crank pin

(1) Cracking

If cracking of the crank journal or crank pin is suspected, thoroughly clean the crankshaft and perform a color check on the shaft, or run a candle flame over the crankshaft and look for oil seepage from cracks. If any cracks are detected, replace the crankshaft.

(2) Crank pin and crank journal outside diameter measurement.

When the difference between the maximum wear and minimum wear of each bearing section exceeds the wear limit, replace the crankshaft. Also check each bearing section for scoring. If the scoring is light, repair it with emery cloth.

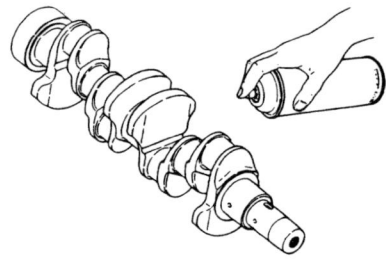

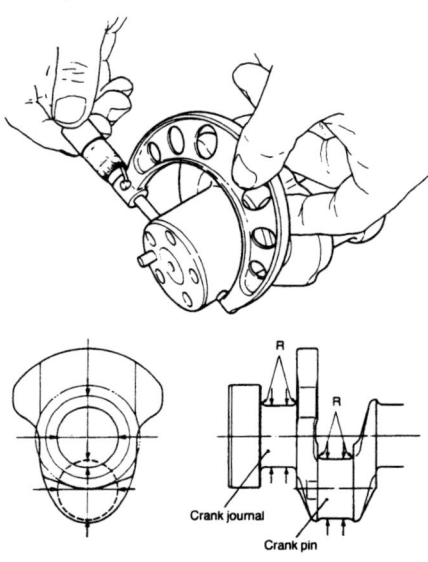

mm (in.)

|  |  | Standard | Wear limit |
|---|---|---|---|
| Crank pin | Outside dia. | Ø61.950~61.964  (Ø2.4390~2.4395) | Ø61.90 (Ø2.4370) |
|  | Bushing inside dia. | Ø62.00~62.045  (Ø2.4409~2.4427) | Ø62.12 (Ø2.4457) |
|  | Crank pin and bushing oil clearance | 0.036~0.095  (0.0014~0.0037) | 0.2 (0.0079) |
| Crank journal | Outside dia. | Ø70.950~70.964  (Ø2.7935~2.7939) | Ø70.90 (Ø2.7913) |
|  | Bushing inside dia. | Ø70.00~70.045  (Ø2.7559~2.7577) | Ø70.117 (Ø2.7605) |
|  | Crank journal and bushing oil clearance | 0.036~0.095  (0.0014~0.0037) | 0.2 (0.0079) |

## Chapter 2 Basic Engine
### 6. Crankshaft

(3) Bending of the crankshaft

Support the crankshaft with V-blocks at both ends of the journals. Measure the deflection of the center journal with a dial gauge while rotating the crankshaft to check the extent of crankshaft bending.

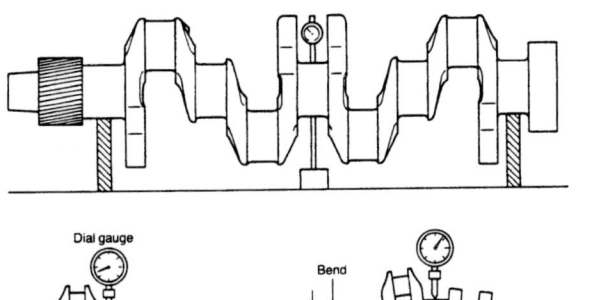

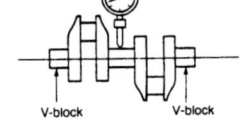

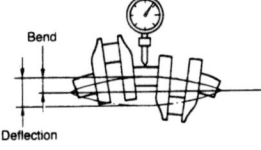

| Crankshaft bend | Less than 0.02mm (0.0007 in.) |
|---|---|

### 6-2.2 Side gap

Checking side clearance of the crankshaft

After assembling the crankshaft, tighten the main bearing cap to the specified torque, and move the crankshaft to one side, placing a dial gauge on one end of the shaft to measure thrust clearance.

This measurement can also be effected by inserting the gauge directly into the clearance between the thrust bearing and crankshaft thrust surface.

Replace the thrust bearing if it is worn beyond the limit.

mm (in.)

|  | Standard | Wear limit |
|---|---|---|
| Crankshaft side gap | 0.12 ~ 0.21 (0.0047 ~ 0.0083) | 0.28 (0.0110) |

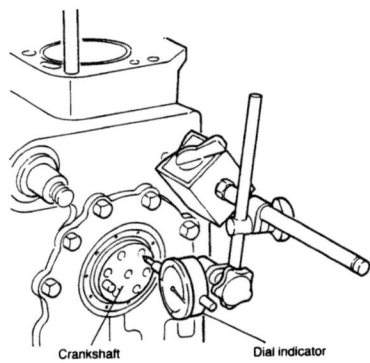

## 6-2.3 Main bearings

(1) Inspecting the main bearing
Check for flaking, seizure or burning of the contact surface and replace if necessary.

(2) Measuring the inner diameter of the metal
Tighten the cap to the specified torque and measure the inner diameter of the metal.

| Bearing cap bolt tightening torque | 19 ~ 21 kg-m (137.42 ~ 151.68 ft-lb) |
|---|---|

NOTE: When assembling the bearing cap, keep the following in mind.
1) The lower metal (cap side) has no oil groove.
2) The upper metal (cylinder block side) has an oil groove.
3) Check the cylinder block alignment No.
4) The "FW" on the cap lies on the flywheel side.

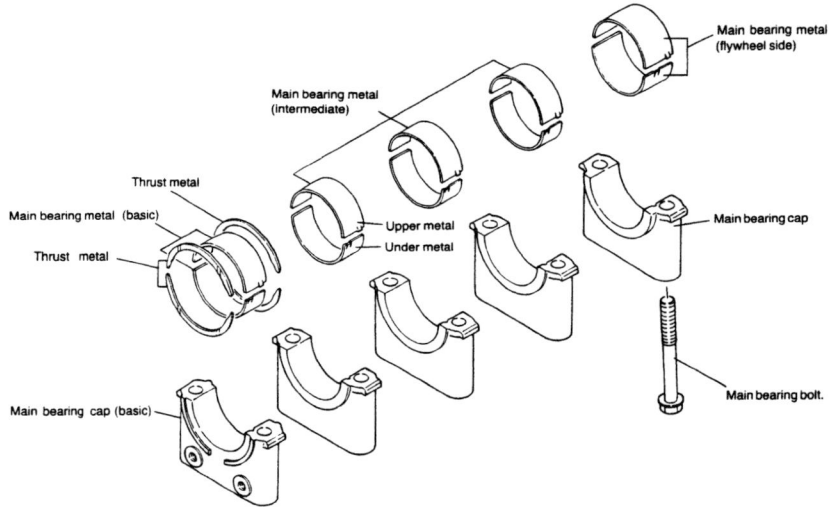

(3) Underside bearing
Listed specifications below are available.

| | |
|---|---|
| Main Bearing | 0.25 u.s. |
| | 0.50 u.s. |
| Main Bearing | 0.25 u.s. |
| | 0.50 u.s. |
| Main Bearing | 0.25 u.s. |
| | 0.50 u.s. |
| Thrust Metal | 0.25 u.s. |
| | 0.50 u.s. |

## 6-3 Rear oil seal

### 6-3.1 Inspection

Check the rear oil seal for damage, and replace as necessary

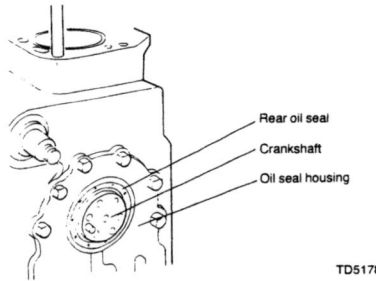

### 6-3.2 Replacement

(1) Remove the eight cap screws and the oil seal housing from the cylinder block.
(2) Remove the oil seal with a pry bar.

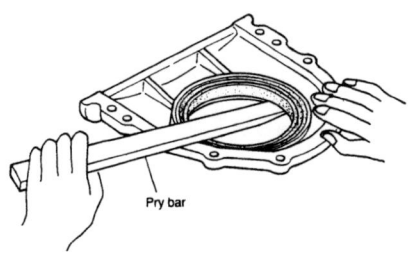

(3) Clean the oil seal seating area, and install a new oil seal into the housing.
(4) Be sure that the insertion direction of the oil seal is correct. Insert so that the main lip mounting the spring is on the inside (oil side).

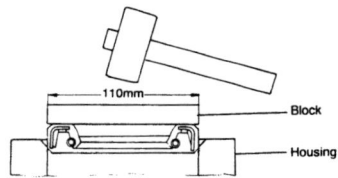

(5) Never tap the oil seal directly as in the diagram below.

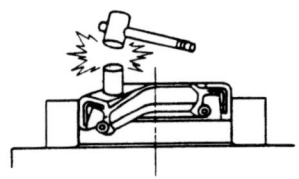

(6) Install the oil seal housing and tighten the cap screws to 2.6 kg-m (18.8 ft-lb)

### 6-4 Crankshaft installation precautions

When installing the crankshaft, align the timing marks on the crankshaft gear and camshaft gear

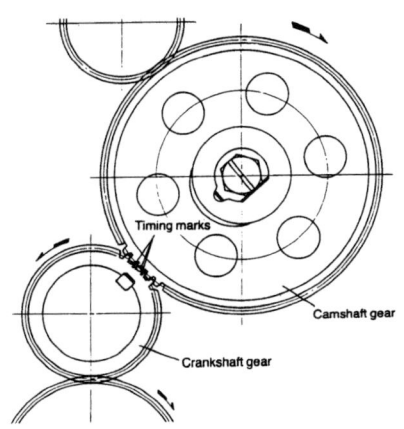

# 7. Camshaft

## 7-1 Camshaft construction

The camshaft, an integral camshaft with intake and exhaust cams, is driven by the camshaft gear and may be timed individually.

A tappet is mounted on top of the intake and exhaust cams. The tappet moves up and down with the rotation of the cam and opens and closes the intake and exhaust valves with the pushrod and rocker arm.

During high speed operation the cam surface is exposed to a strong inertial force from the moving valves and spring load, and comes in contact with the tappet at high surface pressure.

Therefore, to reduce wear the surface is tempered by high frequency hardening, and the cam form selected to decrease the force of inertia. Since the intake and exhaust cam profile of this engine is that of a parabolic acceleration cam with a buffering curve, movement of the valve at high speed is smooth, and this improves the durability of the intake and exhaust valve seats.

Also, the fuel injection pump roller tappet from the cylinder side comes into contact with the fuel cam and moves the fuel injection pump plunger. A fuel cam is provided between the intake and exhaust cams for each cylinder.

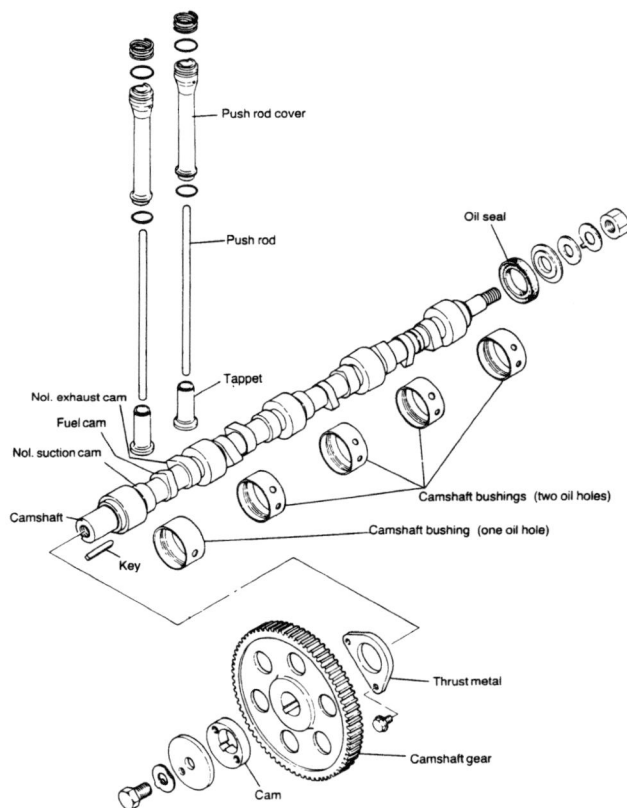

## Chapter 2 Basic Engine
## 7. Camshaft

### 7-2 Checking the camshaft side gap

The load is received by the standard bearing near the end of the camshaft, causing rapid wear of the end of the bearing and enlargement of the side gap. Therefore, measure the thrust gap before disassembly. As the cam gear is shrink-fitted to the cam, be careful when replacing the thrust bearing.

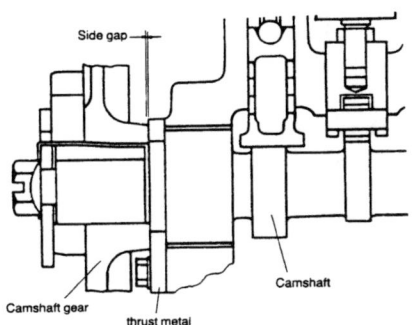

| | Standard | Wear limit |
|---|---|---|
| Camshaft side gap | 0.05 ~ 0.20<br>(0.0019 ~ 0.0079) | 0.3<br>(0.012) |

mm (in.)

### 7-3 Valve curve

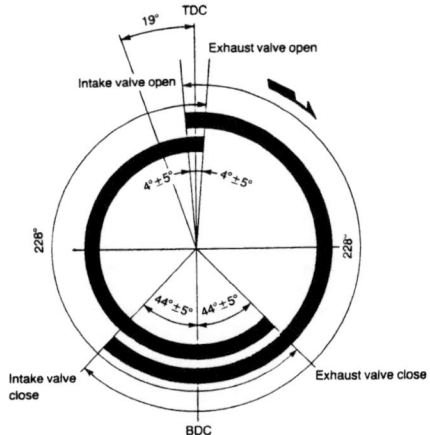

| | 0.22 ~ 0.28mm<br>(0.0087~0.0110 in.) |
|---|---|
| Intake and exhaust valve head clearance | |
| Intake valve open b. TDC | 4°±5° |
| Intake valve close a. BDC | 44°±5° |
| Exhaust valve open b. BDC | 44°±5° |
| Exhaust valve close a. TDC | 4°±5° |

### 7-4 Inspection

#### 7-4.1 Cam height

(1) Since the cam surface is tempered and ground, there is almost no wear. However, measure the height of the intake and exhaust cams, and replace the camshaft when the measured value exceeds the wear limit.

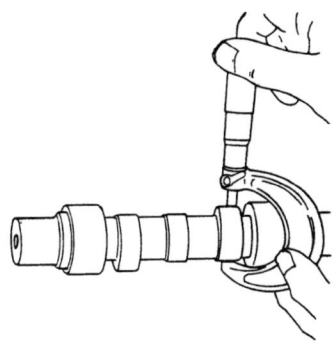

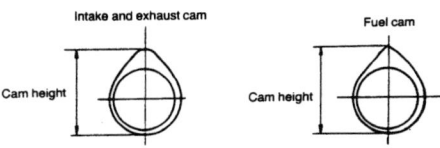

mm (in.)

| | | Maintenance standard | Wear limit |
|---|---|---|---|
| Camshaft height | Intake and exhaust cam | 42.47~42.53<br>(1.6720~1.6744) | 42.4<br>(1.669) |
| | Fuel cam | 39.47~39.53<br>(1.5539~1.5563) | 39.4<br>(1.551) |
| Camshaft side clearance | | 0 | — |

#### 7-4.2 Camshaft journals and bearings

Measure the outside diameter of the journals and the inside diameter of the bearings, and replace the bearings as necessary.

mm (in.)

| Item | Maintenance standard | Maximum allowable clealance |
|---|---|---|
| Camshaft journals O.D. (all) | 49.950 ~ 49.975<br>(1.9665 ~ 1.9675) | — |
| Bearings I.D. (all) (after installation) | 50.020 ~ 50.090<br>(1.9693 ~ 1.9720) | — |
| Oil clearance | 0.045 ~ 0.140<br>(0.0018 ~ 0.0055) | 0.25<br>(0.0098) |

## Chapter 2 Basic Engine
## 7. Camshaft

### 7-4.3 Bending of the camshaft

Support both ends of the camshaft with V-blocks, place a dial gauge against the central bearing areas and measure bending. Replace if excessive.

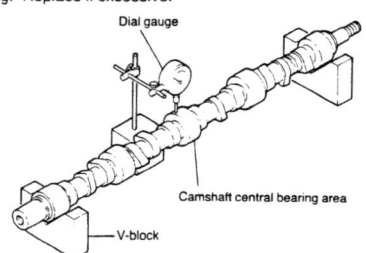

NOTE: The reading on the dial gauge is divided by two to obtain the extent of bending.

mm (in.)

|  | Wear limit |
|---|---|
| Camshaft deflection | 0.02 (0.0007) |

### 7-5 Tappets

These mushroom type tappets feature a special iron casting with chill-hardened contact surfaces for high wear resistance. The center of the cam surface width and the center of the tappet are offset to prevent eccentric wear of the contact surface.

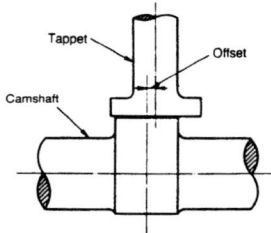

#### 7-5.1 Tappet disassembly precautions

The cylinder number and intake and exhaust must be clearly indicated when disassembling the camshaft and tappets.

#### 7-5.2 Tappet stem wear and contact

Measure the outside diameter of the tappet stem, and replace the tappet when the wear limit is exceeded or contact is uneven.

mm (in.)

| | | |
|---|---|---|
| Tappet stem outside diameter | ⌀19.94 ~ 19.96 (⌀0.7850~0.7858) | — |
| Guide hole inside diameter | ⌀20.00 ~ 20.02 (⌀0.7874~0.7882) | — |
| Tappet stem and guide hole clearance | 0.04 ~ 0.08 (0.0016 ~ 0.0031) | 0.17 (0.0067) |

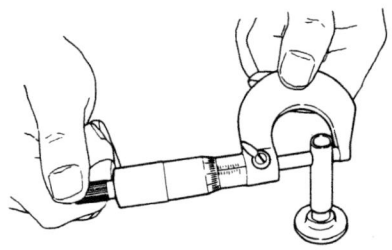

#### 7-5.3 Tappet and cam contact surface

Since the tappet and cam are offset, the tappet rotates in an up and down movement during operation, so there is no uneven contact.
Since eccentric wear will occur if the cam tappet contact is poor, replace the tappet if there is any uneven contact or deformation.

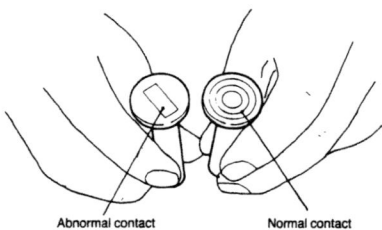

Contact surface conditions are shown in the following:

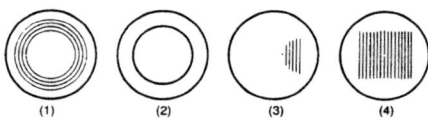

*(1), (2)* Traces when the tappet is rotating normally.
*(3), (4)* Traces when the tappet does not rotate, the contact surface remains still and only the point of contact wears away excessively. Discover the reason for the lack of rotation and replace the tappet.

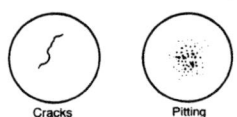

Also, there may be perforated pittings or cracks on the contact surface of the tappet. In such cases, discover the reason for the abnormality and replace the tappet.

## 7-6 Push rods

The push rods are sufficiently rigid and strong to prevent bending.
Place the push rod on a stool or flat surface, measure the clearance between the center of the push rod and the flat surface, and replace the push rod if the wear limit is exceeded.

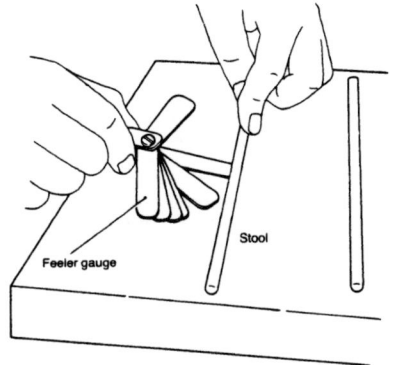

Check both ends for wear and peeling, and replace the push rod if faulty.

mm (in.)

|  | Standard | Wear limit |
|---|---|---|
| Push rod length | 258 ~ 260 (10.157 ~ 10.236) | — |
| Push rod bend | Less than 0.03 (0.0011) | 0.1 (0.0039) |
| Push rod dia. | Ø8.88 ~ 9.12 (Ø0.3496 ~ 0.3591) | — |

## 7-7 Push rod cover installation

Install the push-rod guide with the diamond mark facing forward.

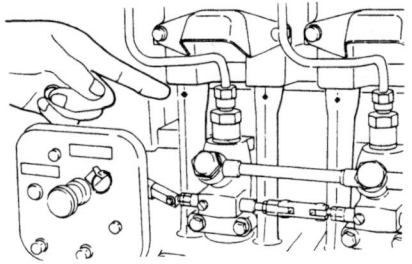

## 7-8 Oil seal

Check the camshaft oil seal for damage, and replace as necessary.

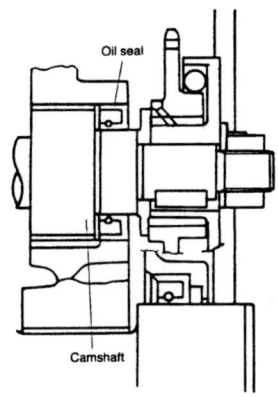

## 7-9 Camshaft installation precautions

When installing the camshaft, align the timing marks on the crankshaft and camshaft gears.

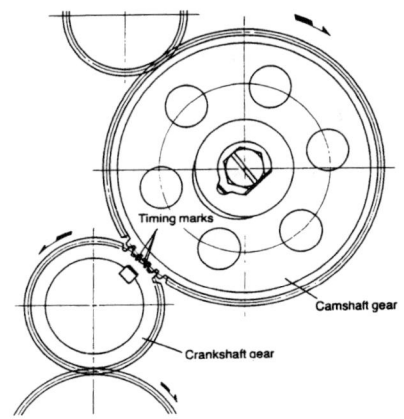

# 8. Timing Gears

The timing gears are used to spur the gear and are specially treated for high durability.

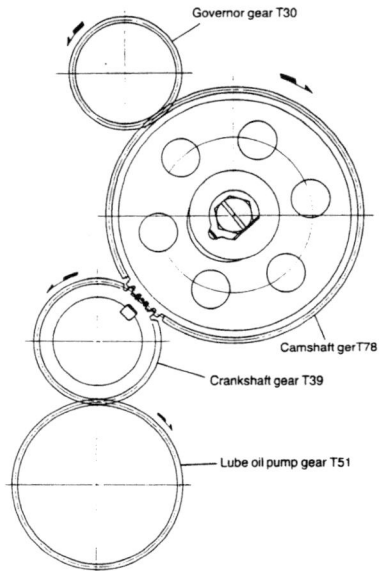

Governor gear T30
Camshaft ger T78
Crankshaft gear T39
Lube oil pump gear T51

## 8-1 Inspection

Inspect the gears and replace if the teeth are damaged or worn.

### 8-1.1 Inspecting the gear tooth surface

Check the tooth surface for damage caused by pitching and check tooth contact. Repair if the damage is light. Also inpect the gears for cracking and corrosion.
When gear noise becomes high because of wear or damage, replace the gears as a set.

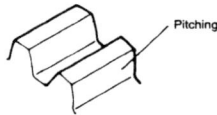

Pitching

### 8-1.2 Inspecting the gear boss

Check for play between each gear and the gear shaft, burning caused by play, key damage, and for cracking at the edge of the key groove. Replace the gears when faulty.

### 8-1.3 Measuring gear backlash

Unsuitable backlash will cause excessive wear or damage at the tooth tops and abnormal noise during operation. Moreover, in extreme cases, the valve and fuel injection timing will deviate and the engine will not run smoothly.
When the backlash exceeds the wear limit, repair or replace the gears as a set.

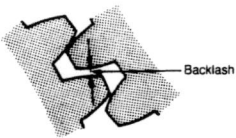

Backlash

(1) Lock one of the two gears to be measured and measure the amount of movement of the other gear by placing a dial gauge on the tooth surface.

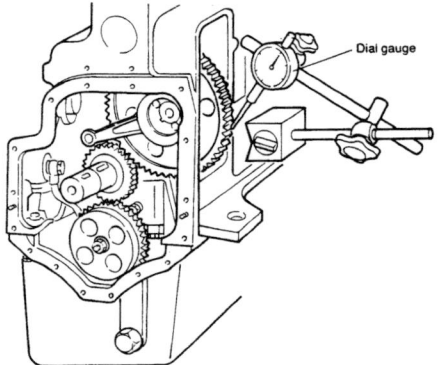

Dial gauge

mm (in.)

| Gears | Backlash |
|---|---|
| Lube oil pump gear | 0.08 ~ 0.16 (0.00315 ~ 0.00236) |
| Crankshaft gear | 0.08 ~ 0.16 (0.00315 ~ 0.00236) |
| Camshaft gear | |
| Governor gear | 0.08 ~ 0.16 (0.00315 ~ 0.00236) |

NOTE: If backlash is excessive, it will not only result in excessive noise and gear damage, but also lead to bad valve and fuel injection timing and a drop in engine performance.

# Chapter 2 Basic Engine
## 8. Timing Gears

### 8-2 Disassembly and reassembly precautions

Timing marks are provided on the crankshaft gear and camshaft gear to adjust the timing between opening and closing of the intake and exhaust valves and fuel injection when the piston is operated.
Always check that these timing marks are aligned when disassembling and reassembling the timing gear.

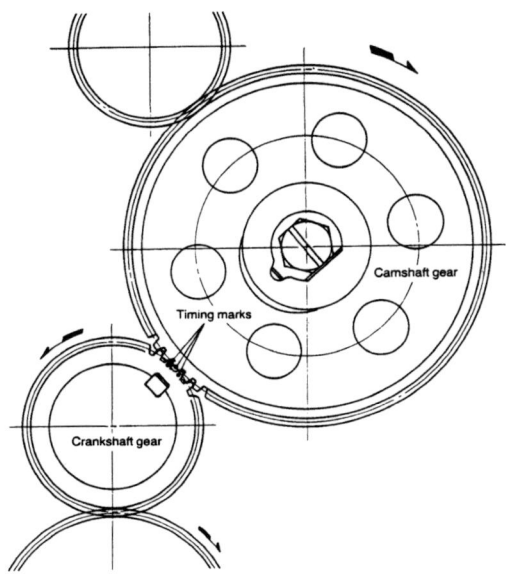

# 9. Flywheel and Housing

The function of the flywheel is, through inertia, to rotate the crankshaft in a uniform and smooth manner. It absorbs the turning force created during the combustion stroke of the engine, and compensates for the decrease in turning force during the other strokes.

The flywheel is mounted and secured by 6 bolts on the crankshaft end at the opposite end to the gear case.

The flywheel's unbalanced force on the shaft center must be kept below the specified value for the crankshaft as the flywheel rotates with the crankshaft at high speed. To achieve this, the balance is adjusted by drilling holes in the side of the flywheel, and the unbalanced momentum is adjusted by drilling holes in the circumference.

A flywheel with a ring gear is used for electric starting.

The ring gear is shrink fitted onto the circumference of the flywheel, and this ring gear serves to start the engine by meshing with the starter motor pinion.

The stamped letter and line which indicate top dead center of each cylinder are positioned on the flywheel circumference, and by matching these marks with the arrow mark at the hole of the flywheel housing, the rotary position of the crankshaft can be ascertained in order to adjust tappet clearance or fuel injection timimg.

## 9-1 Specifications

|  | Chain starting | Electric starting |
|---|---|---|
| Flywheel outside dia. | 460mm (18.11 in.) | 465 mm (18.31 in.) [460mm (18.11 in.) without ring gear] |
| Flywheel width | 85 mm (3.35 in.) | 85mm (3.35 in.) attaching righ gear |
| Flywheel weight | 53.4 kg (117.5 lb) | 53.4 kg (117.5 lb) attaching ring gear |
| Ring gear center dia. | — | 459 mm (18.07 in.) |
| Number of ring gear teeth | — | 153 |

## 9-2 Top dead center position and fuel injection timing

(1) Marking

1) 2TM, 4TM

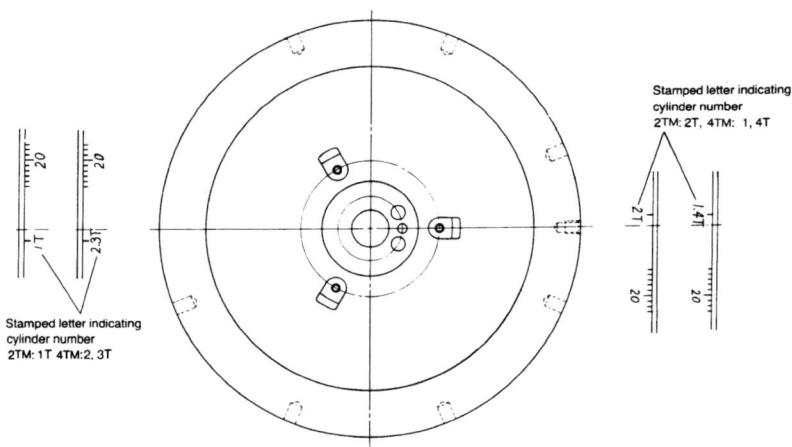

## Chapter 2 Basic Engine
### 9. Flywheel and Housing

2) 3TM

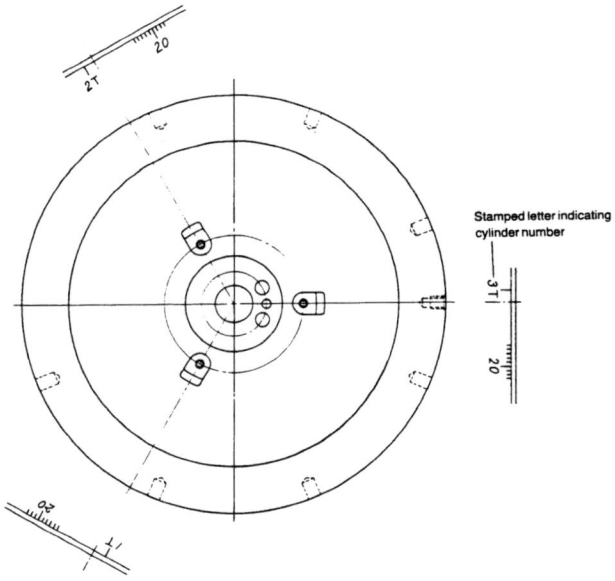

(2) Matching mark

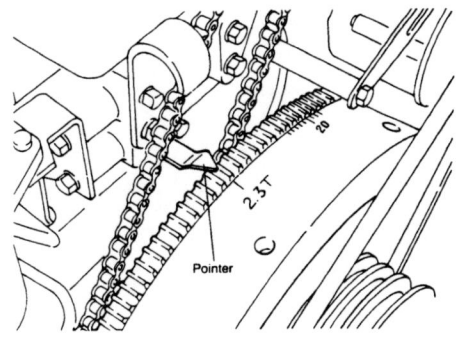

## Chapter 2 Basic Engine
## 9. Flywheel and Housing

### 9-3 Removal and Installation of flywheel
#### 9-3.1 Removal
Remove the flyweel mounting bolts and then the flywheel.

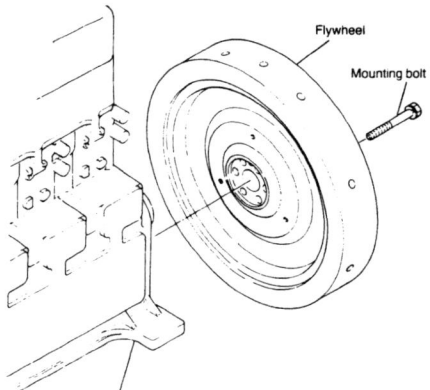

#### 9-3.2 Installation
(1) Coat the flywheel mounting bolt threads with engine oil.
(2) Align the positioning pin with the pin hole, and tighten the flywheel bolts to the specified torque.

| Flywheel mounting bolt tightening torque | 19 ~ 21 kg-m (135.4 ~ 151.8 ft-lb) |
|---|---|

### 9-4 Ring gear (electrical starting)
When replacing the ring gear due to excessive wear or damaged teeth, heat the ring gear evenly at its circumference, and after it has expanded drive it gradually off the flywheel by tapping it with a hammer, copper bar or some similar tool around the whole circumference.

mm (in.)

| Interference of ring gear | 0.158 ~ 0.250 (0.0062 ~ 0.0098) |
|---|---|

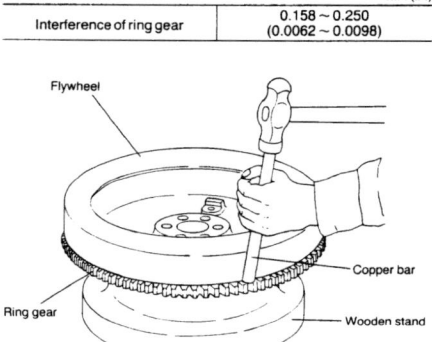

## CHAPTER 3
# FUEL SYSTEM

1. Fuel Supply System ............................................................. 3-1
2. Injection Pump ................................................................... 3-3
3. Governor and Linkage ......................................................... 3-9
4. Fuel Injection Nozzle .......................................................... 3-13
5. Fuel Feed Pump ................................................................ 3-17
6. Fuel Filter ......................................................................... 3-18
7. Water Separator ................................................................ 3-21
8. Fuel Tank (Option) ............................................................. 3-22

## 1. Fuel Supply System

The fuel oil system consists of the fuel injection pump, fuel injection pipe, fuel injection nozzle, fuel filter, oil/water separator, fuel tank, fuel feed pump, and their accessory parts. The fuel injection pump is driven by the fuel cam of the cam shaft, and is controlled by the governor.

Dirt and other impurities in the fuel are removed by the filter and the clean fuel is sent to the injection pump, which applies the necessary pressure for injection nozzle and atomizes the fuel by passing it through the injection nozzle. A governor in the injection pump also controls the amount of fuel injected and the injection timing according to the engine load and speed.

The injection pump feeds the fuel to the injection nozzle through a high pressure pipe. The pressurized fuel is atomized and injected by the injection nozzle into the combustion chamber.

Fuel that overflows the injection nozzle is returned to the fuel tank through the fuel return pipe. The quality of the equipment and parts comprising the fuel injection system directly affects combustion performance and has a considerable effect on engine performance. Therefore, this system must be inspected and serviced regularly to ensure top performance.

*Chapter 3 Fuel System*
*1. Fuel Supply System* _____ *TM*

**1-2 Fuel oil circuit**

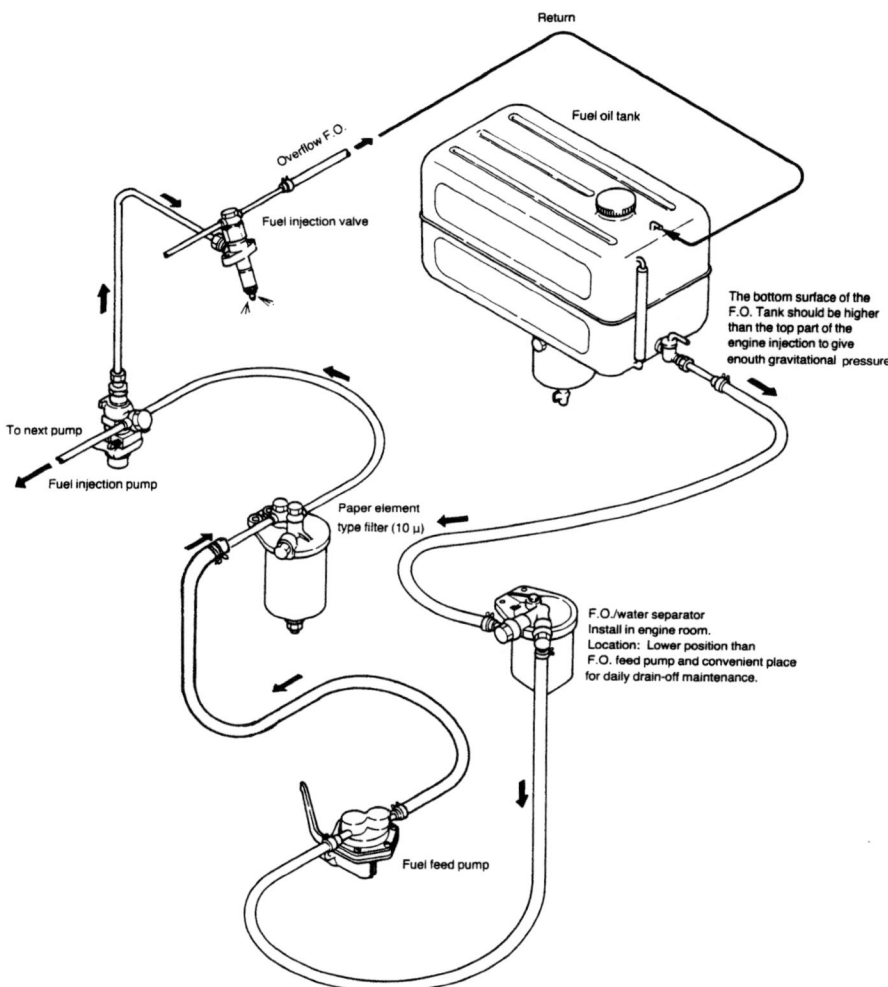

Note) Mount the F.O. tank so that the tank bottom is higher than the F.O. pump.

# 2. Injection Pump

## 2-1 Construction

The injection pump is the most important part of the fuel system. This pump feeds the proper amount of fuel to the engine at the proper time in accordance with the engine load.

In the TM series, a fuel injection pump is installed for each cylinder. i.e., two for 2TM, three for 3TM, and four pumps for 4TM. The injection pumps are geared and operated by the connecting rod which is installed at the end of the rack.

The pump is designed and manufactured by Yanmar, and is ideal for the fuel system of this engine.
Since the injection pump is subjected to extemely high pressures and must be accurate as well as deformation- and wear-free, stringently selected materials are used and precision finished after undergoing heat treatment.
The injection pump must be handled carefully. Since the delivery valve and delivery valve holder and the plunger and plunger barrel are lapped, these must be changed as pairs.
The fuel injection pump is constructed from the following main parts.
(1) Pump parts which compress and deliver the fuel: plunger, plunger barrel.
(2) Parts which move the plunger: camshaft, tappet, plunger spring, plunger spring retainer.
(3) Parts which control the injection amount: control rack, control pinion, control sleeve.
(4) Parts which prevent back flow and dripping during injection: delivery valve.

## 2-2 Specifications

| Type | |
|---|---|
| Injection pressure | 200 kg/cm$^2$ (2844 lb/in.$^2$) |
| Plunger diameter × stroke | ⌀9.5mm × 9.5mm (⌀0.3740 in. × 0.3740mm) |
| Delivery valve suction capacity | 51mm$^3$/st (0.031 in.$^3$/st) |
| Fuel injection limited volume at 1100 rpm | 51 ± 0.5mm$^3$/1000 st (0.031 ± 0.00003 in.$^3$/1000 st) |

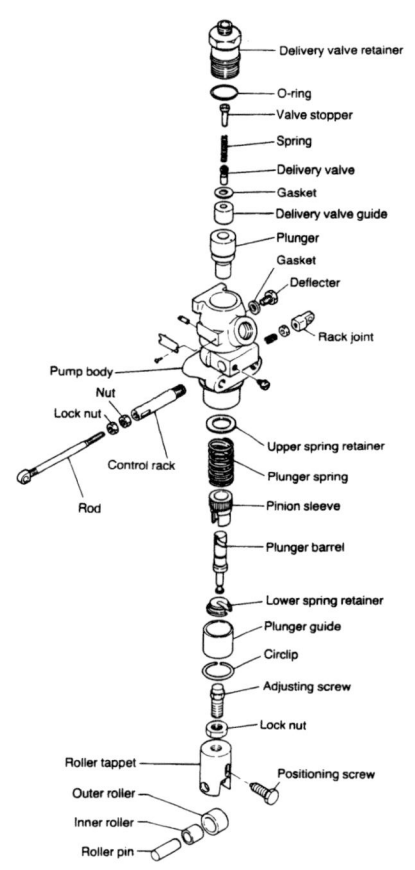

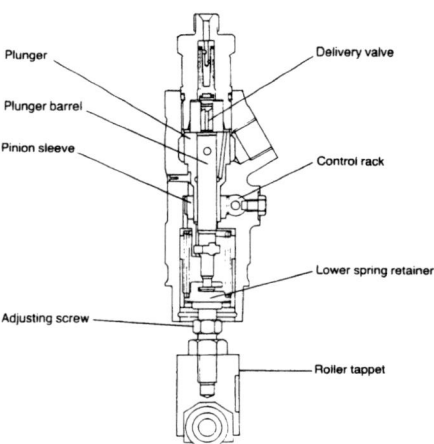

Chapter 3 Fuel System
2. Injection Pump

## 2-3 Operation principles
### 2-3.1 Plunger

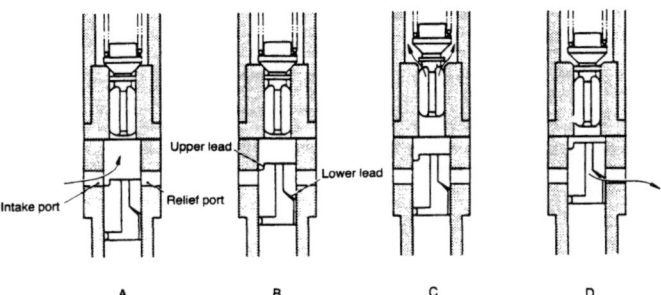

A. When the plunger reaches its lowest position (when the fuel cam reaches the base circle), the top and vertical grooves of the plunger are filled with fuel from the intake port.

B. When the plunger rises to the position at which the upper lead closes the intake port, the fuel begins to push the delivery valve upward.

C. As the plunger rises further, the delivery valve is pushed up and the fuel is sent through the delivery valve and high pressure pipe to the injection nozzle.

D. The plunger continues to rise until the lower lead closes the discharge port. At this point the fuel is discharged from the vertical groove through the relief port, the delivery valve is pushed back, and fuel feed is halted.

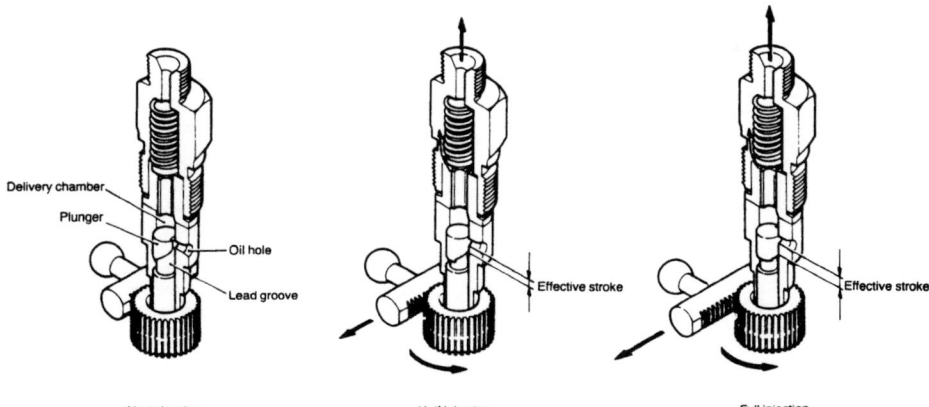

The amount of fuel and the injection timing are adjusted by rotation of the plunger with the control sleeve and by changing the relative positions of the upper lead, lower lead, and ports. In other words, the amount of fuel and the injection timing are adjusted by changes of the plunger stroke, from the closing of the intake port by the upper lead to the opening of the relief port by the lower lead.

NOTE: The plunger is an integral part of the plunger barrel and takes in and compresses fuel by reciprocating inside the plunger barrel. The plunger and plunger barrel are precisely machined, and because the plunger is driven in an extremely small space the two should be used together and should not be changed with other cylinders.

## Chapter 3 Fuel System
## 2. Injection Pump

### 2-3-2 Delivery valve

(1) Delivery valve fuel suction collar

The delivery valve of this engine is equipped with a piston (collar), as shown in the figure. This collar prevents injection cutting and dripping — caused by a lowering of the pressure inside the pipe. It sucks back the fuel in the high pressure pipe when the delivery valve drops at the end of the plunger stroke.

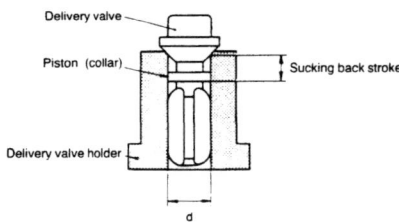

Amount of fuel sucked back: $\pi/4 \ d^2 \ell = 51.0 \ mm^3/stroke$
$(0.0031 \ in.^3/st.)$

(2) Operation of delivery valve

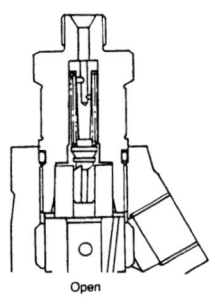

Open

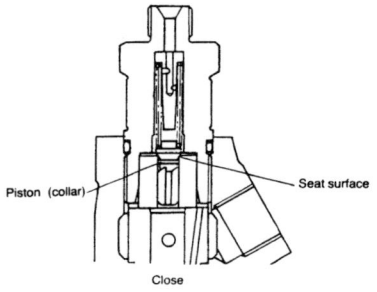

Close

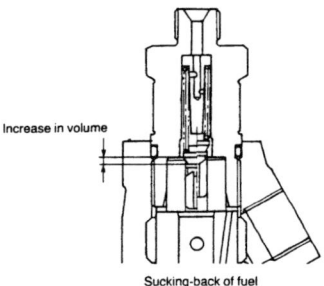

Increase in volume

Sucking-back of fuel

1) The delivery valve is pressed against the seat surface by the delivery valve spring. When fuel is pressurized by the rising of the plunger, the pressure forces open the valve and fuel is delivered to the injection pipe.
2) Next, after the plunger pressurizes and delivers the fuel, the pressure of the plunger side decreases and the valve is depressed by the spring.
   At the same time, the piston in the delivery valve also descends, lowering the hydraulic pressure inside the injection pipe and sucking back the fuel. This improves the disconnection of injection at the nozzle and prevents dripping.
3) The valve is depressed further, and when it rests on the seat surface, back flow of fuel on the plunger side is prevented and a fixed after-pressure is maintained.

### 2-4 Testing

#### 2-4-1 Measuring the fuel injection volume

(1) Fix the fuel injection pump to the pump tester, and deliver fuel to the pump after the adjusting rack is set at the increased injection volume side. Then measure the delivery pressure resistance.
The plunger of the pump is working normally if the reading on the pressure gauge indicates above 500 kg/cm²

(2) Next, discontinue the delivery action of the pump and check the pressure withstanding time, observing the pressure gauge. If the pressure withstanding time is extremely short, there is a malfunction in the delivery valve of the pump. If any part of the pump is found to be defective, the following disassembly and repairs are necessary.

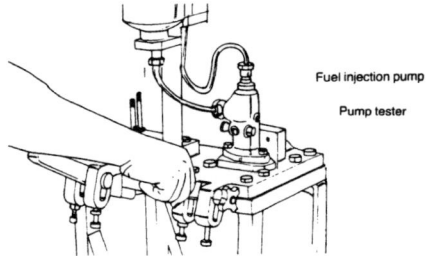

Fuel injection pump

Pump tester

## Chapter 3 Fuel System
## 2. Injection Pump

Fuel injection volume measuring conditions

| Nozzle | $5 - \phi 0.27$ |
|---|---|
| Nozzle holder | TM type |
| Injection pressure | $200 \text{kg/cm}^2 (2840 \text{ lb/in.}^2)$ |
| High pressure line | $\emptyset 1.8 \times 550$ mm |
| Used fuel | JIS No.2 |
| Feed pressure | $0.2 \text{kg/cm}^2 (2.84 \text{ lb/in.}^2)$ |

Fuel injection volume specifications

| Camshaft R.P.M. | 1100 rpm |
|---|---|
| Rack mark injection volume | 51cc/1000 st. |
| Allowable error between cylinders | ±0.5cc/1000 st. |

### 2-5 Disassembly

(1) Remove the delivery valve retainer with the valve stopper, and the spring, gasket, delivery valve, delivery valve guide and plunger barrel.
(2) Remove the circlip, plunger guide lower retainer, plunger, pinion sleeve, plunger spring and upper retainer.
(3) Remove the set screw and control rack.
(4) Remove the positioning screw and roller tappet ass'y from the engine.

### 2-6 Inspecting injection pump parts
#### 2-6.1 Plunger

(1) Inspect the plunger for wear, scoring and discoloration around the lead. If any problems are found, conduct a pressure test and replace the plunger and plunger barrel assembly.

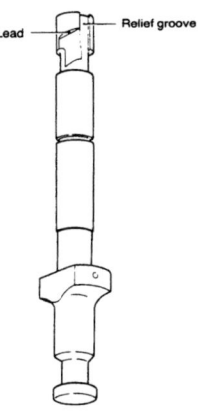

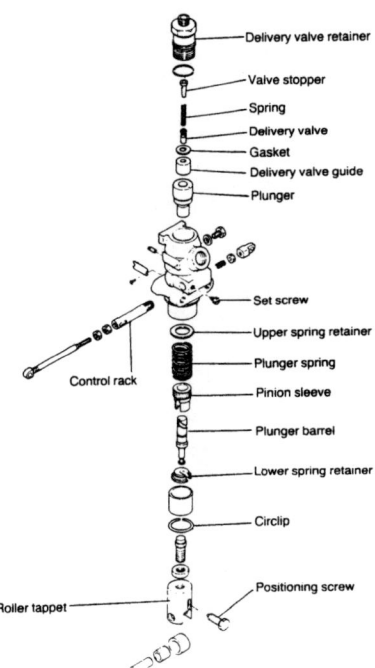

(2) Inspect the outside sliding surface of the plunger with a magnifying glass. Lap or replace the plunger and plunger barrel assembly when corrosion, hairline cracks, staining and/or scoring are detected.
(3) Check the clearance between the plunger collar and control sleeve groove. Replace these parts when wear exceeds the specified limit.
(4) After cleaning the plunger, tilt it approximately 60°, as shown in the figure, and slowly slide it down. Repeat this several times while rotating the plunger. The plunger should slide slowly and smoothly. If it slides too quickly, or binds along the way, repair or replace it.

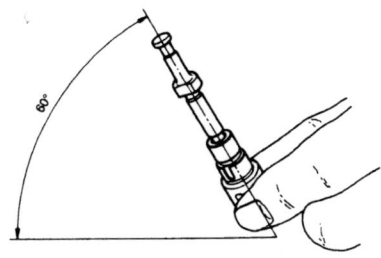

## Chapter 3 Fuel System
## 2. Injection Pump

### 2-6.2 Delivery valve

(1) Replace the delivery valve if the return collar and seat are scored, dented or worn.

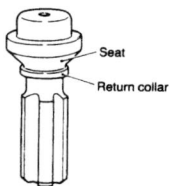

(2) After thoroughly washing the delivery valve, block the bottom of the valve seat with your finger, and push the valve lightly in the manner shown in the figure. Remove your finger. The valve should return. If it doesn't, the return collar is heavily worn and must be replaced.

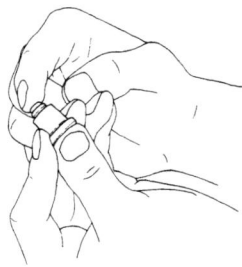

### 2-6.3 Plunger spring and delivery valve spring

Inspect the plunger spring and delivery valve spring for fractured coils, rust, inclination and permanent strain. Replace the spring when faulty.

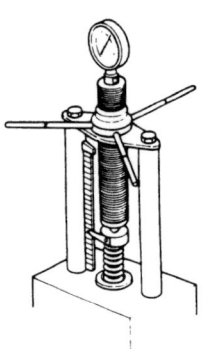

### 2-6.4 Plunger guide

Inspect the sliding face of the plunger guide for damage and wear. Replace the spring when faulty.

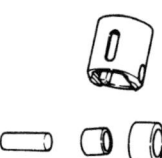

### 2-6.5 Tappet

Inspect the cam sliding surface of the tappet roller for wear, scoring and peeling; replace the tappet and roller assembly when the total tappet and roller play exceeds 0.2mm (0.0079 in.)

### 2-6.6 Control rack and pinion

If the control rack does not move smoothly when a force of within 60g is applied, replace the rack and pinion assembly.

### 2-7 Reassembly

It is very important to pay attention to handling the various parts of the fuel injection pump as they are precision machined and may not be scratched or scarred. Prior to reassembling them, be sure to wash them well in flushing oil, and particularly do not allow any dirt to enter the plunger and plunger barrel. It is recommended that lube oil be applied to these parts for rust prevention purposes.

Reverse the disassembly steps to reassemble the parts. Note the reassembly instructions below.

(1) Pay special attention to the copper gaskets between the delivery valve holder and the delivery valve spring holder, and the deflecter.
(2) When installing the pinion sleeve, align the matching marks on the pinion sleeve and the control rack.

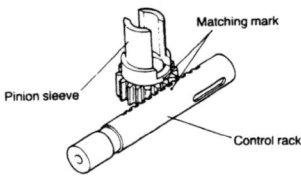

## Chapter 3 Fuel System
## 2. Injection Pump

(3) Align the matching marks when installing the plunger into the plunger barrel.

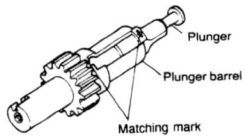

Plunger
Plunger barrel
Matching mark

### 2-8 Fuel injection timing adjustment

When deviation of the No.1, (and other cylinder), injection interval occurs at the pump, the injection timing of at least one of the pumps is incorrect. Therefore, the injection pump must be mounted on the engine, and the injection timing of each cylinder adjusted.

(1) Remove the high pressure pipe from the pump.
(2) Install a measuring pipe on the delivery valve spring holder.

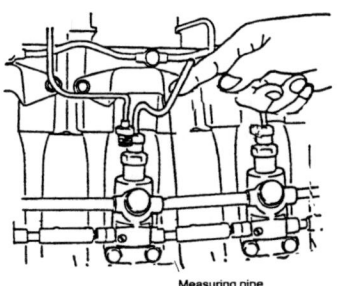

Measuring pipe

(3) Bleed the air from the injection pump.
(4) Fix the 1-point mark of the control rack on the A-side of the pump body.
(5) Turn the flywheel to the normal rotating direction.
(6) Check the angle on the flywheel at the moment when the fuel is discharged from the measuring pipe. (The proper angle is b.T.D.C 18 − 20 degrees).

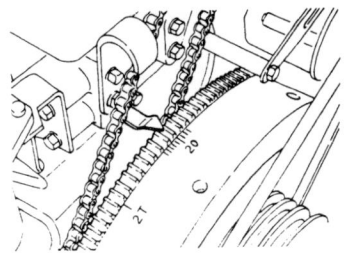

(7) Open the adjustment port at bottom of the fuel pump.
(8) Loosen the lock nut and turn the adjusting screw either clockwise to retard the timing or counter clockwise to advance the timing.
(9) After adjustment, tighten the lock nut.
(10) In the same manner, adjust the timing of the remaining injection pumps.

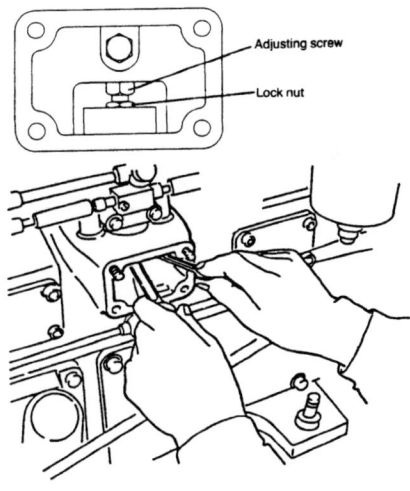

Adjusting screw
Lock nut

# 3. Governor and Linkage

## 3-1 Construction

The governor serves to keep the engine speed constant by automatically adjusting the amount of fuel supplied to the engine according to changes in the load. This protects the engine against sudden changes in load, such as sudden disengagement of the clutch, the propeller leaving the water in rough weather, or other cases where the engine is suddenly accelerated.

## 3-2 Operating principles

The positions of the three governor weights (open and closed) are regulated by the speed of the engine.

The centrifugal force of the governor weights pivots around the governor weight pin and is changed to axial force that acts on the sleeve. This force is transmitted to the governor lever and the lever shifts the fuel control rack to increase or decrease the fuel supply. The governor lever is stabilized at the point at which the force produced by the governor weight is balanced with the load of the regulator spring connecting the regulator and governor levers.

When the speed is reduced by application of a load, the force of the regulator spring pushes the governor sleeve in the "fuel increase" direction, stabilizing the engine speed by changing the position of the regulator lever

## 3-3 Disassembly

(1) Remove the regulator spring.
(2) Remove the link.
(3) Remove the governor cover together with the lever assembly.
(4) Loosen the governor positioning union, and remove the governor as an assembly. (You might feel this is rather too tight to remove, but it can be removed manually.)

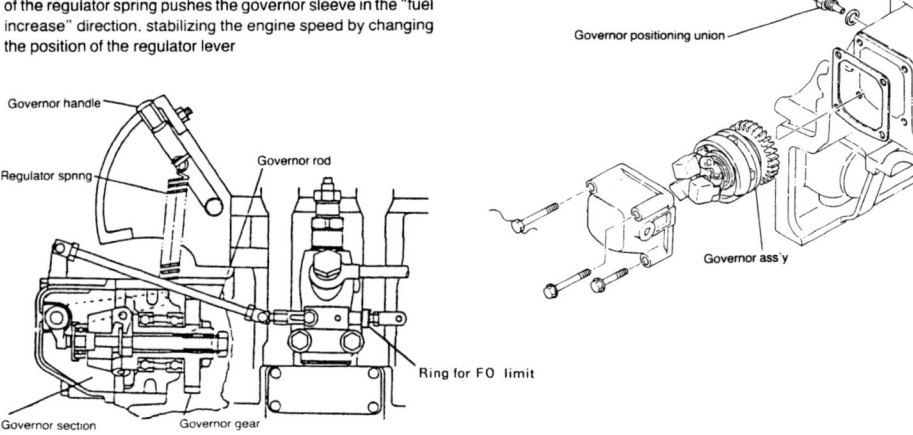

## 3-4 Inspection

### 3-4.1 Governor weight

Check contact with the sleeve and wear.

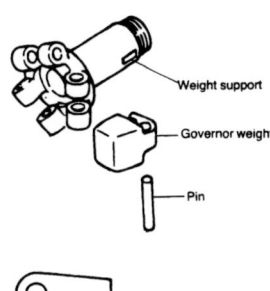

### 3-4.2 First lever and bearing retainer

Check the first lever contact with the bearing retainer for wear.

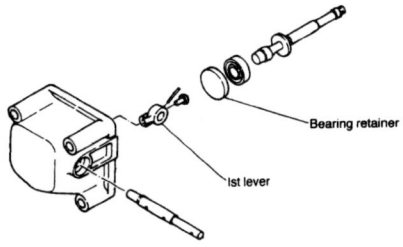

### 3-4.3 Regulator spring

Measure the free length and tension of the spring.

mm (in.)

| Regulator spring | Standard | Wear limit |
|---|---|---|
| Free length | 90 (3.54) | 91 (3.58) |
| Load when attached | 91 (3.58) | 92 (3.62) |

## 3-5 Reassembly

For reassembly, follow the disassembly procedures in reverse order. When inserting the governor assembly, in particular ensure that the governor gear and the cam shaft gear mesh with each other by controlling the union position, and then insert the governor.

# Chapter 3 Fuel System
## 1. Governor and Linkage

### 3-6 Adjustment
#### 3-6.1 Connecting links between cylinders

(1) Lower and raise the governor handle several times, and confirm that the fuel control rack easily shifts to right and left.

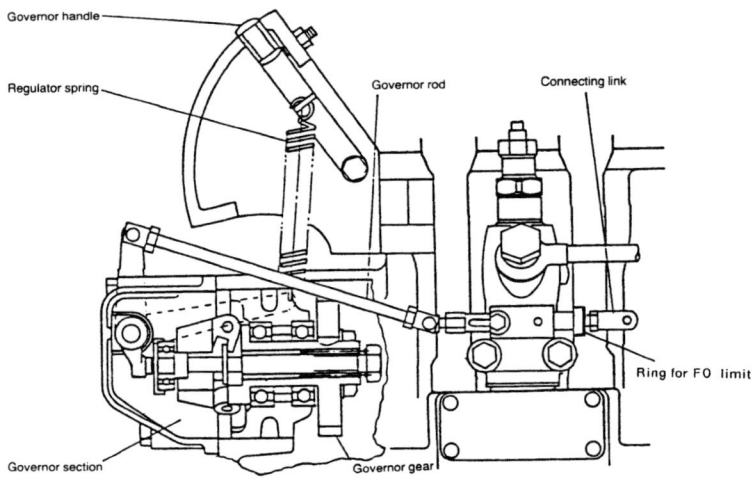

(2) Loosen the lock nut on the adjusting nut of the control rack for each cylinder so that identical adjusting nut lengths are retained for the rack and adjusting lever of the adjusting shaft control on all cylinders.

(3) Adjust the adjusting shaft so that the single point mark, engraved on each control rack matches with the A surface of the fuel injection pump for all such shafts, taking any one of the cylinders as a base, and then tighten the lock nut. In other words, adjust the connecting section of the governor so that the single mark engraved on each control rack comes to the A surface of each injection pump at the same time.

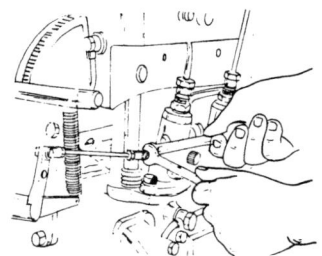

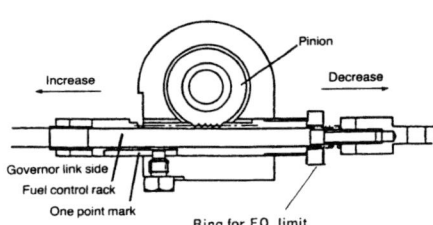

## Chapter 3 Fuel System
### 1. Governor and Linkage

(4) Set the governor handle to the full speed position.
(5) Loosen the lock nuts from the ends of the governor rod.
(6) Pull the fuel injection limiting pin from the fuel injection pump of each cylinder, and turn the governor rod until the left end of the control rack comes in contact with the adjusting nut, provided that the control rack is at the extreme left (or its single point mark aligns with the A surface of the injection pump body). At this position, tighten up the lock nuts of the governor rod. That is, when the governor handle is set at the full speed position, without pulling the limiting pin of the injection pump, push the governor link by hand to the right (or in the direction of decreased fuel injection). This will give a clearance of about 1mm between the left end of the control rack and the adjusting nut. Then pull the limiting pin, which will shift the control rack to the left side, narrowing the clearance. The adjustment is completed when this clearance reaches zero.

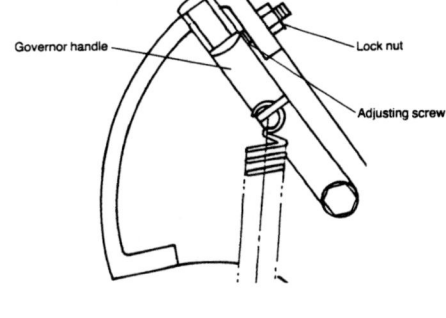

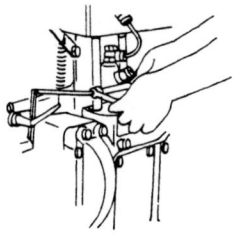

NOTE: *When the control rack is moved to the extreme left by pulling the limiting pin, the fuel injection volume limiting ring must be so adjusted and set that the A surface of the injection pump and the single-point mark of the adjusting rack are aligned.*

#### 3-6.2 Maximum idling speed

(1) Start the engine and place the clutch lever in neutral.
(2) Fully raise the governor handle.
(3) Measure the engine R.P.M. and compare the readings with the specifications below.

| Maximum engine R.P.M. | 2400 ~ 2450 rpm |
|---|---|

(4) To increase R.P.M, loosen the lock nut and turn the adjusting screw counterclockwise. To decrease, turn it clockwise.

# 4. Fuel Injection Nozzle

## 4-1 Construction

When fuel oil pumped by the fuel injection pump reaches the injection nozzle, it pushes up the nozzle valve (held down by a spring), and is injected into the combustion chamber at high pressure.

The fuel is atomized by the nozzle to mix uniformly with the air in the combustion chamber. How well the fuel is mixed with high temperature air directly affects combustion efficiency, engine performance and fuel economy.

Accordingly, the fuel injection nozzles must be kept in top-condition to maintain performance and operating efficiency.

## 4-3 Functioning

Fuel from the fuel injection pump passes through the oil port in the nozzle holder, and enters the nozzle body reservoir.

When oil reaches the specified pressure, it pushes up the nozzle valve (held by the nozzle spring), and is injected through the small hole on the tip of the nozzle body.

The nozzle valve is automatically pushed down by the nozzle spring and closed after fuel is injected.

Oil that leaks from between the nozzle valve and nozzle body goes through the hole on top of the nozzle spring and the oil leakage fitting and back into the fuel tank.

Adjustment of injection starting pressure is effected with the adjusting shims.

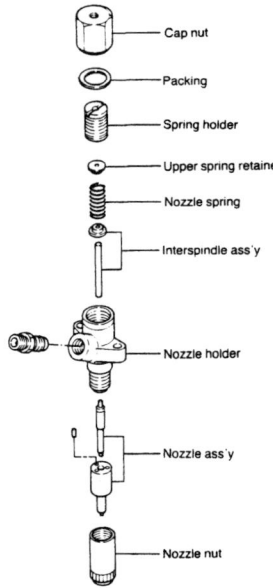
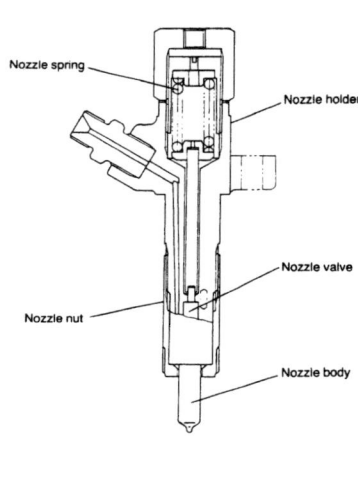

## 4-2 Specification

| | |
|---|---|
| Nozzle valve opening pressure | $200 \sim 205 \text{kg/cm}^2$ |
| Injection angle | 140° |
| No. of injection holes × hole dia. | $5 \times 0.26 \sim 0.28 \text{mm}$ |
| Hallmark No. | 140S275X1 |
| Nozzle type | YDLLA |

## Chapter 3 Fuel System
## 4. Fuel Injection Nozzle

(3) Nozzle body identification number
The type of nozzle can be determined from the number inscribed on the outside of the nozzle body.
1) Hole type fuel injection nozzles

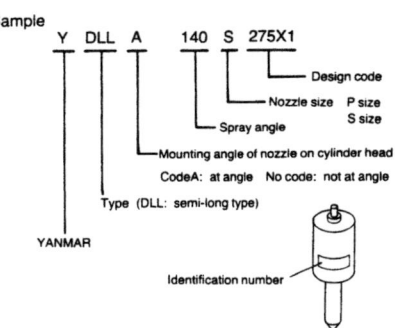

Sample
Y DLL A 140 S 275X1
- Design code
- Nozzle size  P size
- Spray angle  S size
- Mounting angle of nozzle on cylinder head
  CodeA: at angle  No code: not at angle
- Type (DLL: semi-long type)
YANMAR
Identification number

### 4-4 Disassembly

NOTE: 1. Disassemble fuel injection nozzle in a clean area, as for fuel injection pump.
2. When disassembling more than one fuel injection nozzle, keep the parts for each injection nozzle separate for each cylinder (i.e. the nozzle for cylinder 1 must be remounted in cylinder 1).

(1) When removing the injection nozzle from the cylinder head, remove the high pressure fuel pipe, fuel leakage pipe, etc., the injection nozzle retainer nuts, and then the fuel injection nozzle.

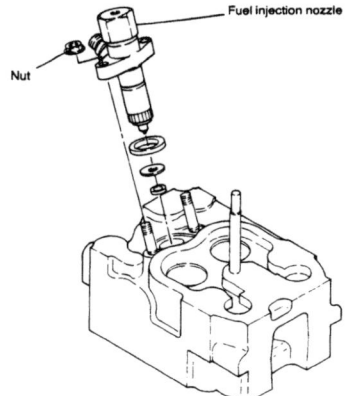

(2) Put the nozzle in a vise
NOTE: Use the special nozzle holder for the hole type injection nozzle so that the high pressure mounting threads are not damaged.

(3) Remove the nozzle nut.

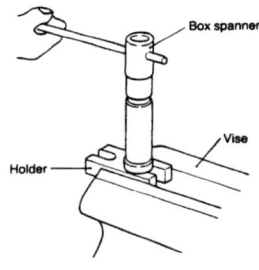

NOTE: Use a special box spanner for the hole type (the thickness of the two nozzle nuts is 27mm (1.0630 in.)

(4) Remove the inner parts
NOTE: Be careful not to loosen the spring seat, adjusting shims or other small parts.

### 4-5 Cleaning and Inspection
#### 4-5.1 Washing

(1) Be sure to use new diesel oil to wash the fuel injection nozzle parts.)
(2) Wash the nozzle in clean diesel oil with the nozzle cleaning kit.

1) Diesel Kiki nozzle cleaning kit:
Type NP-8486B No.5789-001
2) Anzen Jidosha Co., Ltd. nozzle cleaning kit:
Type NCK-001

(3) Clean off the carbon on the outside of the nozzle body with a brass brush.

## Chapter 3 Fuel System
### 4. Fuel Injection Nozzle

(4) Clean the nozzle seat with cleaning spray.

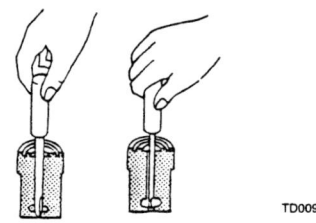

TD0092

(5) Clean off the carbon on the tip of the nozzle with a piece of wood.
(6) Clean hole type nozzles with a nozzle cleaning needle.

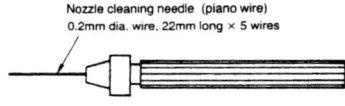

Nozzle cleaning needle (piano wire)
0.2mm dia. wire, 22mm long × 5 wires

| Part code no. | 2810-000010 |
|---|---|

#### 4-5.2 Inspection

(1) Inspect for scratches/wear
Inspect oil seals for abnormal scratches or wear and replace the nozzle if the nozzle sliding surface or seat are scratched or abnormally worn.

(2) Check nozzle sliding
Wash the nozzle and nozzle body in clean diesel oil, and make sure that when the nozzle is pulled out about half way from the body, it slides down by itself when released. Rotate the nozzle a little; replace the nozzle/nozzle body as a set if there are some places where it does not slide smoothly.

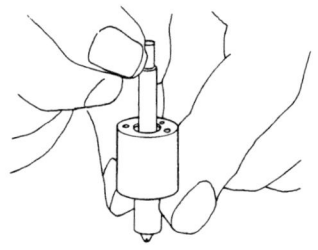

(3) Inspecting stop plate (inter-piece)
Check for scratches/wear in seals on both ends, Check for abnormal wear on the surface where it comes in contact with the nozzle; replace if the stop plate is excessively worn.

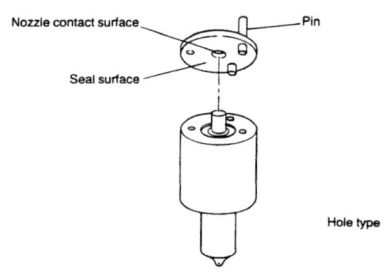

mm (in.)

| Nozzle contact surface wear limit | 0.1 (0.0039) |
|---|---|

(4) Inspecting the nozzle spring
Replace the nozzle spring if it is extremely bent, or the surface is scratched or rusted.

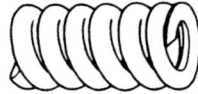

(5) Nozzle holder
Check the oil seal surface for scratches/wear; replace if wear is excessive.

### 4-6 Reassembly

The fuel injection nozzle is reassembled in the opposite order to disassembly.
(1) Insert the adjusting shims, nozzle spring and nozzle spring seat in the nozzle holder, mount the stop plate with the pin, insert the nozzle body/nozzle set and tighten the nut.
(2) Use the special holder when tightening the nut for the hole type nozzle, as in disassembly.

Nozzle nut tightening torque

kg-m (ft-lb)

| Hole type nozzle | 6.5 ~ 7.5 (47.0 ~ 54.2) |
|---|---|

# Chapter 3 Fuel System
## 4. Fuel Injection Nozzle

### 4-7 Adjustment

#### 4-7.1 Adjusting opening pressure

Mount the fuel injection nozzle on the nozzle tester and use the handle to measure injection starting pressure. If it is not at specified pressure, use the adjusting shims to increase/decrease pressure (both hole and pintle types).

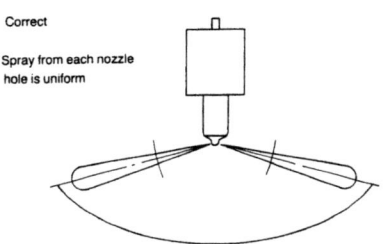

Correct

Spray from each nozzle hole is uniform

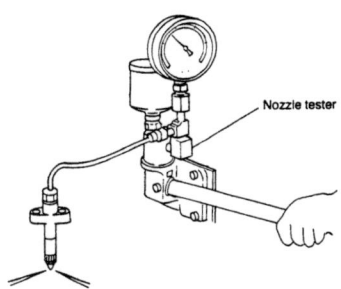

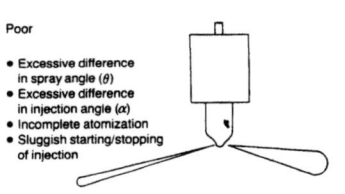

Poor

- Excessive difference in spray angle ($\theta$)
- Excessive difference in injection angle ($\alpha$)
- Incomplete atomization
- Sluggish starting/stopping of injection

Injection starting pressure

| Injection starting pressure | kg/cm² (lb/in.²) |
|---|---|
| Injection starting pressure | 200 ~ 210 (2844 ~ 2986) |

#### 4-7.2 Injection test

After adjusting the nozzle to the specified starting pressure, check seat oil tightness and fuel spray condition.

(1) Seat oil tightness

After two or three injections, gradually increase the pressure up to 20 kg/cm² (284 lb/in.²). Before reading the starting pressure, maintain the pressure for 5 seconds, and make sure that no oil is dripping from the tip of the nozzle.

Test the injection with a nozzle tester; retighten and test again if there is excessive oil leakage from the overflow coupling.

Replace the nozzle as a set if oil leakage is still excessive.

(2) Injection spray condition

Operate the nozzle tester lever once to twice a second and check for abnormal injection.

1) Hole type nozzles

Replace hole type nozzles that do not satisfy the following conditions:
- Proper spray angle ($\theta$)
- Correct injection angle ($\alpha$)
- Complete atomization of fuel
- Prompt starting/stopping of injection

### 4-8 Installation

(1) Apply paste lubricant containing MOS₂ (molibdenum disulfide YANMAR Part No.97775-500500), Rocole paste 50 gr (Part No.97775-400050), or the equivalent to the nozzle and other major parts at the time of assembly. Without this, disassembly of the parts may become impossible by the time of overhauling.

(2) Replace the adiabatic packing whenever the fuel valve is removed.

(3) Tighten the two fuel valve fixing nuts lightly and evenly with a 100mm length wrench (see illustration). (Tightening torque: 1 kg-m)

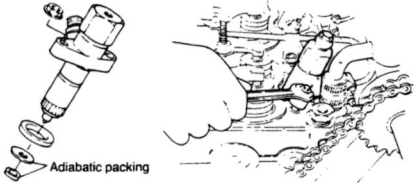

Adiabatic packing

Chapter 3 Fuel System
5. Fuel Feed Pump

# 5.Fuel Feed Pump

## 5-1 Construction

The fuel pump feeds the fuel from the fuel tank to the injection pump through the fuel filter. When the fuel tank is installed at a higher position than the fuel filter and injection pump, the fuel will be fed by its head pressure, but if the fuel tank is lower than the filter and injection pump, a fuel pump is required.

The fuel pump of this engine is diaphragm type and is installed on the side cover of the cylinder body.

The diaphragm is operated by the movement of a lever by the fuel feed pump cam at the P.T.O. shaft.

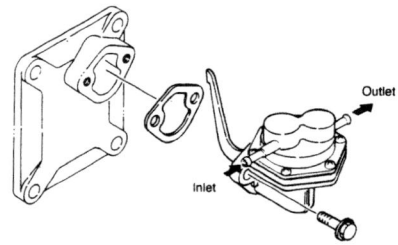

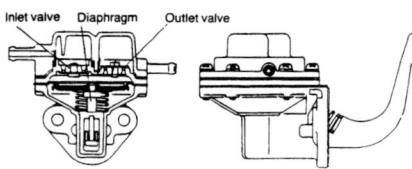

## 5-2 Specifications

| Head | 0.5 m |
|---|---|
| Discharge volume | Cam revolutions 1,000 rpm<br>Delivery pressure 0.25 – 0.35 kg/cm² |
| Closed off pressure | Below –100mmHg<br>(at 250 rpm cam revolutions) |

## 5-3 Disassembly and reassembly

### 5-3.1 Disassembly

(1) Remove the fuel feed pump mounting nut, and take the fuel feed pump off the side cover.
(2) Clean the fuel feed pump assembly with fuel oil.
(3) After checking the orientation of the arrow on the cover, make match marks on the upper body and cover, remove the small screw, and disassemble the cover, upper body and lower body.

### 5-3.2 Reassembly

(1) Clean all parts with fuel oil, inspect, and replace any defective parts.
(2) Replace any packings on parts that have been disassembled.
(3) Make sure that the intake valve and discharge valve on upper body are mounted in the proper direction, and that you don't foreget the valve packing.
(4) Assemble the diaphragm into the body, making sure the diaphragm mounting holes are lined up (do not force).
(5) Align the match marks on the upper body of the pump and cover, and tighten the small screws evenly.

|  | kg-cm (ft-lb) |
|---|---|
| Tightening torque | 25 ~ 35 (1.80 ~ 2.52) |

## 5-4 Inspection

(1) Place the fuel feed pump in kerosene, cover the discharge port with your finger, move the priming lever and check for air bubbles (Repair or replace any part which emits air bubbles).

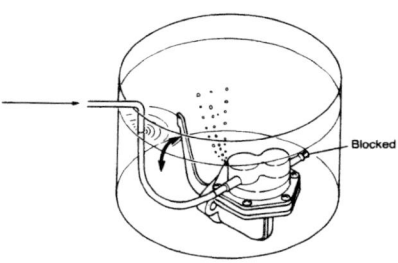

(2) Attach a vinyl hose to the fuel feed pump intake, keep the pump at the specified depth from the fuel oil surface, move the priming lever by hand and check for sudden spurts of fuel oil from the discharge port. If oil is not spurted out, inspect the diaphragm and diaphragm spring and repair/replace as necessary.

## 6. Fuel Filter

## 6-1 Fuel filter

### 6-1.1 Construction

This fuel filter is installed between the pre-fuel filter, explained on the previous page, and the fuel injection pump, and works to remove further contamination and impurities from the fuel that can't be removed by the pre-filter.

The fuel filter incorporates a replaceable filter paper element. Fuel from the fuel tank enters the outside of the element and passes through the element under its own pressure. As it passes through, the dirt and impurities in the fuel are filtered out, allowing only clean fuel to enter the interior of the element. The fuel exits from the outlet at the top center of the filter and is sent to the injection pump.

A hexagonal head bolt for air bleeding and a threaded hole for fuel return are provided in the fuel filter body. The surplus fuel at the injection nozzle is returned to the fuel filter and then to the injection pump.

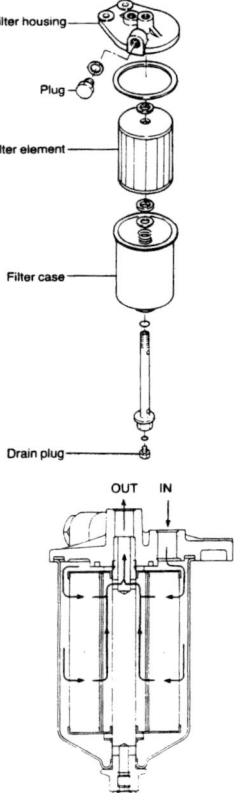

*Chapter 3 Fuel System*
*6. Fuel Filter*                                                                                                     *TM*

### 6-1·2 Specifications

| Filter type | Filter paper type |
|---|---|
| Filtration area | 4000 cm² |
| Max. flow capacity | 2.4/min |
| Pressure loss | 3 ~ 5 mmHg |
| Max. passing particle size | 10 µ |

### 6-1·3 Maintenance

The fuel filter must be periodically inspected. If there is water sediment in the filter, remove all dirt, rust, etc. by washing the filter with clean fuel.

The normal replacement interval for the element is 500 hours, but the element should be replaced whenever it is dirty or damaged. even if the 500-hour replacement period has not elapsed.

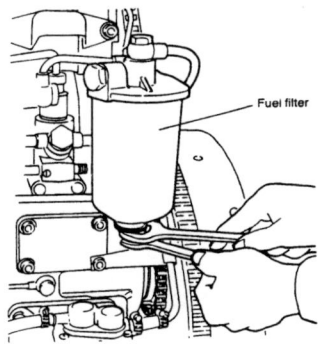

| Filter cleaning | Every 50 hours |
|---|---|
| Filter element replacement | Every 500 hours |

3-20

Chapter 3 Fuel System
7. Water separator

# 7. Water Separator

### 7-1 Construction

Fuel from the tank enters the filter housing inlet and fills the sediment bowl. Water and sediment settle to the bottom of the sediment bowl. The fuel is filtered as it passes through the filter element, leaves the housing at the outlet, and flows to the injection pump.

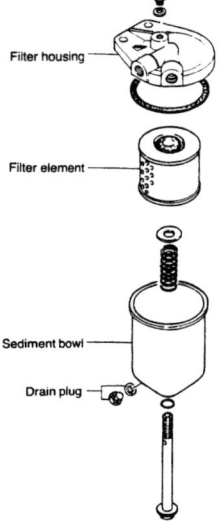

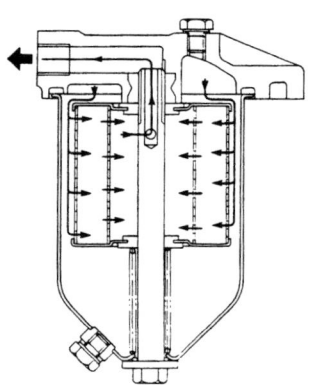

### 7-2 Installation position of oil/water separator

Install the separator so that it is as far below the level of the fuel in fuel tank as possible.

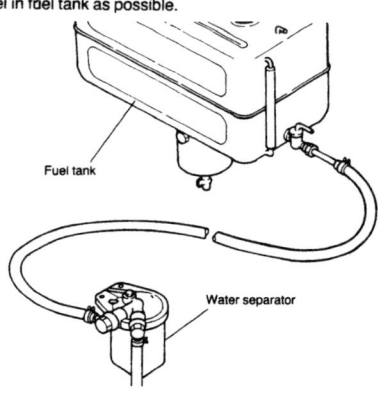

### 7-3 Maintenance

(1) Draining
Every 50 hrs of operation, drain the oil/water separator by removing the drain plug as shown below.

(2) Disassembly and cleaning
Every 500 hrs of operation, pull out the inside filter element and clean it carefully.

*Chapter 3 Fuel System*
*8. Fuel Tank (Option)*                                                                 *TM*

# 8. Fuel Tank (Option)

### 8-1 Construction

Fuel flow can be closed and opened at the fuel cock.
A fuel return connection is provided on top of the tank. A rubber hose can be connected to return fuel from the fuel nozzles.

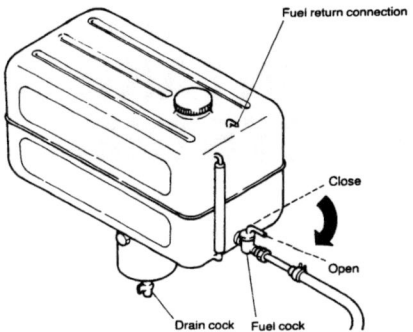

# CHAPTER 4
# INTAKE AND EXHAUST SYSTEM

1. Intake and Exhaust System ................................................... 4-1

# 1. Intake and Exhaust System

## 1-1 Construction

Intake air is introduced from the air intake port of the cylinder head. The exhaust air is collected by the exhaust manifold installed at the outlet of the cylinder head, passed to the exhaust silencer, and then discharged to the open air.

This exhaust silencer is "non-resistance type". It has no resistance in the air barrel. Sound pressure is absorbed by the glassfiber wool lining on the outer circumference of the punching metal. The glassfiber wool is especially effective for absoring unpleasant high frequency sounds. The installation of this silencer results in no adverse effects on engine output.

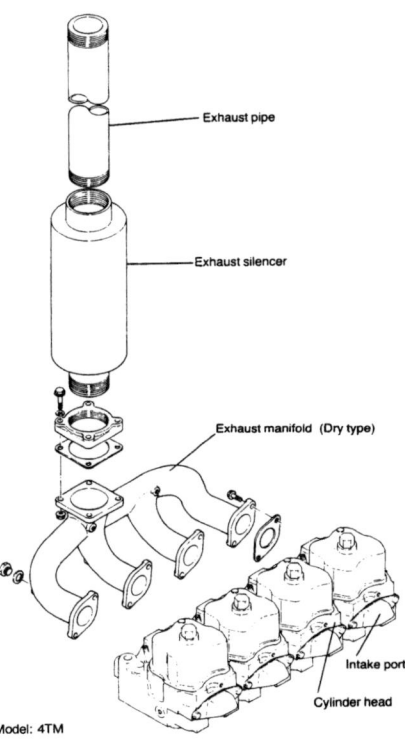

Model: 4TM

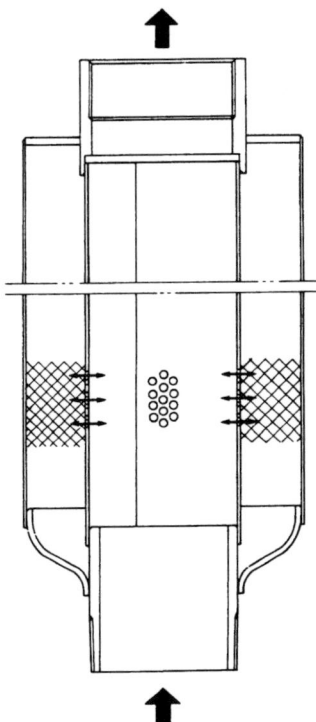

## Chapter 4 Intake and Exhaust System
### 1. Intake and Exhaust System

#### 1-2 Inspection

1) Gasket packing
   Inspect the gasket packing and replace if damaged.
2) Carbon build-up in the exhaust passage
   Remove the exhaust manifold and check the carbon build-up in the exhaust passage. Remove any carbon in the passage. If the carbon build-up is heavy, the exhaust pressure will rise, the cylinders overheat, and starting will be difficult.

(3) It is common for the silencer to become clogged when the engine combustion performance falls. If this happens, clean the inside of the silencer. It is also necessary to check the fuel oil pump and the fuel injection valve.

# CHAPTER 5
# LUBRICATION SYSTEM

1. Lubrication System .................................................................. 5-1
2. Oil Pump ................................................................................ 5-5
3. Oil Filter ................................................................................ 5-8
4. Oil Cooler .............................................................................. 5-9

# 1. Lubrication System

## 1-1 Composition

Engine parts are lubricated by a trochoid pump forced lubrication system. To keep the engine exterior uncluttered and to eliminate vibration damage to piping, exterior piping has been minimized by transporting the lubricating oil through passages drilled in the cylinders and cylinder head. The lubricating oil supplied from the oil filler in the rocker arm cover is collected in the oil pan at the bottom of the cylinder block through the tappet holes.

The lubricating oil is drawn back up through the lubricating oil suction pipe by the trochoid pump and fed to the oil filter, where impurities are filtered out. Then it is adjusted to the prescribed pressure by the oil pressure regulating valve and sent to the main bearing through an oil pipe. The lubricating oil sent to the gear side main bearing flows in two paths: one from the main bearing to lubricate the crank pin through the hole drilled through the crankshaft, and the other to the jet piece to lubricate the gears.

The lubricating oil sent to the flywheel side main bearing also flows in two paths: one from the main bearing to lubricate the crank pin through the hole drilled through the crankshaft, and the other to the rocker arm shaft through the holes drilled through the cylinders and cylinder head.

From the rocker arm shaft, the lubricating oil flows through the small hole in the rocker arm to lubricate the push rods and part of the valve head.

The oil that has dropped to the push rod chamber from the rocker arm chamber lubricates the tappets, cam and cam bearing, and returns to the oil pan.

The pistons, piston pins and contact faces of the cylinder liners are splash lubricated by the oil that has lubricated the crank pin. An oil pressure switch is provided in the lubricating system to monitor normal circulation and the pressure of the lubricating oil.

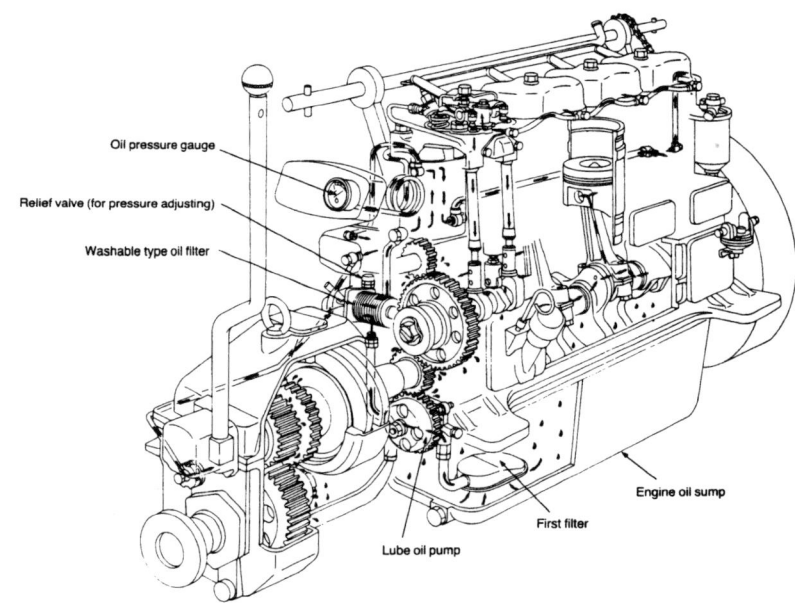

# Chapter 5 Lubrication System
## 1. Lubrication System

**2TM**

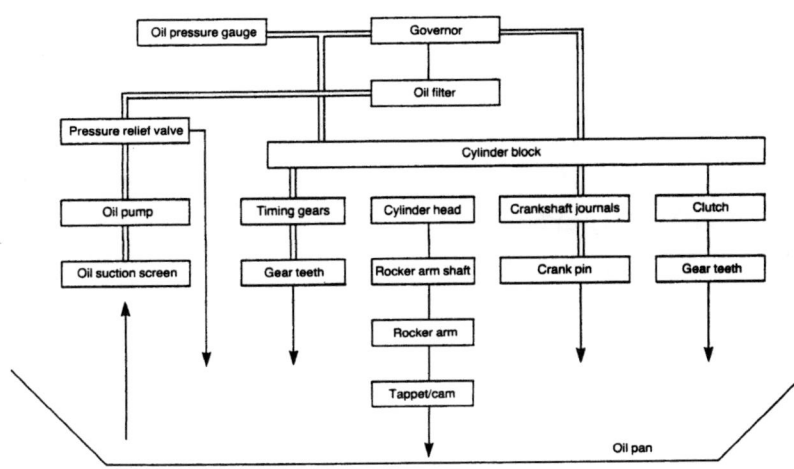

**3TM, 4TM**

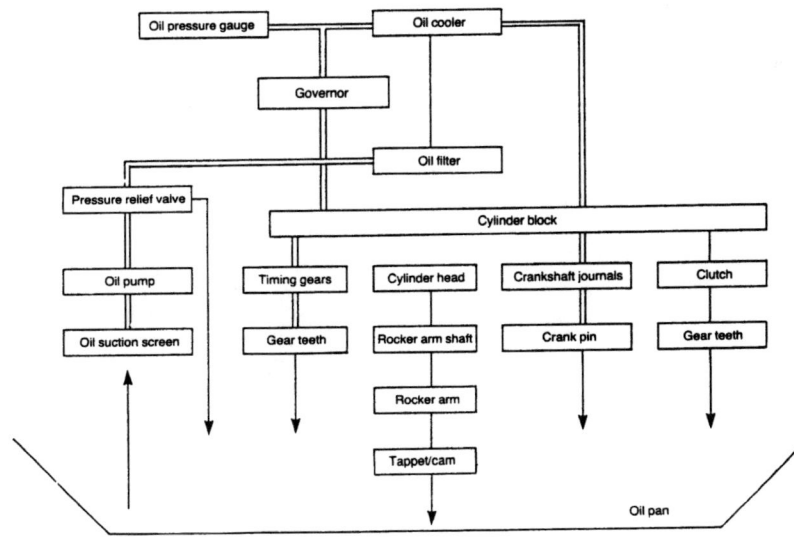

## Chapter 5 Lubrication System
### 1. Lubrication System

**2TM**

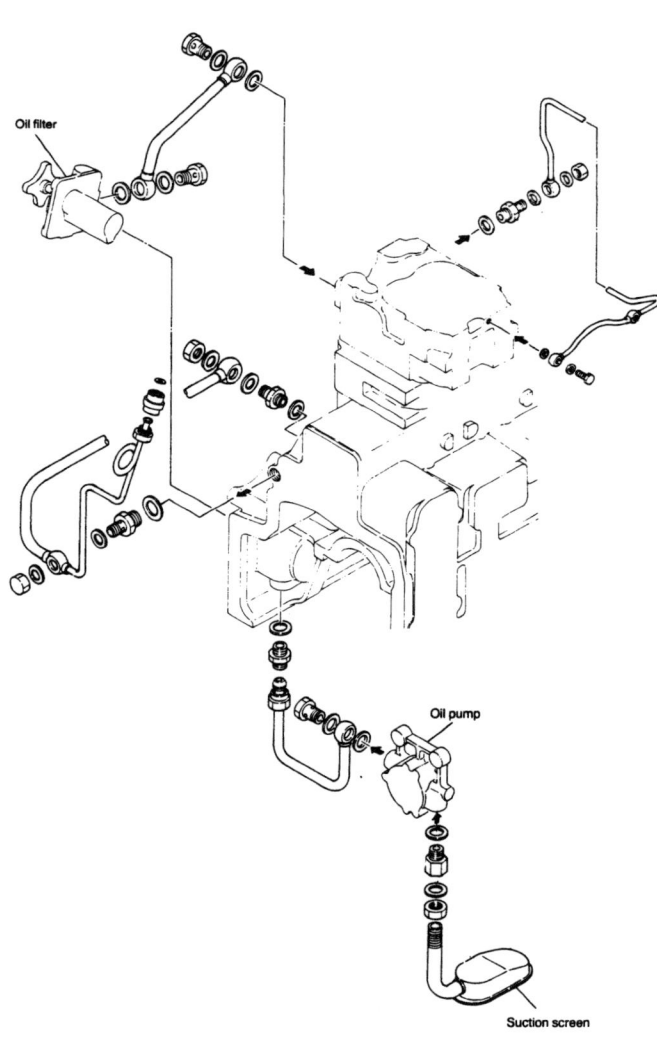

## Chapter 5 Lubrication System
### 1. Lubrication System

*TM*

**3TM, 4TM**

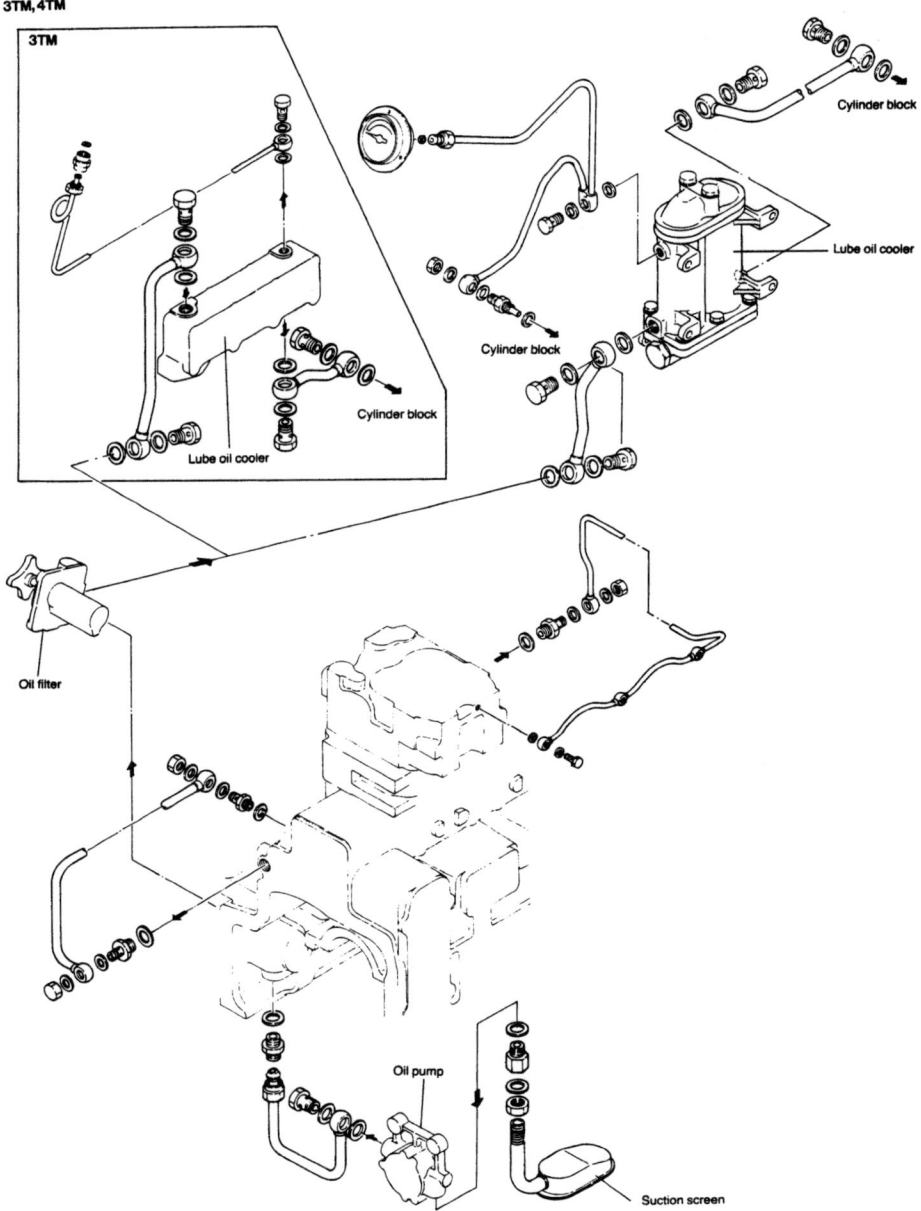

# 2. Oil Pump

## 2-1 Construction

The oil pump is a compact, low pressure variation trochoid pump comprising a trochoid curve inner rotor and outer rotor. Pumping pressure is provided by the change in volume between the two rotors caused by rotation of the rotor shaft. The oil pump is installed under the timing gear case end and is driven by the lubricating pump driving gear.

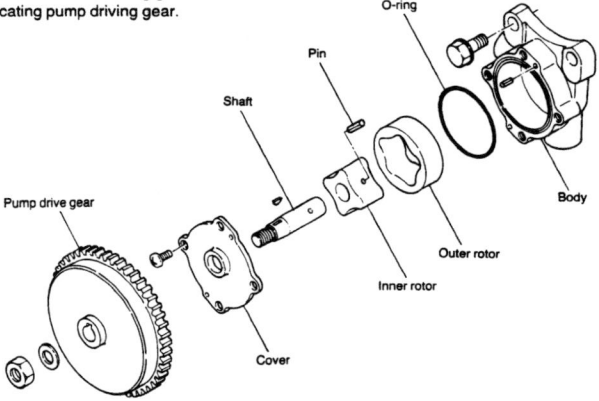

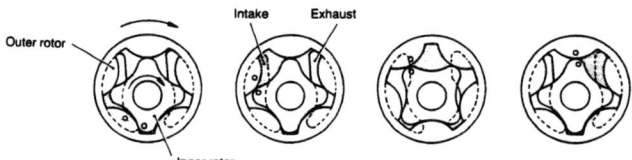

## 2-2 Specifications

|  | 2TM, 3TM | 4TM |
|---|---|---|
| Engine R.P.M. | 2200 rpm | 2200 rpm |
| Gear ratio Crankshaft/Pump shaft | 0.765　39/51 | 0.765　39/51 |
| Pump rev. speed | 1682 rpm | 1682 rpm |
| Delivery capacity | More than 15.8 ℓ/min | More than 25 ℓ/min |
| Delivery pressure | 2.0kg/cm$^2$ | 4.0kg/cm$^2$ |

Chapter 5 Lubrication System
2. Oil Pump
TM

## 2-2 Disassembly

### 2-2.1 Oil pump removal

(1) Remove the reversing gear upper case and the clutch components (refer to page, 8-6 for 2TM and 3TM, 8-20 for 4TM).
(2) Remove the damper disk (For 4TM only).
(3) Remove the two bolts and the oil pump assembly.

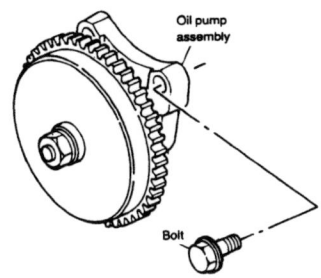

## 2-3 Inspection

When the discharge pressure of the oil pump is extremely low, check the oil level. If it is within the prescribed range, the oil pump must be inspected.

(1) Outer rotor and pump body clearance
    Measure the clearance by inserting a feeler gauge between the outside of the outer rotor and the pump body casing. If the clearance exceeds the wear limit, replace the outer rotor and pump body as a set.

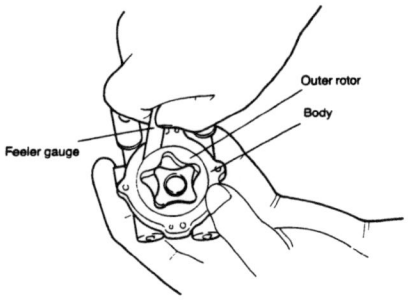

|  | mm (in.) |
|---|---|
| Maintenance standard | 0.10 ~ 0.17 (0.0039 ~ 0.0067) |
| Wear limit | 0.23 (0.0091) |

(2) Outer rotor and inner rotor clearance
    Fit one of the teeth of the inner rotor to one of the grooves of the outer rotor and measure the clearance at the point where the teeth of both rotors are aligned. Replace the inner rotor and outer rotor ass'y if the wear limit is exceeded.

### 2-2.2 Oil pump disassembly

(1) Remove the nut, the washer and the drive gear from the pump shaft.
NOTE: Do not lose the key on the pump shaft.
(2) Remove the four screws and the cover.
(3) Remove the shaft together with the inner rotor and the outer rotor.
NOTE: Do not remove the inner rotor from the shaft.

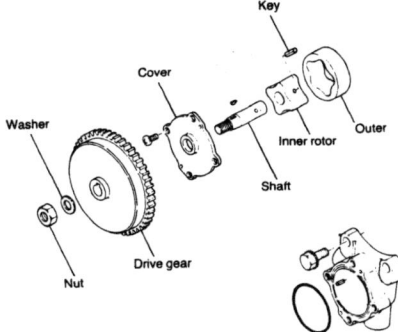

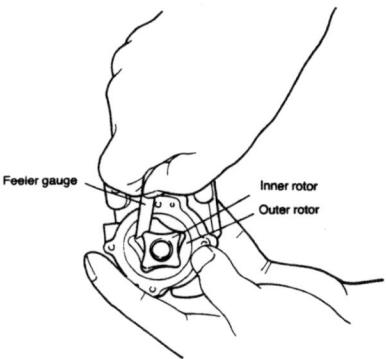

5-6

## Chapter 5 Lubrication System
## 2. Oil Pump

### 2-4 Oil pressure safety valve (4TM)

The safety valve is provided for the L.O. pump of 4 TM. When the L.O. pump inner pressure rises over $9.5 - 10.5 kg/cm^2$, the safety valve opens to release the L.O. outside the pump.

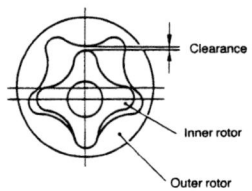

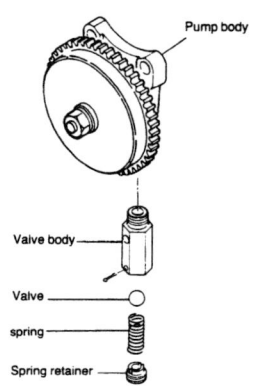

| | mm (in.) |
|---|---|
| Maintenance standard | 0.050 ~ 0.105 (0.00197 ~ 0.00413) |
| Wear limit | 0.15 (0.00591) |

(3) Pump body and inner rotor, outer rotor side clearance.
Install the inner rotor and outer rotor into the pump body casing so that they fit snugly.
Check the clearance by placing a ruler against the end of the body and inserting a feeler gauge between the ruler and the end of the rotor. Replace as a set if the wear limit is exceeded.

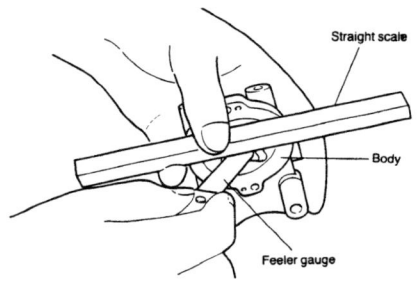

| | mm (in.) |
|---|---|
| Maintenance standard | 0.02 ~ 0.06 (0.0008 ~ 0.0024) |
| Wear limit | 0.09 (0.0035) |

(4) Rotor shaft and body clearance
Measure the outside diameter of the rotor shaft and the inside diameter of the body shaft hole, and replace the rotor shaft and body as an ass'y if the clearance exceeds the wear limit.

| | Maintenance standard | Wear limit |
|---|---|---|
| Rotor shaft outside diameter | 15.966 ~ 15.984 (0.6286 ~ 0.6293) | 15.954 (0.6281) |
| Rotor shaft hole inside diameter | 16.000 ~ 16.022 (0.6299 ~ 0.6308) | 16.094 (0.6336) |
| Clearance when assembled | 0.016 ~ 0.056 (0.0006 ~ 0.0022) | 0.14 (0.0055) |

# 3. Oil Filter

## 3-1 Construction

The oil filter removes dirt and metal particles from the lubricating oil to minimize wear of moving parts. The construction of the oil filter is shown below.

The lubricating oil from the oil pump is passed through the filter paper and distributed to each part as shown by arrow A in the figure.

The lube oil filter is of the "auto-clean" type. Filter clogging can be removed by turning the handle.

| Max. flow capacity | | 2·3TM | 4TM |
|---|---|---|---|
| Filteration | mesh | 150 | |
| Max. flow capacity | ℓ/hr | 1060 | 1306 |
| | cm³ | 12.5 | 15.4 |

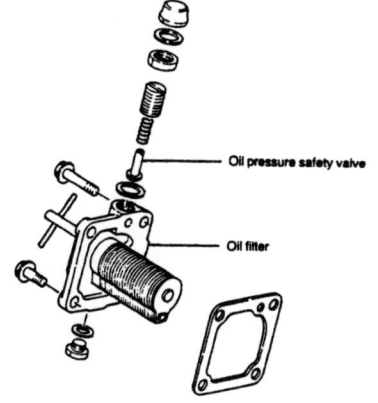

## 3-2 Maintenance

### 3-2.1 Cleaning

Turn the handle 2 or 3 times a day to remove dirt and dust

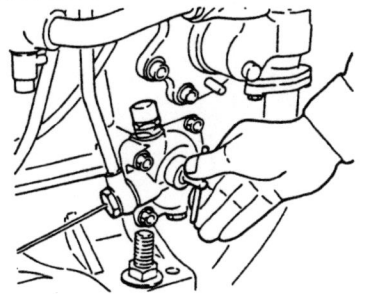

### 3-2.2 Draining

Every 50 hrs. of operation, drain the lube oil filter the plug.

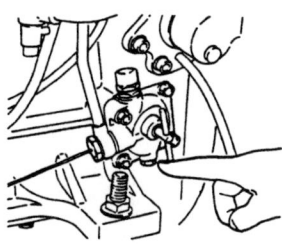

### 3-2.3 Removal and cleaning

Every 250 hrs. of operation, pull out the inside steel-plate assembly and soak it in light oil. Use a brush to remove the sludge from between the steel plates. If necessary, disassemble.

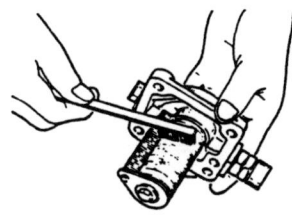

## 3-3 Oil pressure adjustment

Operate the engine at the rated speed, and set the pressure control valve to obtain 3 - 4 kg/cm² pressure at the pressure gauge reading. (Screwing in the valve makes the pressure rise.) If no pressure rise is obtained by screwing in the control valve, check the oil port of the lube oil pump.

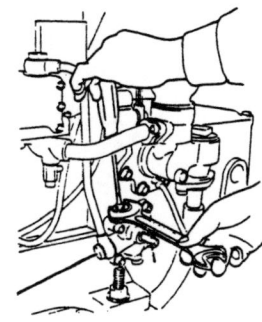

## 4. Oil Cooler

### 4-1 Construction

L.O. passing from the filter is cooled by the sea water direct cooling system.

#### 4-1.1 3TM

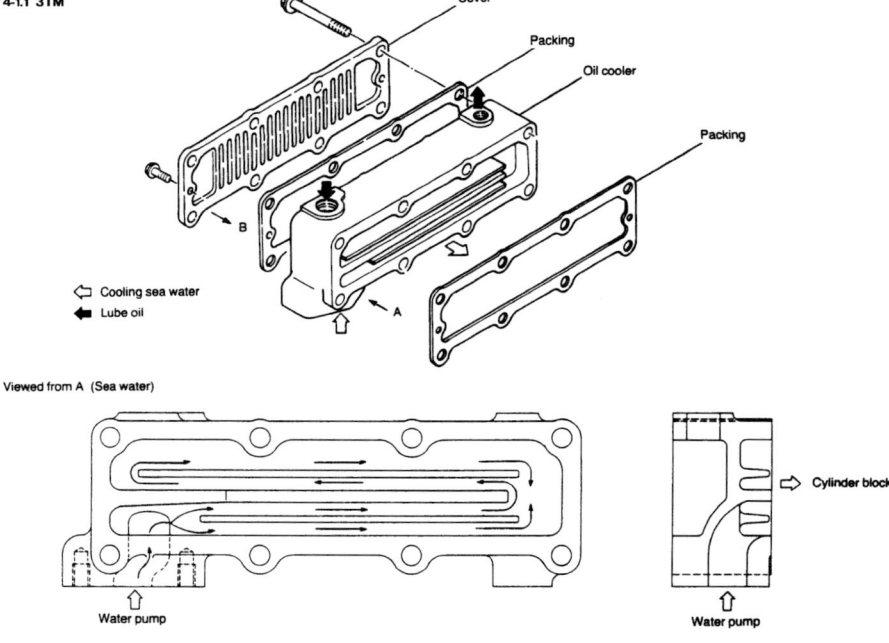

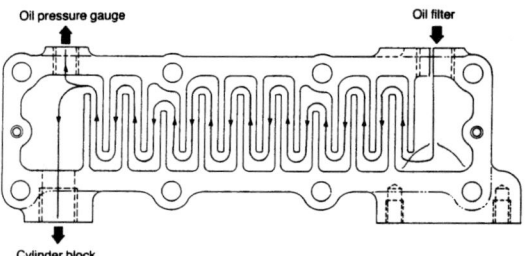

*Chapter 5 Lubrication System*
*4. Oil Cooler* _____*TM*

**4-1.2 4TM**

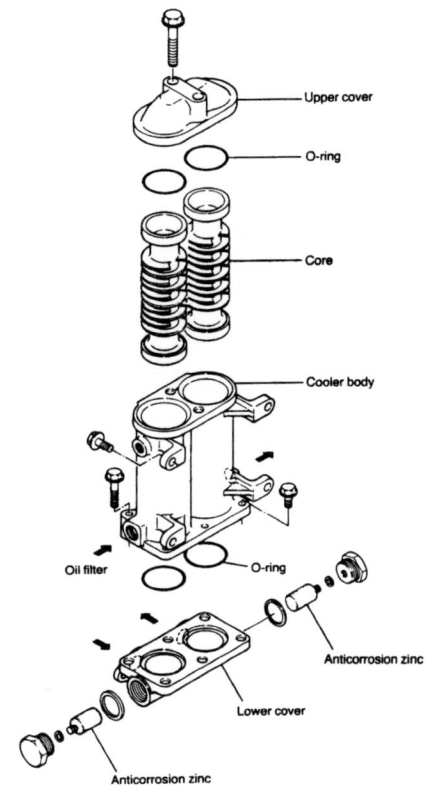

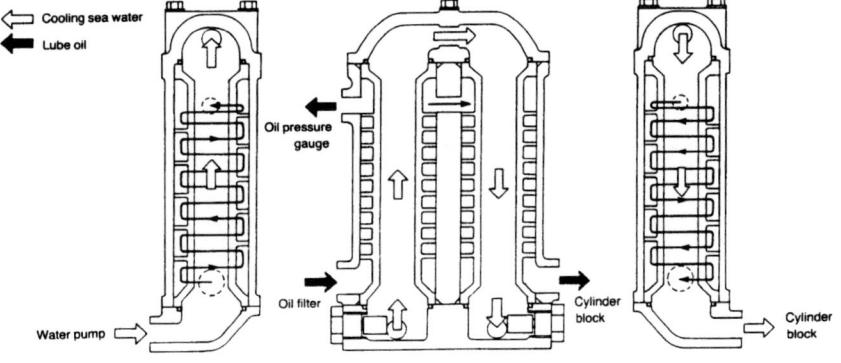

5-10

*Chapter 5 Lubrication System*
*4. Oil Cooler*

### 4-2 Anticorrosion zinc (4TM)

Each piece of zinc plate is installed on the left and right lower covers of the L.O. cooler.

Check the zinc every 3 months or every 500 hrs., whichever comes first. Clean the zinc with a brush. Replace the zinc when it is 1/2 its original size. Replace the O-ring at the same time.

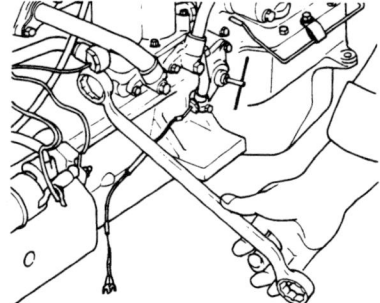

# CHAPTER 6
# COOLING SYSTEM

1. Cooling System .................................................................. 6-1
2. Water Pump ...................................................................... 6-4
3. Kingston Cock .................................................................. 6-7
4. Sea Water Filter (Option) ................................................... 6-8

… TM

# 1. Cooling System

## 1-1 Composition

Sea water direct cooling is provided by use of the reciprocating cooling water pump. Anti-corrosion zinc plates are installed on the parts to protect them from electrolytic corrosion.

A scoop strainer is provided at the water intake Kingston cock to remove dirt and vinyl from the water.

**Model: 4TM**

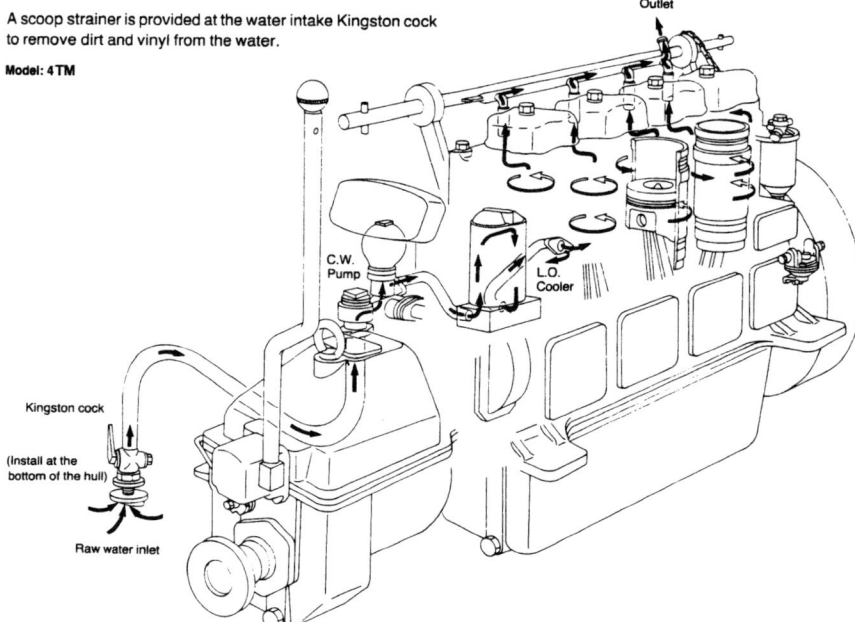

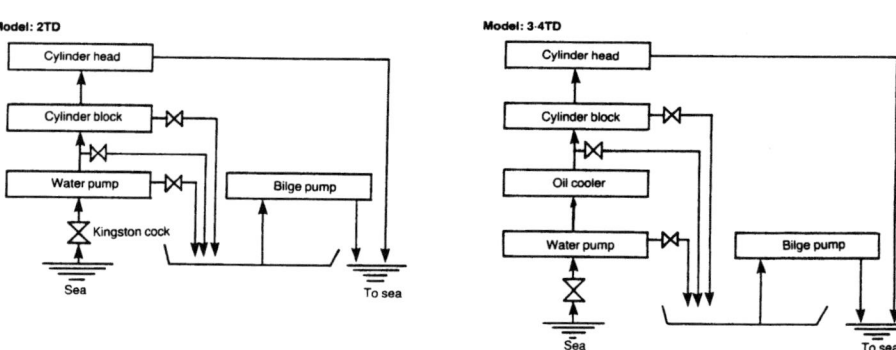

*Chapter 6 Cooling System*
*1. Cooling System* _____ *TM*

**1-2 Drawing (2TM)**

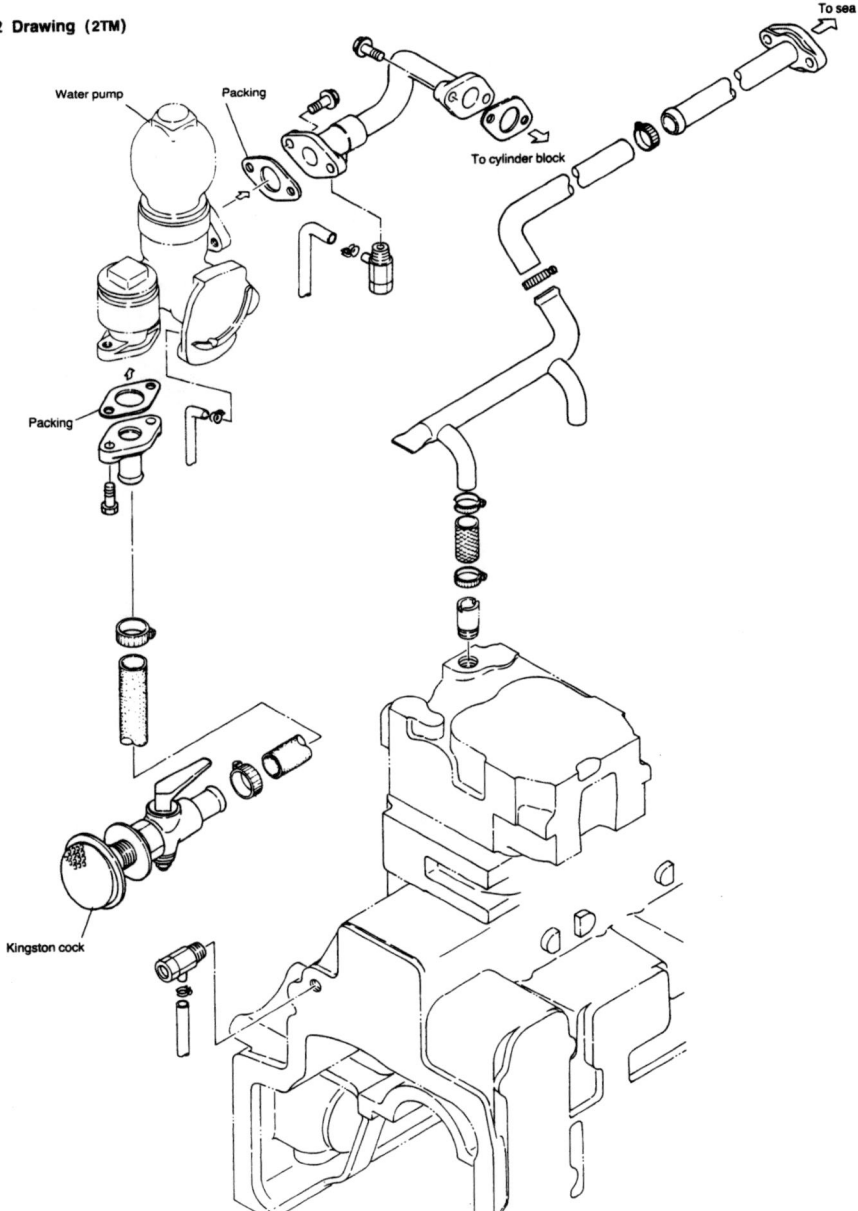

*Chapter 6 Cooling System*
*1. Cooling System*
TM

### 1-3 Drawing (3TM, 4TM)

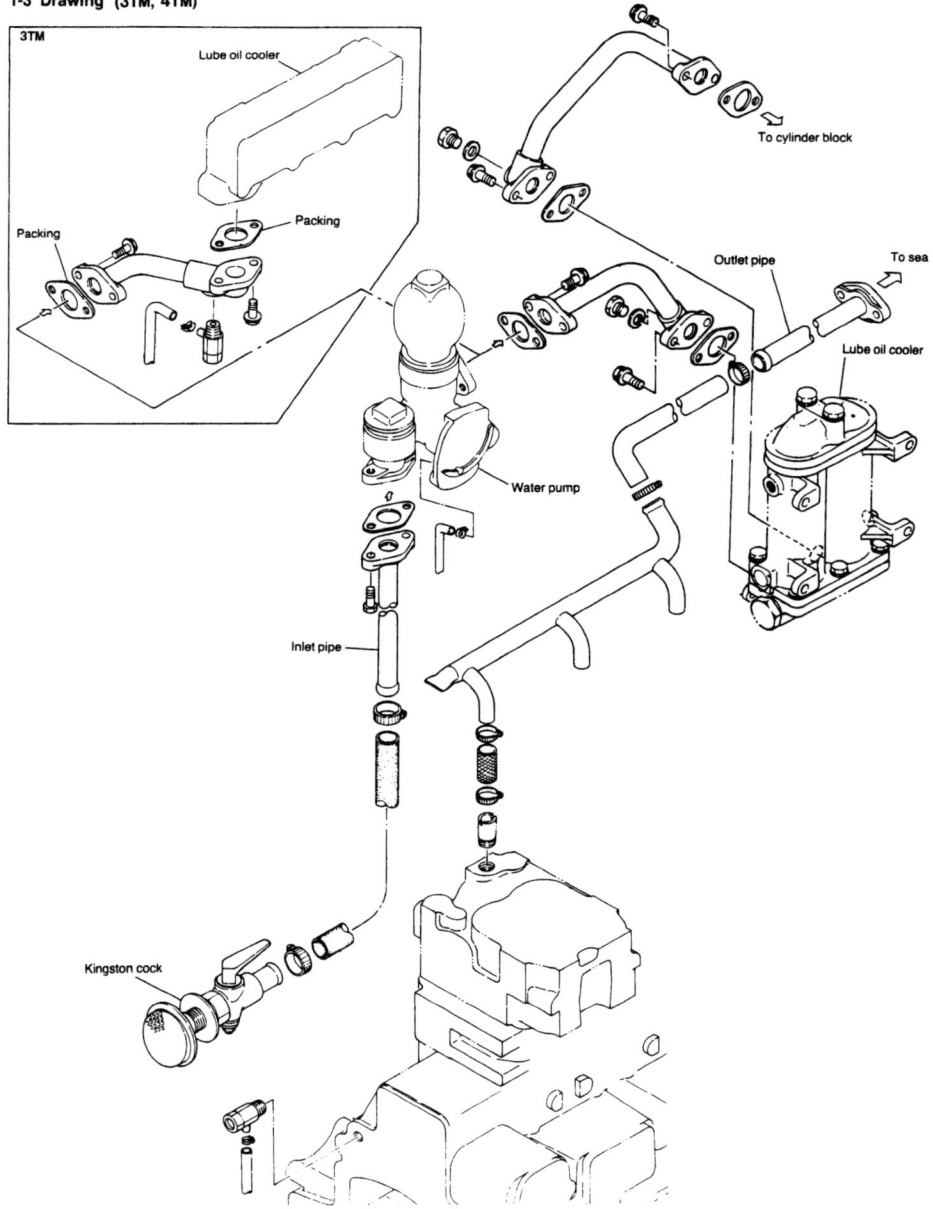

## 2. Water Pump

### 2-1 Construction

The cooling water pump moves the plunger with the cooling water connecting rod installed on the cam shaft end. Suction and discharge of water is done by the opening and closing of the valve.

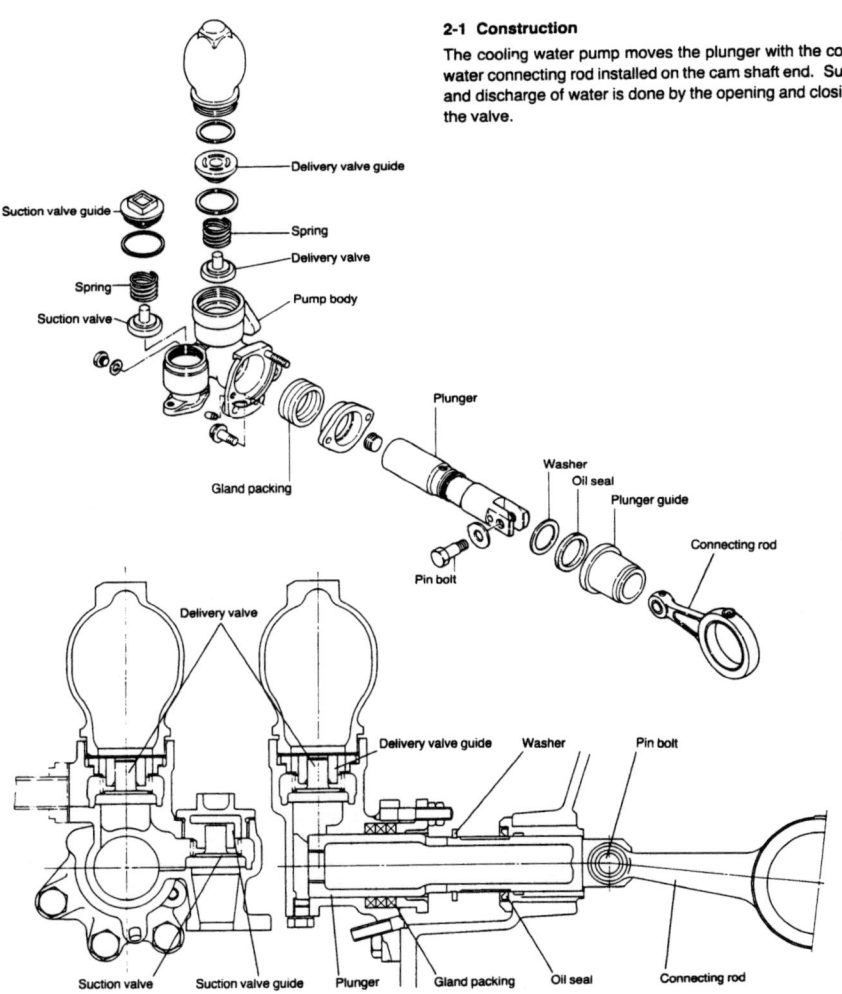

### 2-2 Specifications

|  | 2.3TM | 4TM |
| --- | --- | --- |
| Plunger dia. | 35mm (1.38 in.) | 40mm (1.5748 in.) |
| Stroke | 22mm (0.8661 in.) | 22mm (0.8661 in.) |
| Pump rev. speed | 1050 rpm | 1050 rpm |
| Displacement | 1350 ℓ/hr | 1720 ℓ/hr |

Chapter 6 Cooling System
2. Water Pump

## 2-3 Disassembly
### 2-3.1 Cooling water pump body

(1) Disconnect the inlet and the outlet pipes from the pump body.
(2) Remove the three pump retaining bolts and the pump body.

## 2-4 Inspection and repair
### 2-4.1 Suction and delivery valves and springs

It is not necessary to remove the water pump body from cylinder block for inspection of the suction and delivery valves and springs.

(1) Check that there is no dust in the suction and delivery valves of the pump.
(2) Check the contact of the suction and delivery valves with each valve seat.
(3) Check the sliding of the valve and valve guide.
(4) Check that the valve spring is not weakened.

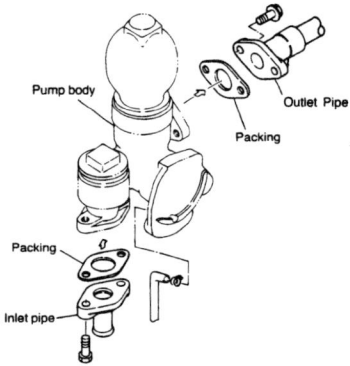

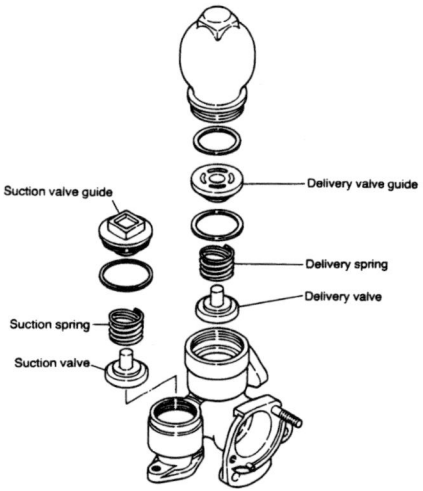

### 2-3.2 Plunger

(1) Remove the reversing gear upper case (refer to page, 8-6 for 2,3TM and 8-20 for 4TM).
(2) Remove the pin bolt from the plunger and connecting rod.
(3) Remove the plunger.

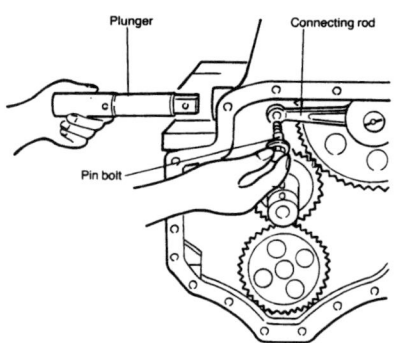

(5) Check the suction and the delivery valve seats for deposits. If necessary, wrap the valves and the seats with fine lapping powder.

NOTE: *When using lapping powder, clean the valves and valve seats so that no powder remains in the pump, and apply oil to the valve seats.*

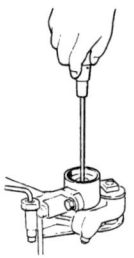

## Chapter 6 Cooling System
## 2. Water Pump

### 2-4.2 Gland packing
(1) Check the gland packing for damage. Replace as necessary.

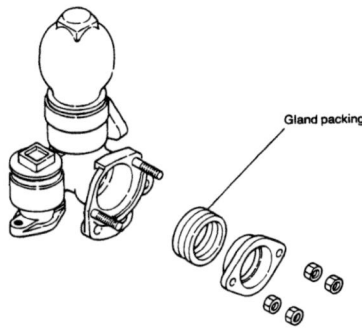

Gland packing

### 2-4.3 Oil seal, washer and rubber
(1) Check the oil seal in the plunge guide, washer and rubber sleeve for damage. Replace as necessary.

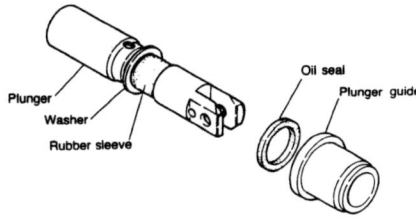

Plunger
Washer
Rubber sleeve
Oil seal
Plunger guide

### 2-4.4 Connecting rod bushings
(1) If replacing bushing(s), make an oil hole on the bushing.

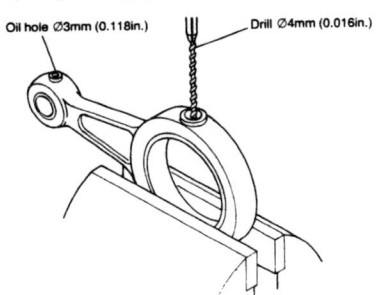

Oil hole Ø3mm (0.118in.)
Drill Ø4mm (0.016in.)

### 2-5 Reassembly
Reverse the disassembly steps described on the preceding pages. Replace any paper packing.

*NOTE: Insert the plunger into the pump assembly. If smooth movement of the plunger cannot be obtained, centering is required.*

### 2-6 Periodic service
#### 2-6.1 Retightening gland packing
After many hours of use, the sealing capacity of the gland packing will drop and cause water leaks. Periodically, retighten the left and right gland packings. After retightening, make sure that there is no overheating caused by excessive tightening.

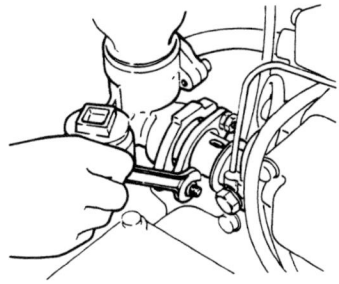

#### 2-6.3 Lubrication of water pump plunger
Every 50 hours of use, apply oil to the pump plunger.

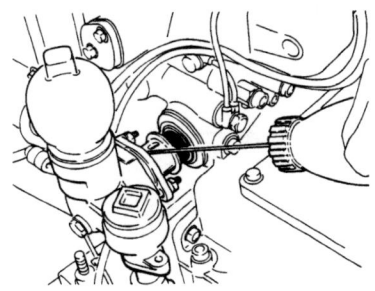

Chapter 6 Cooling System
3. Kingston Cock

# 3. Kingston Cock

### 3-1 Construction

The Kingston cock, installed on the bottom of the hull, controls the intake of cooling water into the boat. The Kingston cock serves to filter the water so that mud, sand, and other foreign matter in the water does not enter the water pump.
Numerous holes are drilled in the water side of the Kingston cock.

### 3-3 Inspection

When the cooling water volume has dropped and the pump is normal, remove the vessel from the water and check for clogging of the Kingston cock.
If water leaks from the cock, disassemble the cock and inspect if for wear, and repair or replace.

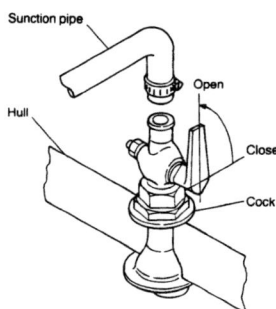

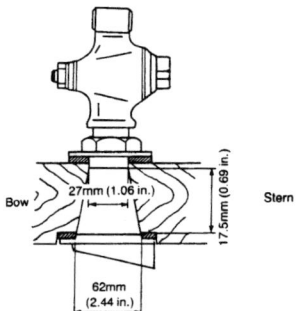

### 3-2 Handling precautions

Caution the user to always close the Kingston cock after each day of use and to confirm that it is open before beginning operation.
If the Kingston cock is left open, water will flow in reverse and the vessel will sink if trouble occurs with the water pump.
On the other hand, if the engine is operated with the Kingston cock closed, cooling water will not be able to get in, resulting in engine and pump trouble.

# 4. Sea Water Filter (Option)

When operating the engine in areas where the sea water contains a large amount of mud, sand or other foreign matter, a sea water filter should be provided between the kingston cock and the sea water pump.
Occasionally inspect the sea water filter and clean the dirt and scale off the element. Remove the dirt and sand from the bottom of the filter.

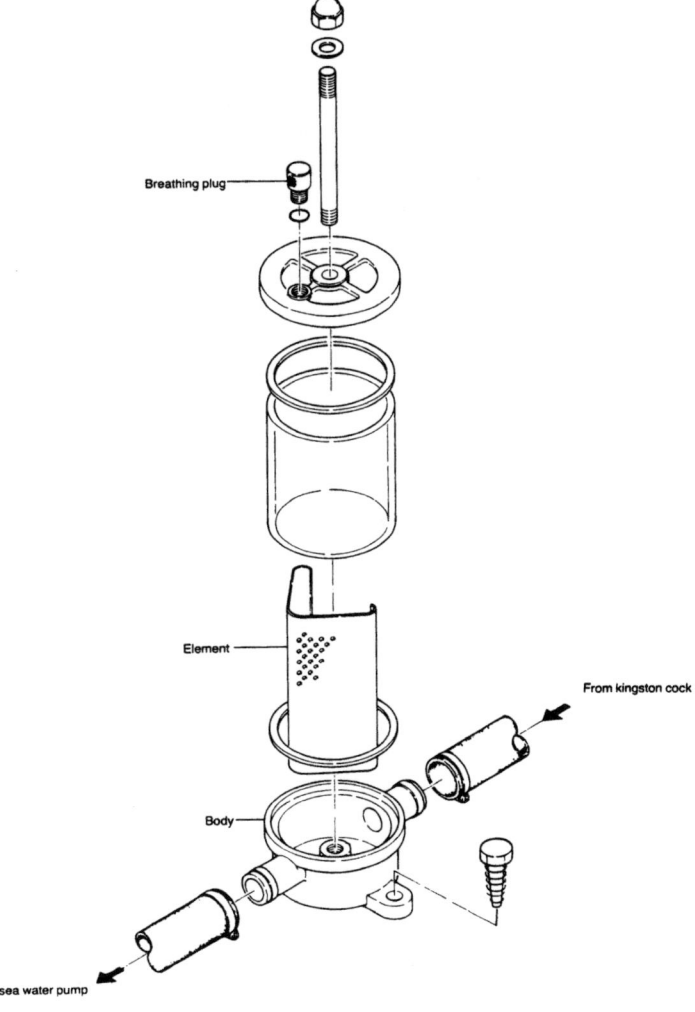

# CHAPTER 7
# CHAIN OVERDRIVE HAND-OPERATED SYSTEM

1. Chain Overdrive Hand-operated System ............................ 7-1

# 1. Chain Overdrive Hand-Operated System

The chain starting device is used for starting the engine. For starting, just operate the handle. This device is convenient when mechanically adjusting the engine.

### 1-1 Construction

The chain starting device consists of a chain and large and small sprockets. The starting handle rotations are transmitted via the small sprocket to the large sprocket, which drives the cam shaft for starting the engine.

The roller clutch at the end of the gear shaft engages only when the shaft is rotated in the proper direction, (when the shaft is rotated in reverse the roller clutch will not engage and the driver gear shaft runs free when the engine starts).

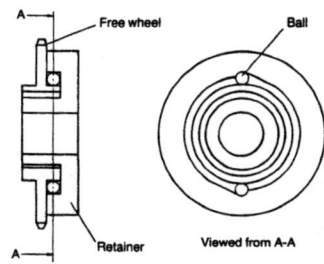

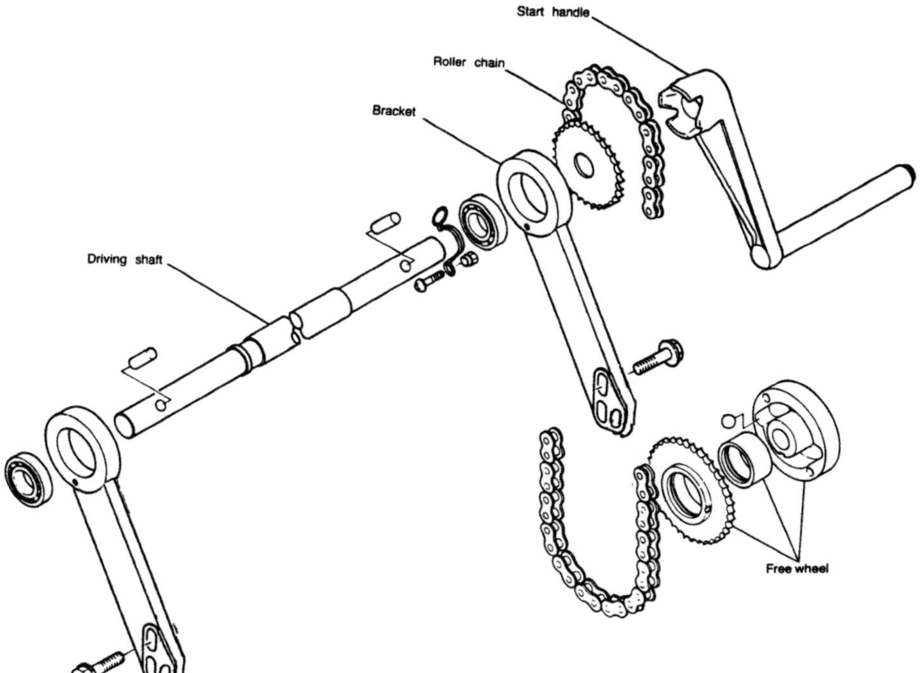

# Chapter 7 Chain Overdrive Hand-Operated System
## 1. Chain Overdrive Hand-Operated System

### 1-2 Specification

$$\text{Speedup ratio} = \frac{\text{rotation of crankshaft}}{\text{rotation of starting shaft}} = 1.73$$

|  | Number of teeth |
|---|---|
| Sprocket wheel (small) | 21 |
| Sprocket wheel (big) | 26 |
| Camshaft gear | 78 |
| Crankshaft gear | 39 |

### 1-3 Roller Chain

|  | mm (in.) |
|---|---|
| A | 12.70 (0.50) |
| B | 7.77 (0.3059) |
| C | 3.40 (0.1339) |
| Length of roller chain | 67 links |

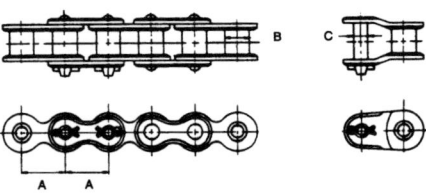

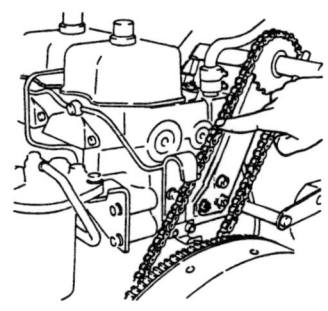

(2) To adjust chain tension, loosen the starting shaft support fixing bolts (2 pcs.), and move the shaft support.

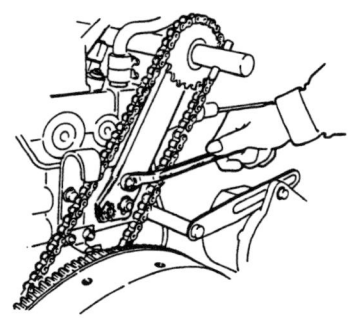

### 1-4 Maintenance
#### 1-4.1 Lubrication of Chain
Every 100 hours of use, apply oil to the chain.

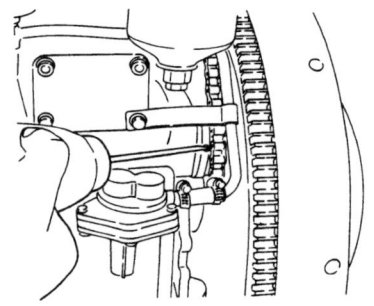

#### 1-4.2 Check and adjust chain tension

(1) Press down on the chain halfway between the freewheel and the starting shaft gear. The chain depression should be about 2-5mm.

# CHAPTER 8
# REDUCTION AND REVERSING GEAR

**[A] FOR MODEL 2TM AND 3TM**
1. Construction .................................................................... 8-1
2. Disassembly .................................................................... 8-6
3. Inspection and servicing ............................................... 8-10
4. Reassembly .................................................................... 8-12
5. Adjustment .................................................................... 8-13

**[B] FOR MODEL 4TM**
1. Construction .................................................................... 8-15
2. Disassembly .................................................................... 8-20
3. Inspection and servicing ............................................... 8-23
4. Reassembly .................................................................... 8-24
5. Adjustment .................................................................... 8-25

[A] For Model 2TM,3TM 1. Construction

# [A] For Model 2TM, 3TM

## 1. Construction

### 1-1 Specifications

| Item | | | Unit | Model Reduction Reversing Gear | | | | | | | | | | | |
|---|---|---|---|---|---|---|---|---|---|---|---|---|---|---|---|
| | | | | Forward | | | | | | Reverse | | | | | |
| Engine model | | | | 2 TM | | | 3 TM | | | 2 TM | | | 3 TM | | |
| Reduction ratio | | | | 2.14 | 2.50 | 3.14 | 2.14 | 2.50 | 3.14 | 2.53 | 2.95 | 3.71 | 2.53 | 2.95 | 3.71 |
| Cont. rating | Output | | PS | 26 | | | 39 | | | 21.30 | | | 31.49 | | |
| | Rev. speed | Input shaft | rpm | 2100 | | | 2100 | | | 2100 | | | 2100 | | |
| | | Output shaft | rpm | 982 | 840 | 670 | 982 | 840 | 670 | 831 | 711 | 567 | 831 | 711 | 567 |
| Service max. | Service max. | | PS | 29 | | | 43 | | | 23.67 | | | 34.59 | | |
| | Rev. speed | Input shaft | rpm | 2200 | | | 2200 | | | 2200 | | | 2200 | | |
| | | Output shaft | rpm | 1029 | 880 | 701 | 1029 | 880 | 701 | 871 | 745 | 594 | 871 | 745 | 594 |
| Input shaft rev. direction | | | | Counter-clockwise viewed from stern | | | | | | | | | | | |
| Output shaft rev. direction | | | | Clockwise viewed from stern | | | | | | Counter-clockwise viewed from stern | | | | | |
| Dry weight | | | kg | 98 | | | | | | | | | | | |

*[A] For Model 2TM,3TM 1. Construction* _____TD

**1-2 Drawing**

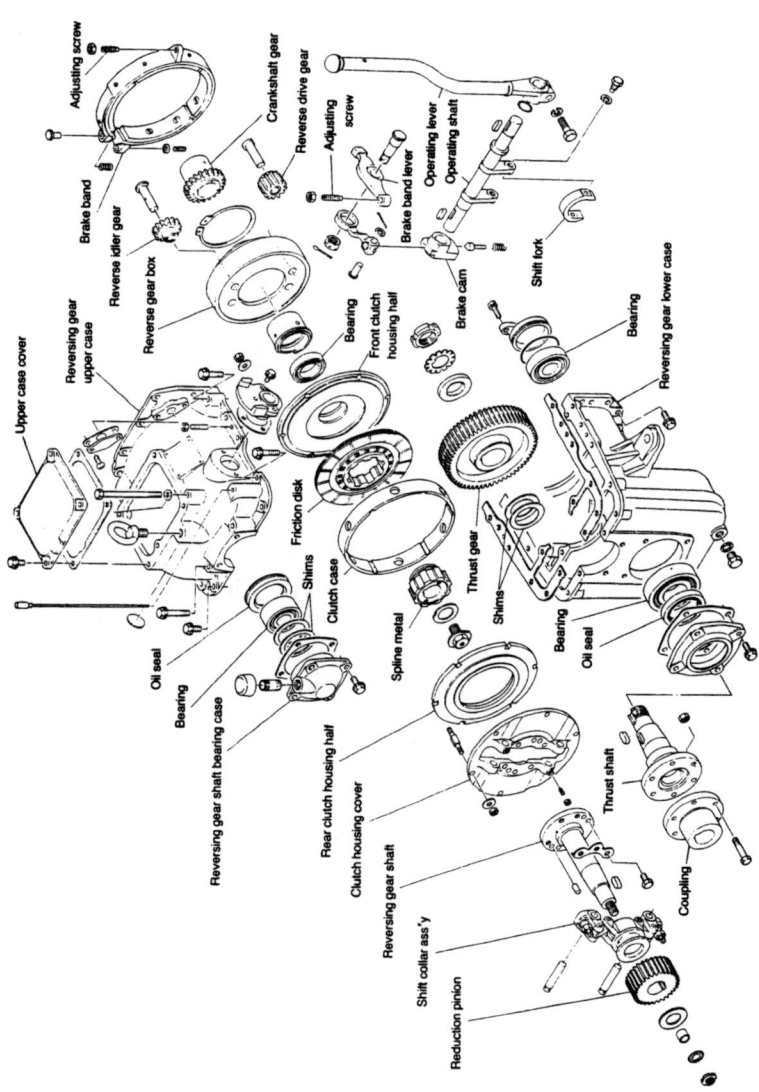

*Chapter 8 Reduction and Reversing Gear*
*[A] For Model 2TM, 3TM 1. Construction*

**1-3 Cross section**

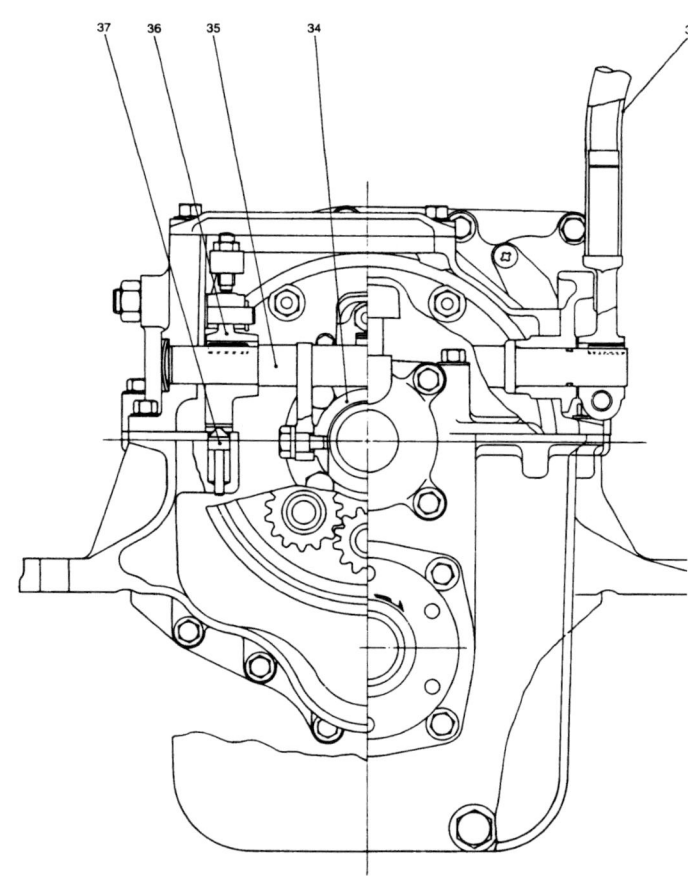

1. Reversing gear upper case
2. Reversing gear lower case
3. Bearing
4. Reversing gear shaft
5. Reduction pinion
6. Oil seal
7. Upper case cover
8. Adjusting screw (brake band)
9. Brake band lever
10. Adjusting screw (friction disk)
11. Brake band
12. Reverse gear box
13. Reverse idler gear
14. Crankshaft gear
15. Crankshaft
16. Bearing
17. Reverse drive gear
18. Spline metal
19. Front clutch housing half
20. Friction disk
21. Rear clutch housing half
22. Clutch case
23. Clutch housing cover
24. Shift collar assembly
25. Bearing
26. Thrust shaft
27. Thrust gear
28. Shims
29. Bearing
30. Thrust shaft rear cover
31. Oil seal
32. Reversing gear shaft bearing case
33. Shims
34. Shift fork
35. Operating shaft
36. Brake cam
37. Neutral pin
38. Operating lever

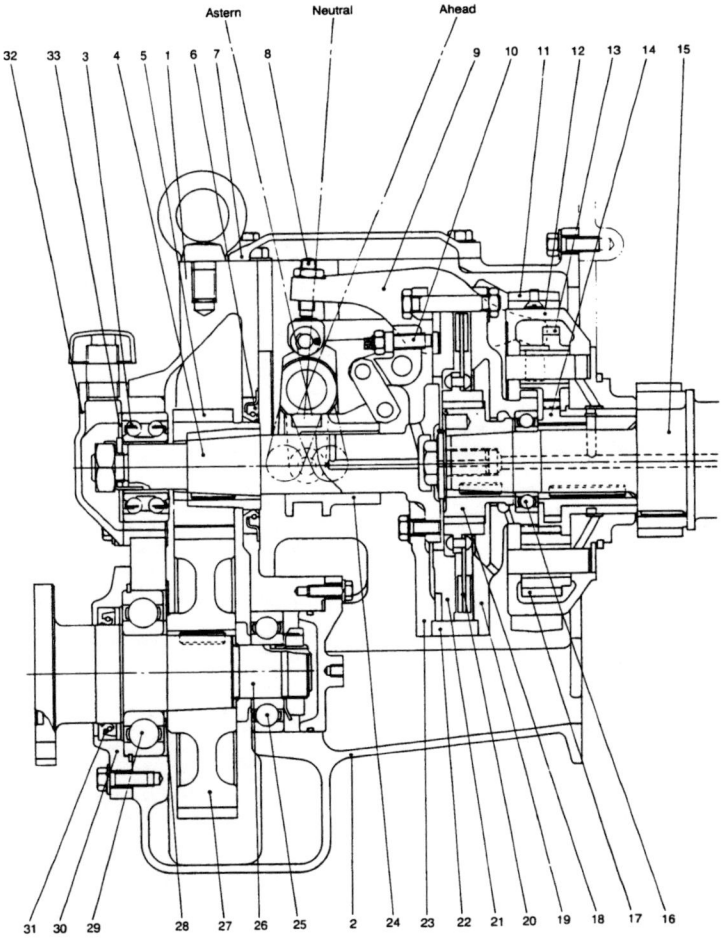

## Chapter 8 Reduction and Reversing Gear
## [A] For Model 2TM, 3TM  1. Construction

### 1-4 Clutch transmission mechanism

The eight gears in the reduction and reversing gear are usually meshed with each other.

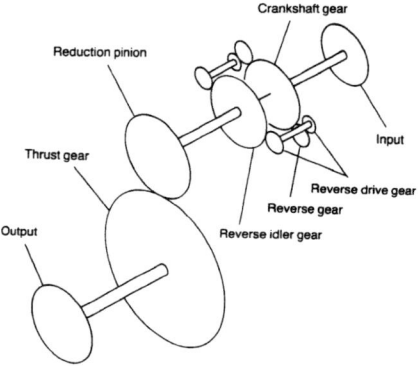

#### 1-4.2 When moving ahead

When the clutch operating lever is moved into ahead position, the friction disk is held by the clutch housing. Then the power is transmitted as described below.

| Crankshaft | → | Friction disk | → | Clutch housing |
| → | Reversing gear shaft | → | Thrust shaft |

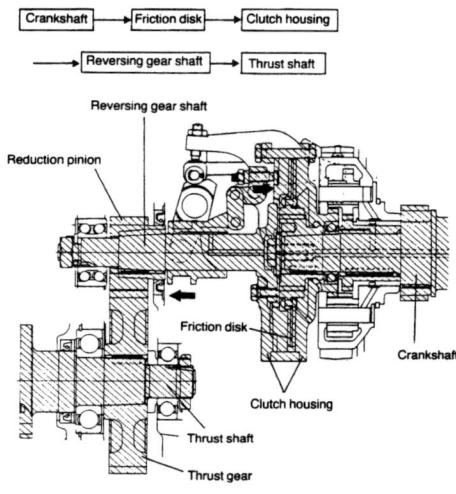

#### 1-4.1 When in neutral position

When the clutch operating lever is placed in neutral, the friction disk is free from the friction surfaces of the clutch housing, and the reverse gear, reduction gear and thrust gear are all stationary. The two reverse idler gears and the two reverse drive gears are planetary around the crankshaft and reverse gears because the power from the crankshaft is not transmitted to the reversing gear shaft.

#### 1-4.3 When moving astern

When the clutch operating lever is moved into astern position, the reverse gear box is held stationary by the brake band. Then the power is transmitted as described below.

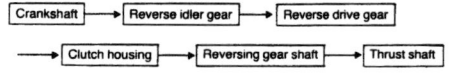

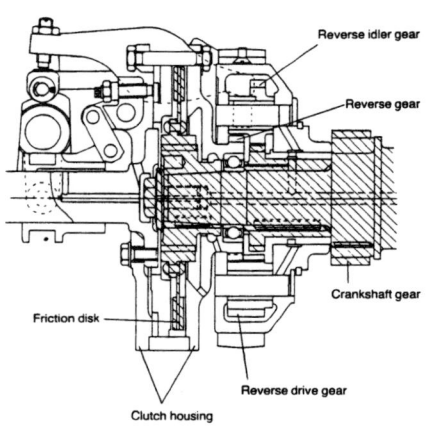

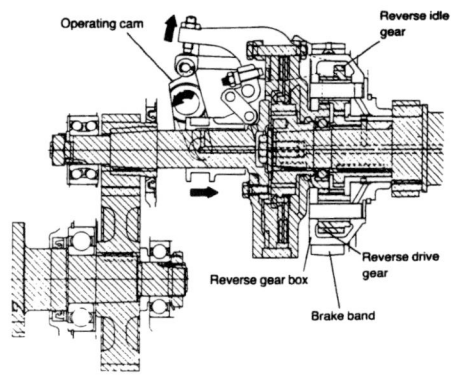

8-5

# 2. Disassembly

### 2-1 Governor assembly

(1) Remove the regulator spring, the pin from governor 2nd lever and the governor rod, and then remove the governor cover.

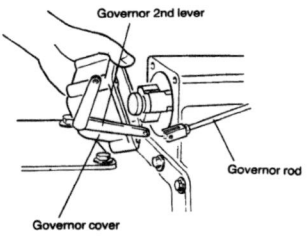

### 2-2 Reversing gear upper case

(1) Remove the tachometer if attached to the reversing gear upper case.

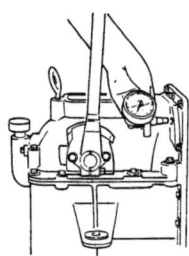

(2) Remove the upper case cover of the reversing gear.
(3) Remove the oil level gauge.
(4) Remove the bolt of the reversing gear shaft bearing case. Take out the case with the removing bolt (plus the clearance adjusting shims of the reversing gear shaft).

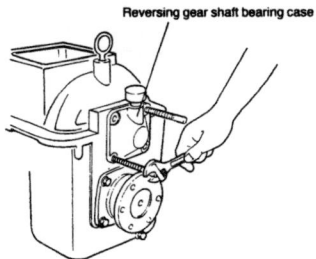

NOTE: Do not lose the adjusting shims.

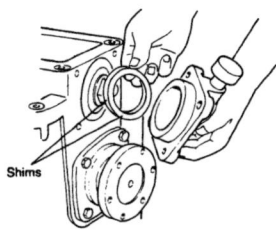

(5) Take out the reversing gear upper case vertically by removing the two positioning taper pins and bolt.

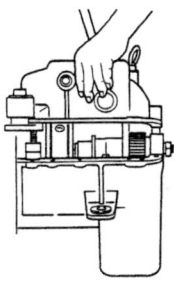

### 2-3 Reversing gear shaft assembly

(1) Remove the reversing gear shaft oil seal by moving it forward.

NOTE: Be sure to remove the oil seal in the shaft direction because the seal's interlocking portion (reversing gear lower case) is not half-split circle type.

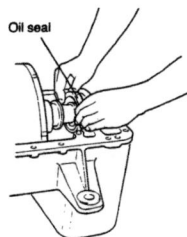

*Chapter 8 Reduction and Reversing Gear*
*[A] For Model 2TM,3TM  2. Disassembly*

(2) Remove the nuts and bend washer on the clutch housing cover located on the opposite side to the flywheel.

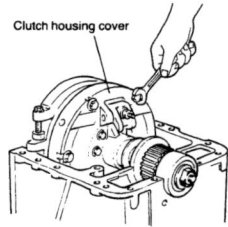

Clutch housing cover

(3) Completely take out the reversing gear shaft by moving it to the opposite side to the flywheel and lifting it.

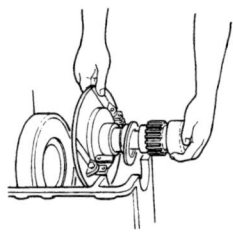

(4) Remove the tightening nut (with bend washer) located on the opposite side to the flywheel of the reversing gear shaft, and take out the reduction pinion and the ball bearing with the gear removing tool.

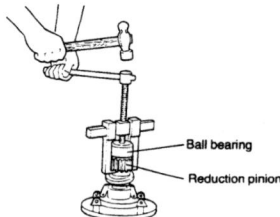

Ball bearing
Reduction pinion

**2-4  Clutch housing and reversing gear box**

(1) Move the rear clutch housing half toward the opposite side to the flywheel and take it out  (fitted to the key bolt).
(2) Move the friction disk and take it out  (fitted to the spline metal).

*NOTE: Be sure to recall the direction of the friction disk.*

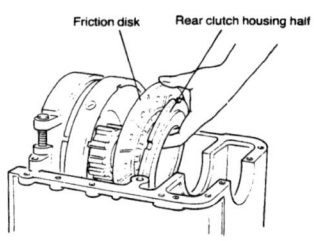

Friction disk      Rear clutch housing half

(3) Remove the clutch case, moving it to the opposite side to the flywheel  (fitted to the key bolt).

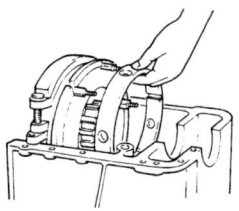

(4) Remove the spline metal locking bolt with the bend washer.

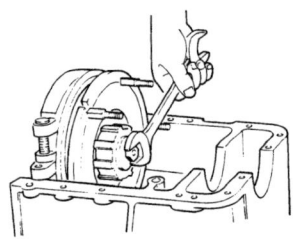

(5) Remove the spline metal

*NOTE: The spline metal is a fitted piece of the crank shaft and taper key. It can be removed by tightening to a removing tool. When hard to remove, a slight shock given to the spline metal will make removal easier.*

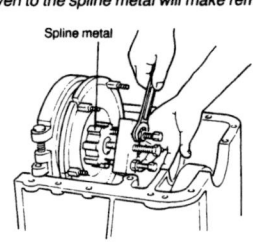

Spline metal

Chapter 8 Reduction and Reversing Gear
[A] For Model 2TM,3TM  2. Disassembly

(6) Remove the front clutch housing by a half twist to the opposite side from the flywheel, using suitable rods.

(9) Lift the brake band and take it out.

NOTE: Do not lose the swivel washer left on the holding side fulcrum.

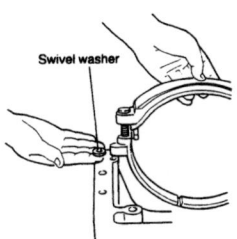

(7) Remove the key for the spline metal.

NOTE: This key should be removed prior to the following procedure for removing the reversing gear box.

### 2-5 Thrust shaft and gear

(1) Remove the bolts of the thrust shaft rear cover.
In case of installation in a boat, remove the reamer bolts and nuts of the coupling, then move the propeller shaft by about 100mm (4 in.) towards the opposite side to the flywheel.

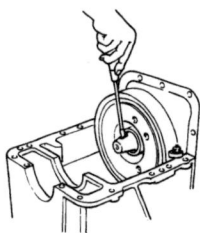

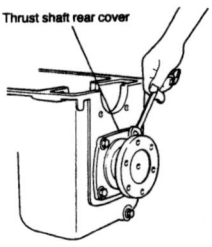

(8) Remove the reverse gear box crank gear and ball bearing toward the opposite side to the flywheel using the removing tool.

(2) Remove the retaining bolt of the thrust shaft front cover.

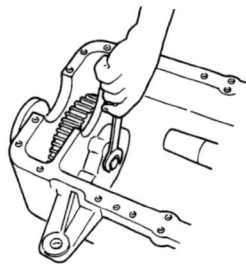

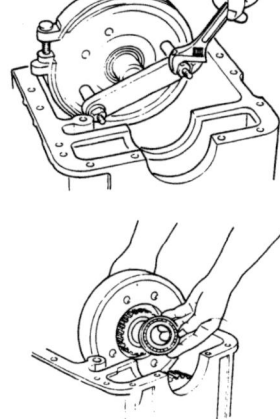

8-8

*Chapter 8 Reduction and Reversing Gear*
*[A] For Model 2TM,3TM  2. Disassembly*

(3) Take out the thrust shaft front cover towards the flywheel side.

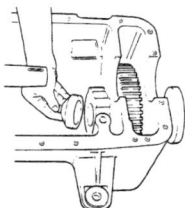

(4) Remove the nut (and bend washer) on the flywheel side, and after removing the washer, place the caulking metal at the head of the thrust shaft. Remove the shaft toward the side opposite the flywheel using a hammer.

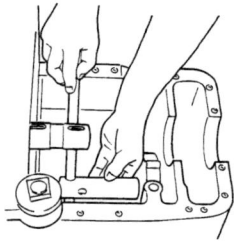

(5) Set the removed nut onto the screw of the thrust shaft and tap. The screw should be protected with a suitable covering.

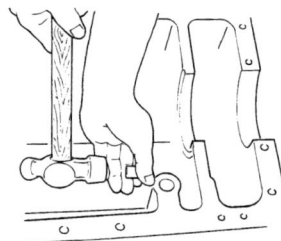

(6) Remove the thrust bearing, rear cover (with oil seal) and the adjusting shims from the case toward the side opposite the flywheel, and the thrust gear, thrust shaft front bearing and spacer can all then be removed.

NOTE: Do not lose the adjusting shims.
It is easier to disassemble the thrust shaft part after the disassembly of the lower case of the reversing gear.

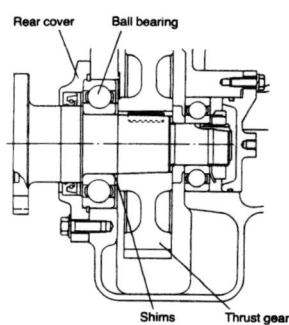

### 2-4 Reversing gear lower case

Remove the lower case of the reversing gear by loosening the fitting bolt from the cylinder block and oil pan.
The lower case is positioned by the two straight pins of the cylinder block.

NOTE: If the engine is installed on a vessel, it is difficult to lift the engine from the engine bed due to the narrow space.
In this case, do not lose the adjusting shim used between the lower case of reversing gear and the engine bed.

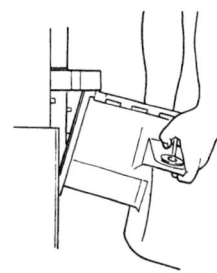

# 3. Inspection and Servicing

### 3-1 Condition of friction surfaces

(1) Check the friction surfaces of the clutch housing for cracks using a test hammer and, if necessary, inspect by color-check. If cracks are noted, replace it with a new one.
(2) Check the bearing housing for burn damage. If any damage is detected, measure the inside diameter. If the inside diameter has reached the wear limit, replace the housing.

mm (in.)

|  | Standard size | Limit of use |
|---|---|---|
| Inside diameter of front clutch housing half | 68.0 ~ 68.046 (2.677~2.6789) | 68.056 (2.6794) |

### 3-2 Condition of each bearing

(1) Check each bearing for damage and rust. If a bearing is rusty or its balls, retainer, etc. are damaged, replace.
(2) Smooth rotation
If the rotation of a bearing is uneven or produces noise, replace it with a new one.

### 3-3 Condition of each gear

(1) Damaged tooth surface
Check the tooth surface of each gear for cracks, scratches and pitching. Replace when serious damage is found.
(2) Wear of tooth surface
Check the tooth surface of each gear for wear.
If the wear is less than 70% of the face width, find out why this has happened, and, if necessary, replace the gear. Neither the tooth top nor the tooth flank should have any wear.
(3) Check the fitted part of shafts or key grooves for cracks and burn damage and replace, when necessary.
(4) Gear backlash

mm (in)

|  | Standard value |
|---|---|
| Crankshaft gear and reverse idler gear | 0.12 ~ 0.2 (0.0047 ~ 0.0079) |
| Reverse gear and reverse drive gear | |
| Reduction gear and thrust gear | |

(5) Replace the gear when gear noise becomes too loud.
(6) Side gap

mm (in.)

|  | Standard size | Limit of use |
|---|---|---|
| Thrust shaft | 0.11 ~ 0.40 (0.0043 ~ 0.0157) | 0.41 (0.0161) |

### 3-4 Friction disk

(1) Check the friction disk for cracks, burn damage or fracture, and repair any damage. Replace if discolored or seriously damaged.

(2) Check the friction disk for wear.
If its thickness is less than the values listed below, replace.

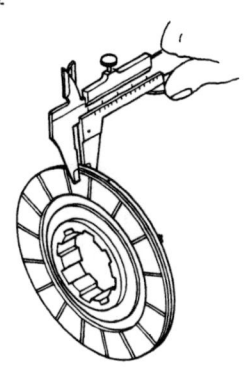

mm (in.)

|  | Standard value | Wear limit value |
|---|---|---|
| Thickness of friction disk | 10.15 ~ 10.35 (0.3996 ~ 0.4075) | 9.45 (0.3720) |

## 3-5 Clearance between reverse gear shafts and bushings.

(1) Check the oil clearance between the reverse idler gear shaft and bushing, and the reverse drive gear shaft and bushing. If the clearance exceeds the allowable limit, replace the bushing.

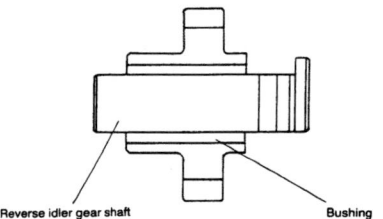

Reverse idler gear shaft — Bushing

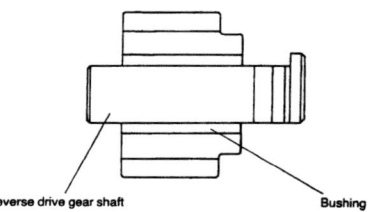

Reverse drive gear shaft — Bushing

mm (in)

| | Standard dimensions | Clearance at assembly | Maximum allowable clearance |
|---|---|---|---|
| Outside diameter of reverse idler gear shaft | ⌀16.003 ~ ⌀16.018 (0.63004 ~ 0.63063) | 0.020 ~ 0.072 | 0.15 |
| Inside diameter of bushing | ⌀16.038 ~ ⌀16.075 (0.63142 ~ 0.63287) | (0.00079 ~ 0.00283) | (0.00591) |
| Outside diameter of reverse drive gear shaft | ⌀16.003 ~ ⌀16.018 (0.63004 ~ 0.63063) | 0.020 ~ 0.072 | 0.15 |
| Inside diameter of bushing | ⌀16.038 ~ ⌀16.075 (0.63142~0.63287) | (0.00079 ~ 0.00283) | (0.00591) |

# 4. Reassembly

Reverse disassembly steps described on the preceding pages. Note the reassembly instructions below.

(1) If any oil is left on the friction surfaces, thoroughly clean.
(2) If removed, replace any paper packing.
(3) Note torque specifications below.

| | | kg-m | (ft-lb) |
|---|---|---|---|
| Clutch housing cover-to-front Clutch housing half nuts | w3/8 | 4.5~5.5 | (32.63~39.88) |
| Spline metal retaining bolt | | 13.5 | (97.88) |
| Reversing gear shaft-to-clutch housing cover bolts | w3/8 | 4.5~5.5 | (32.63~39.88) |
| Reversing gear shaft lock nut | | 25 | (181.25) |
| Thrust shaft lock nut | | 25~28 | (181.25~203) |
| Thrust shaft rear cover retaining bolts | M10 | 4.5~5.0 | (32.63~36.25) |
| Lower case-to-oil pan and cylinder block bolts | M10 | 4.5~5.0 | (32.63~36.25) |
| Upper case-to-lower case bolts | M10 | 4.5~5.0 | (32.63~36.25) |
| Upper case-to-cylinder block bolts | M10 | 4.5~5.0 | (32.63~36.25) |
| Reversing gear shaft bearing housing retaining bolts | M10 | 4.5~5.5 | (32.63~39.88) |

(4) Bend over any lock washer after tightening the locknut.
(5) Be sure the thrust gap of the thrust shaft is 0.138 ~ 0.392mm (0.00543 ~ 0.01543 in.).

NOTE: *Remove or attach shims between the rear bearing and thrust gear to adjust the thrust gap.*

(6) Be sure the thrust gap of the reversing gear shaft is 0.2 ~ 0.4mm (0.008 ~ 0.016 in.).

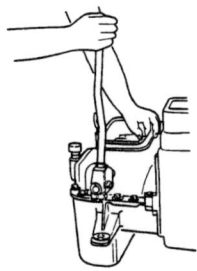

NOTE: *Removing or attaching shims between the bearing and bearing case.*

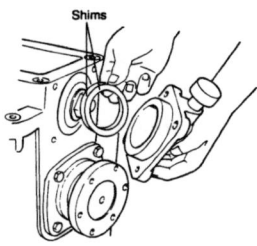

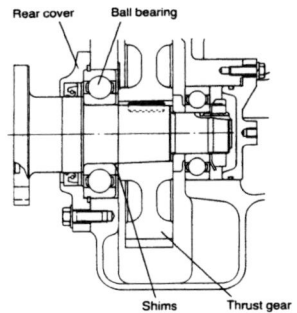

*Chapter 8 Reduction and Reversing Gear*
*[A] For Model 2TM,3TM 5. Adjustment*

TM

# 5. Adjustment

### 5-1 Adjustment of ahead adjusting screws
(1) Set the operating lever to neutral, and detach the upper case cover.
(2) Loosen these adjusting screws completely.
(3) Shift the lever to ahead.
(4) Without use of a spanner, tighten the two screws as much as you can with your fingers.
(5) Again return the lever to neutral.
(6) Retighten each of the two adjusting screws another ¾ of one turn, and be sure to lock them up with the lock nut.

### 5-3 Adjustment by Retightening
Adjustments of the reversing gear after many hours of engine running have already been described.
However, usually a short-cut method is employed. Slightly retighten the two ahead adjusting screw evenly and also the adjusting screw of the astern mode brake band tightening lever. With this method, care should be taken not to tighten the bolts too much as the lever may not shift smoothly into the ahead or astern.

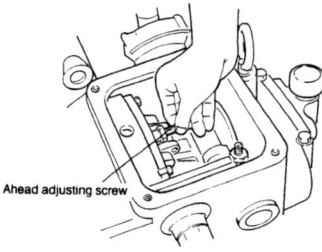

Ahead adjusting screw

### 5-2 Adjustment of astern brake band
(1) Set the operating lever to neutral, and remove the upper case cover.
(2) Loosen the adjusting screw of the brake band tightening lever.
(3) Shift the lever to the astern setting.
(4) Tighten the adjusting screw until there is no gap between the brake band and the gear box.

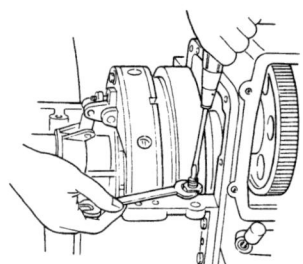

(5) Return the lever to neutral. Then tighten the adjusting screw another one and one half turns, and lock with the lock nut.
Since the brake band should be in contact with the gear box all around its circumference. if required remove the reversing gear upper case and adjust the brake band supporting bolts.

# [B] For Model 4TM

## 1. Construction

### 1-1 Specifications

| Item | | | Unit | Model Y-15M Reduction Reversing Gear | | | | | | | |
|---|---|---|---|---|---|---|---|---|---|---|---|
| | | | | Forward | | | | Reverse | | | |
| Engine model | | | | 4TM | | | | | | | |
| Reduction ratio | | | | 3.80 | 3.22 | 2.59 | 2.13 | 3.93 | 3.33 | 2.68 | 2.20 |
| Cont. rating | Output | | PS | 52 | | | | 39 | | | |
| | Rev. speed | Input shaft | rpm | 2100 | | | | 1974 | | | |
| | | Output shaft | rpm | 553 | 653 | 810 | 986 | 502 | 593 | 736 | 896 |
| Service max. | Output | | PS | 57 | | | | 42.75 | | | |
| | Rev. speed | Input shaft | rpm | 2200 | | | | 2068 | | | |
| | | Output shaft | rpm | 579 | 684 | 849 | 1033 | 526 | 621 | 771 | 939 |
| Input shaft rev. direction | | | | Counter-clockwise viewed from stern | | | | | | | |
| Output shaft rev. direction | | | | Clockwise viewed from stern | | | | | | | |
| Dry weight | | | kg | 100 | | | | | | | |

Chapter 8 Reduction and Reversing Gear
[B] For Model 4TM 1. Construction
TM

**1-2 Drawing**

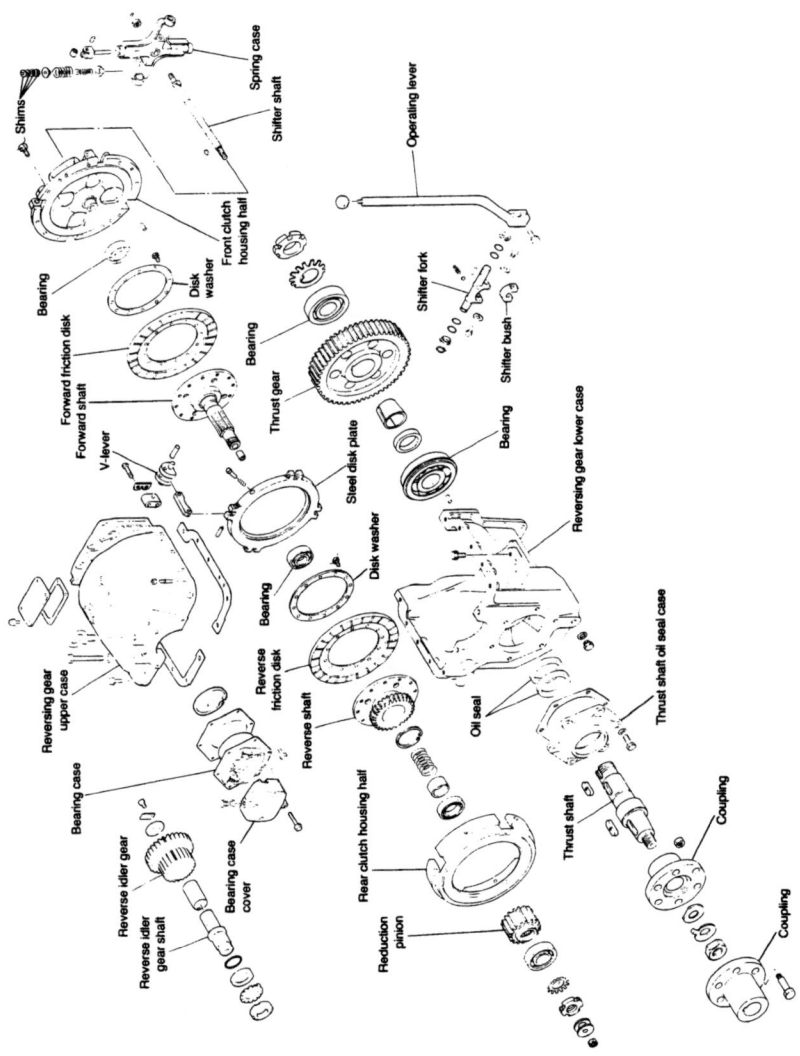

8-16

*Chapter 8 Reduction and Reversing Gear*
*[B] For Model 4TM 1. Construction*

**1-3 Cross section**

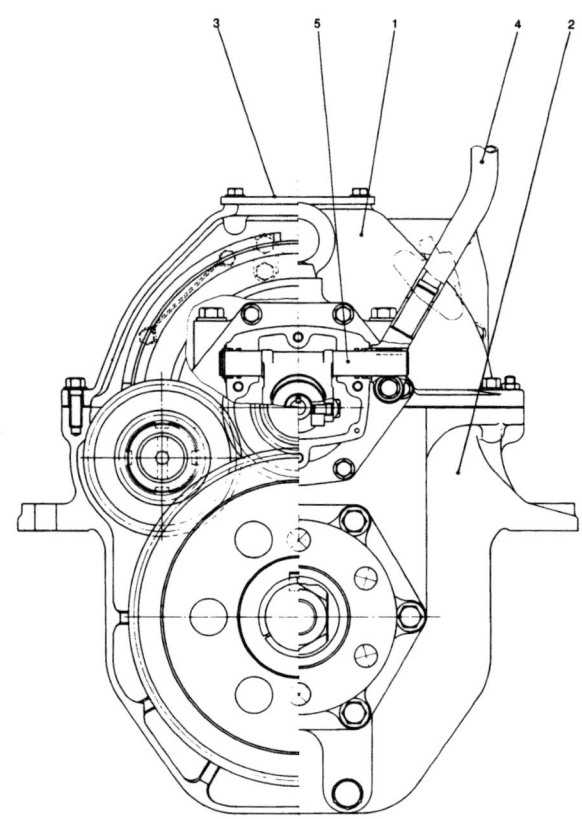

1. Reversing gear upper case
2. Reversing gear lower case
3. Upper case cover
4. Operating lever
5. Shifter fork
6. Shifter collar
7. Shifter bush
8. Shifter shaft
9. Rear clutch housing half
10. Reverse friction disk
11. Steel disk plate
12. Forward friction disk
13. Front clutch housing half
14. V-lever
15. V-lever holder
16. Spring case
17. Reverse idler gears
18. Crankshaft
19. Input flange
20. Bearing
21. Forward shaft
22. Reverse shaft
23. Reduction pinion
24. Bearing
25. Thrust shaft
26. Thrust gear
27. Bearing
28. Thrust shaft oil seal case
29. Oil seals
30. Coupling
31. Neutral pin
32. Bearing case
33. Bearing case cover

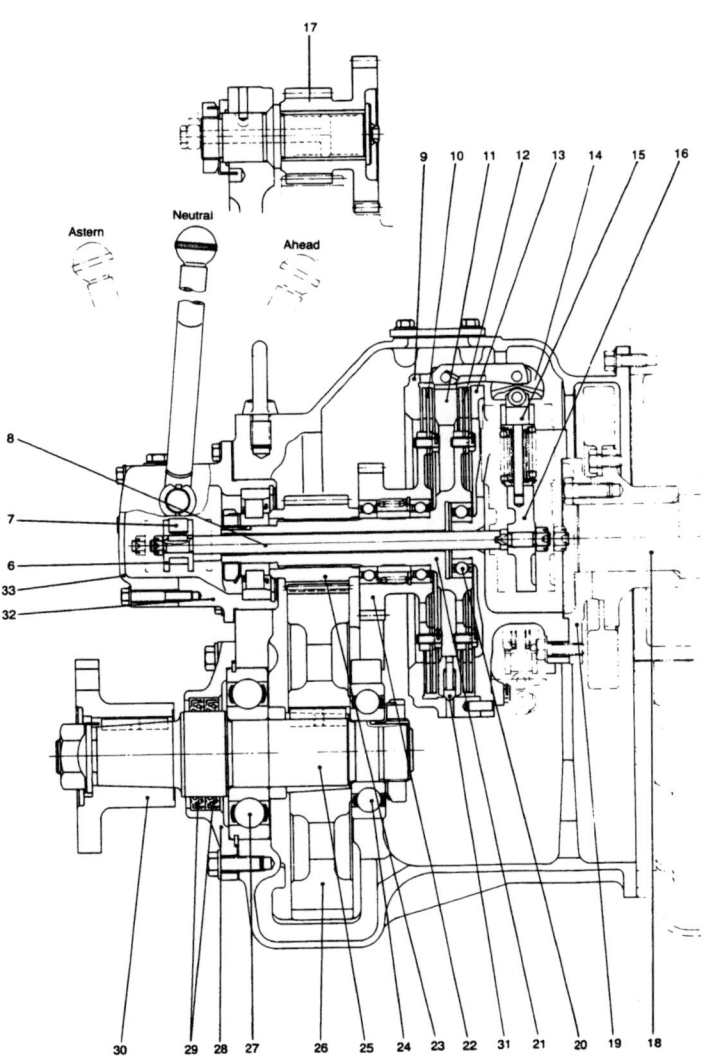

## 1-4 Clutch Transmission Mechanism

The four gears in the reduction and reversing gear are usually meshed with each other.

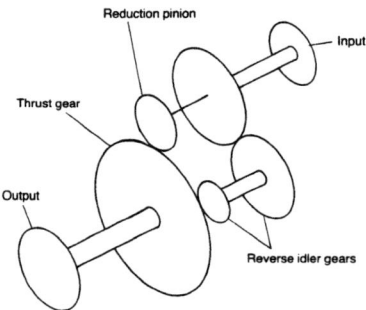

### 1-4.1 When in neutral position:

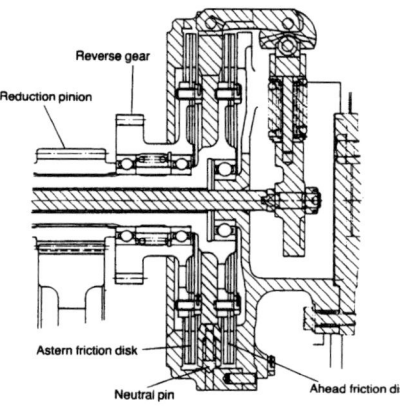

The two friction disks are free from the friction plate, and the reverse gears, reduction pinion and thrust gear are all stationary even when the engine is running. A neutral pin is furnished so as not to transmit power between the friction plate and the friction disks. Therefore, "accompaniment" does not occur with the propeller shaft while the mechanism is in its neutral position.

### 1-4.2 When moving ahead

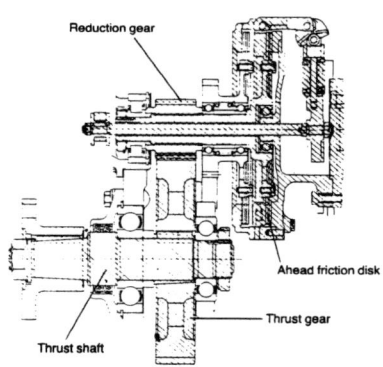

There are two friction disks. The power is transmitted to the ahead friction disk, then from the reduction pinion to the thrust gear to drive the thrust shaft.

### 1-4.3 When moving astern

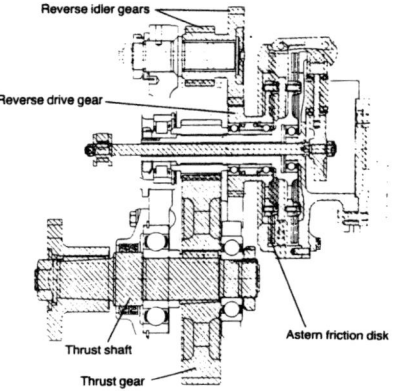

Power is transmitted to the astern friction disk, and in turn to the reverse drive gear, reverse idler gears and thrust gear, to drive the thrust shaft.

Thus, when the gear lever is operated, the ahead and astern friction disks are used as appropriate, depending upon the transmission mode.

## 2. Disassembly

### 2-1 Dismantling of the governor assembly

(1) Remove the governor bearing, and the positioning union (L.O. pipe joint).
(2) Remove the governor case.
(3) Pull out the governor weight, governor gear, and the bearing assemblies.

### 2-3 Disassembly of the reversing gear upper case

(1) Remove the upper case cover.
(2) Remove the tachometer gear unit.
(3) Remove the left and right positioning knock pins for the reversing gear upper case.
(4) Remove the fixing bolts of the case (M12 × 100 2 pcs.; M10 × 30 10 pcs.; M10 × 25 18 pcs.)
(5) Remove the bearing case fixing bolts (M8 × 25 6 pcs.).
(6) Insert the minus driver into the joint of the case, pry up the case, and remove.

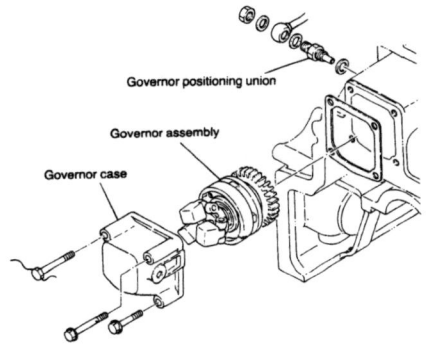

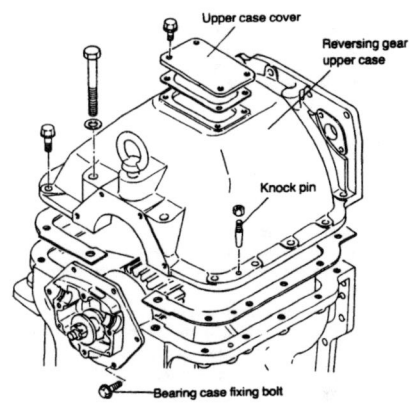

### 2-2 Disassembly of the operating lever and shifter

(1) Remove the bearing case cover, and remove the operating lever, fork, and shifter bush.

NOTE: Take care not to lose the spring and steel balls at the rear of the fork.

### 2-4 Disassembly of the clutch

(1) Remove the fixing bolts (M10 × 30 8 pcs.) of the front clutch housing half unit which is installed to the input shaft flange at the end of the crankshaft.
(2) Bring up the clutch assembly and remove.

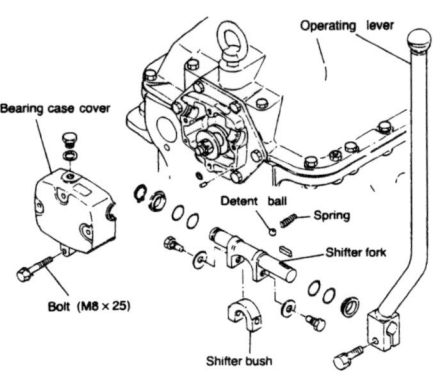

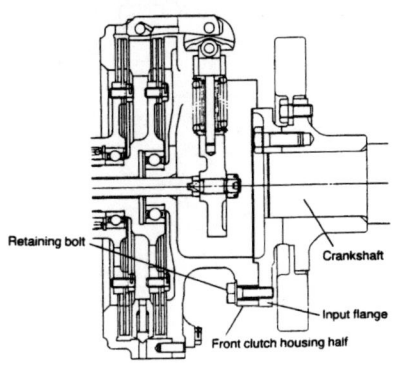

Chapter 8 Reduction and Reversing Gear
[B] For Model 4TM 2. Disassembly

### 2-5 Disassembly of the intermediate shaft and the gear assembly

(1) Straighten the bend washer.
(2) Remove the intermediate shaft lock nut, bend washer, spacer, and O-ring.
(3) Pull out the intermediate shaft and gear assemblies from the clutch case.

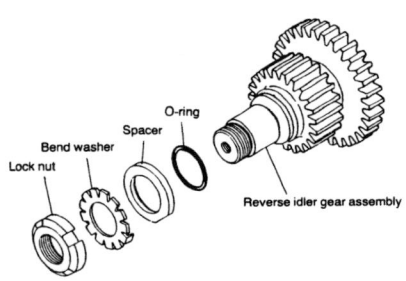

### 2-7 Clutch assembly

(1) Remove the cotter pin and the nut from front end of the shifter shaft.
(2) Remove the V-lever supports from front clutch housing half, and remove the spring case from the shifter shaft

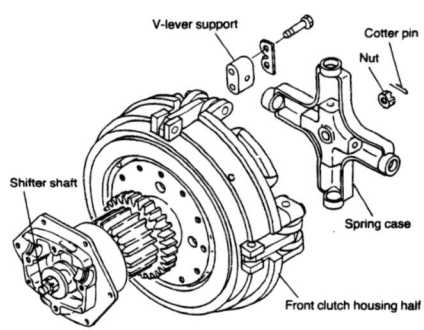

### 2-6 Disassembly of the thrust shaft

(1) Remove the thrust shaft cover (oil seal case) fixing bolts (M12 × 35 6 pcs.), and pry up the cover.
(2) Straighten the lock washer at the end of the front thrust shaft.
(3) Loosen the thrust shaft lock nut.
(4) Place a wooden block to the thrust shaft end inside the reversing gear lower case, and knock it with a hammer. The thrust shaft can be removed leaving the large gear inside the case.
(5) Knock out the ball bearing (#6411NR, #6310) from inside the case.

(3) Remove the snap ring from the bearing case, and remove the bearing case.
(4) Remove the cotter pin, the nut and the shifter sleeve from the shifter shaft.
(5) Remove the shifter shaft from the components.

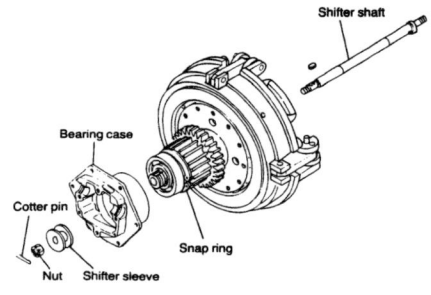

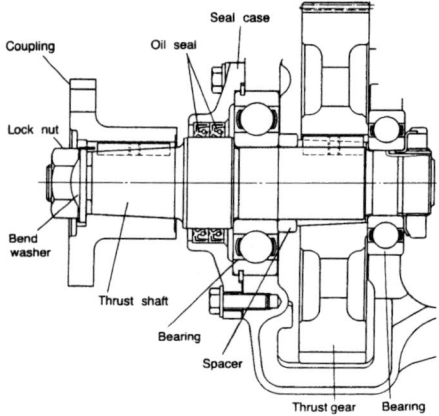

## Chapter 8 Reduction and Reversing Gear
### [B] For Model 4TM 2. Disassembly

(6) Straighten the ears of the lock washer and remove the nut and the lock washer.
(7) Remove the bearing, the remaining snap ring and reduction pinion from the shaft.

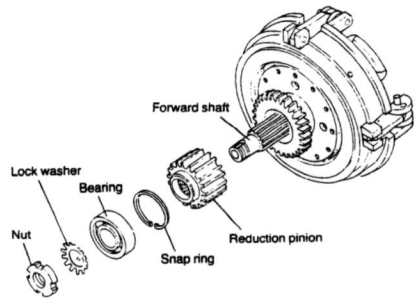

(8) Cut the wire, remove the 12 bolts, and separate the rear clutch housing half from the front half.

NOTE: *Make matching marks on the clutch housing and the steel disk plate for reassembly.*

NOTE: *Do not lose the neutral pins and springs. When removing the rear clutch housing, the four neutral pins and four springs may jump out.*

(9) Remove the reverse shaft assembly and the steel disk plate from the forward shaft assembly.

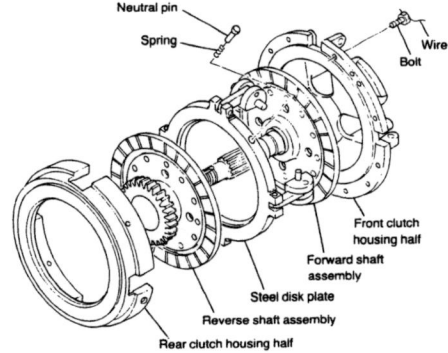

# 3. Inspection and Servicing

### 3-1 Condition of friction surfaces

(1) Check the clutch case for cracks using a test hammer and, if necessary, inspect by color-check. If cracks are noted, replace it with a new one.
(2) Check each bearing housing for burn damage. If any damage is detected, measure the inside diameter. If the inside diameter has reached the wear limit, replace the housing.

### 3-2 Condition of each bearing

(1) Check each bearing for damage and rust. If a bearing is rusty or its balls, retainer, etc. are damaged, replace.
(2) Smooth rotation
If the rotation of a bearing is uneven or produces noise, replace it with a new one.

### 3-3 Condition of each gear

(1) Damaged tooth surface
Check the tooth surface of each gear for cracks, scratches and pitching. Replace when serious damage is found.
(2) Wear of tooth surface.
Check the tooth surface of each gear for wear.
If the wear is less than 70% of the face width, find out why this has happened, and, if necessary, replace the gear. Neither the tooth top nor the tooth flank should have any wear.
(3) Check the fitted part of shafts or key grooves for cracks and burn damage and replace, when necessary.
(4) Gear backlash

|  | mm (in) |
|---|---|
|  | Standard value |
| Forward gear and idler gear | 0.12 ~ 0.2 |
| Reverse gear and idler gear | (0.0047 ~ 0.0079) |
| Idler gear and large gear |  |

Replace the gear when gear noise becomes too loud.

(5) Side gap

|  |  | mm (in.) |
|---|---|---|
|  | Standard size | Limit of use |
| Thrust shaft | 0.11 ~ 0.40 (0.0043 ~ 0.0157) | 0.41 (0.0161) |

### 3-4 Friction disks

(1) Check the friction disks for cracks, burn damage or fracture, and repair any damage. Replace all discolored or seriously damaged friction disks.
(2) Check the friction disks for wear.
If the thickness is less than the values listed below, replace.

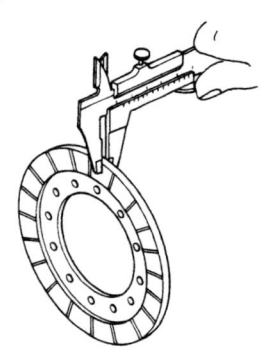

|  |  | mm (in.) |
|---|---|---|
|  | Standard value | Wear limit value |
| Thicknesses of friction disks (both ahead and astern) | 10.15 ~ 10.35 (0.3996 ~ 0.4075) | 9.45 (0.3720) |

# 4. Reassembly

Reverse disassembly steps on preceding pages.
Note reassembly instructions below.
(1) If any oil is on the friction surfaces, thoroughly clean.
(2) If removed, replace any paper packing.

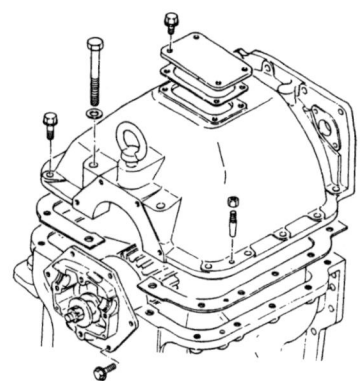

(3) Note torque specifications below.

| | | kg-m (ft-lb) | |
|---|---|---|---|
| Friction disk retaining bolts (both) | M8 | 2.8 | (20.3) |
| Front-to-rear clutch housing bolts | M8 | 2.2~2.8 | (15.9~20.3) |
| Forward shaft lock nut | M30 | 25 | (181.25) |
| Front end of shifter shaft lock nut | M12 | 6.0 | (43.5) |
| Rear end of shifter shaft lock nut | M10 | 4.5~5.5 | (32.625~39.875) |
| Front end of thrust shaft lock nut | M50 | 70 | (507.5) |
| Reverse idler gear shaft lock nut | M35 | 25 | (181.25) |
| Lower case-to-cylinder block and oil pan | M10 | 4.5~5.5 | (32.625~39.875) |
| Front clutch housing half-to-crankshaft input flange bolts | M10 | 4.5~5.5 | (32.625~39.875) |
| Upper case-to-lower case bolts | M10 | 4.5~5.5 | (32.625~39.875) |
| Upper case-to-cylinder block bolts | M10 | 4.5~5.5 | (32.625~39.375) |
| Bearing case retaining bolts | M8 | 2.2~2.8 | (15.95~20.3) |
| Thrust shaft oil seal case retaining bolts | M12 | 9.0 | (65.25) |
| Thrust shaft coupling nuts | w5/8 | 25 | (181.25) |

(4) Bend over any lock washer after tightening the lock nut.

# 5. Adjustment

In the case of V-lever type mechanical marine gears, inadequate adjustment of the V-lever ~ the roller clearance is likely to cause slippage of, or cracks in, the marine gear friction plate.

### 5-1 Measurement of shifter shaft motion

If the occurs, check the alignment of the marine gear thrust shaft and the propeller shaft, and also check the V-lever ~ the roller clearance according to the following procedures.
Before checking, remove the clutch assembly.

(1) Check that the all the V-levers pushed up by the roller move concurrently when the shifting shaft is shifted. If even one V-lever moves faster than the others, the pressure on the friction plate is sure to be uneven. This can cause the slippage or cracking of the friction plate.

(2) Check that the clearance between the V-lever and the roller is 0.60–1.06mm (0.024–0.042 in.) when the marine gear is in the neutral position. It is hard to make this measurement directly, so measure the play of the shifting shaft, instead.

The play of the shifting shaft: the distance of V-lever displacement when the clutch is moved to forward or reverse from neutral, and the V-roller comes into contact with the V-lever to set the V-lever in motion.

Standard play of the shifting shaft:
1.0–2.0mm (0.04–0.08 in.)
Measure the play with the dial gauge as an illustration:

(3) Adjustment of V-lever clearance
To adjust, add or remove shims on the V-lever holder. Adding shim(s) makes the clearance smaller.

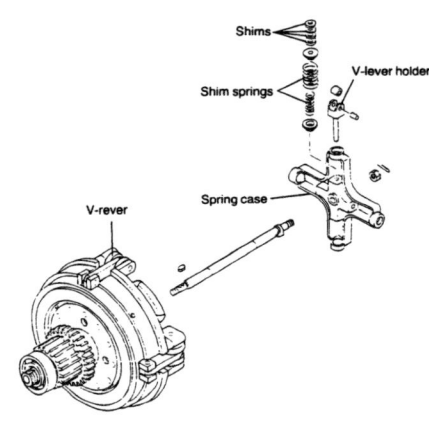

**CHAPTER 9**
# ELECTRICAL SYSTEM

1. Composition ............................................................................ 9-1
2. Battery .................................................................................... 9-2
3. Starter Motor ......................................................................... 9-5
4. Alternator, Option .................................................................. 9-16

*Chapter 9 Electrical System*
*1. Composition*

# 1. Composition

## 1-1. Composition

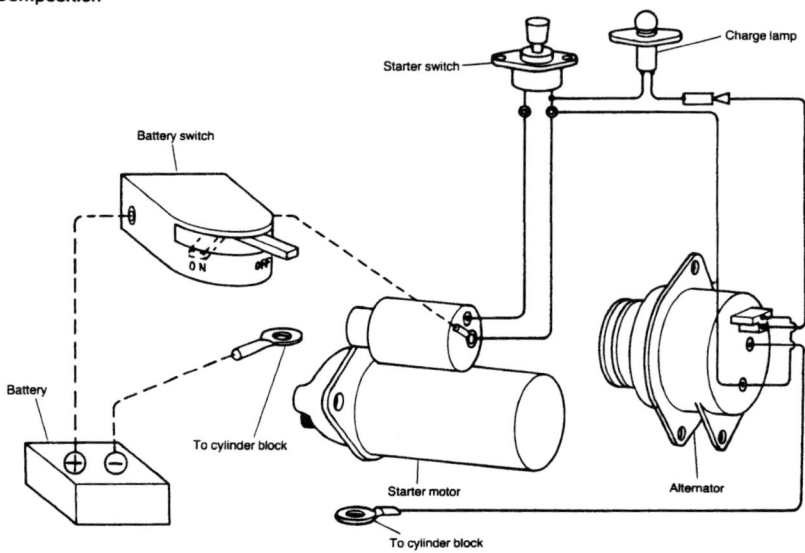

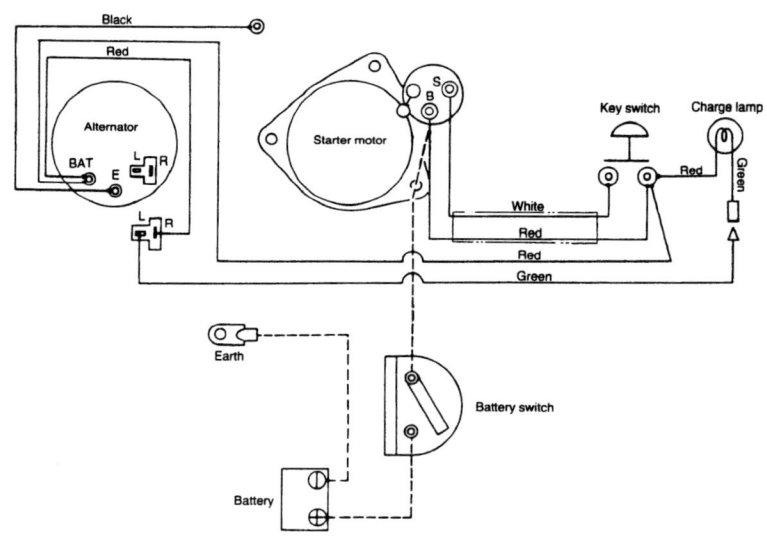

# 2. Battery

## 2-1 Construction

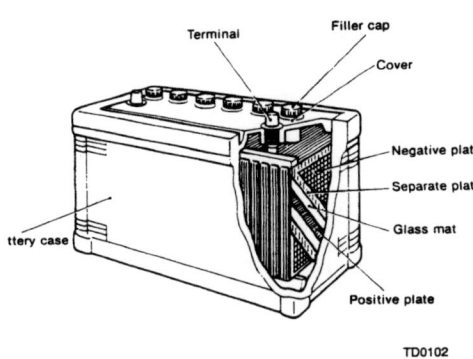

TD0102

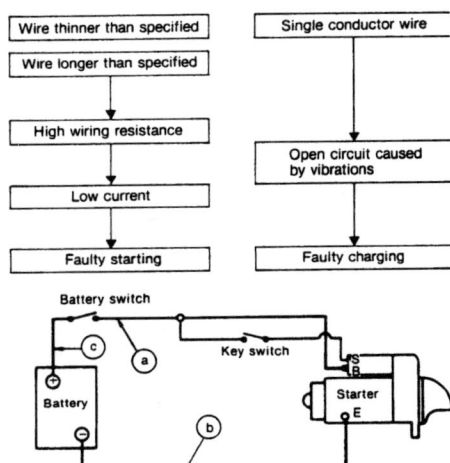

The battery utilizes chemical action to convert chemical energy to electrical energy. This engine uses a lead acid battery which stores a fixed amount of power that can be used when required. After use, the battery can be recharged and used again.
As shown in the figure, a nonconductive container is filled with dilute sulfuric acid electrolyte. Lead dioxide positive plates and lead dioxide negative plates separated by glass mats are stacked alternately in the electrolyte. The positive and negative plates are connected to their respective terminals.
Power is removed from the battery by connecting the load across these two terminals.
When the battery is discharging, an electric current flows from the positive plates to the negative plates. When the battery is being charged, electric current is passed through the battery in the opposite direction by an external power source.

## 2-2 Battery capacity and battery cables

### 2-2.1 Battery capacity
Since the battery has a minimum capacity of 12V, 70AH, it can be used for 100 ~ 150AH.

| Minimum battery capacity | 12V 120AH |
|---|---|
| Fully charged specific gravity | 1.280 |

### 2-2.2 Battery cable
Wiring must be performed with the specified electric wire. Thick, short wiring should be used to connect the battery to the starter, (soft automotive low-voltage wire [AV wire]). Using wire other than that specified may cause the following troubles:

The overall lengths of the wiring between the battery (+) terminal and the starter (B) terminal, and between the battery (−) terminal and the starter (E) terminal should be based on the following table.

| Voltage system | Allowable wiring voltage drop | Conductor cross-section area | a+b+c allowable length |
|---|---|---|---|
| 12V | 0.2V or less/100A | 20mm² (0.0311 in.²) | Up to 2.5m (98.43 in.) |
| | | 40mm² (0.062 in.²) | Up to 5m (196.87 in.) |

NOTE: *Excessive resistance in the key switch circuit (between battery and start (S) terminals) can cause improper pinion engagement. To prevent this, follow the wiring diagram exactly.*

## 2-3 Inspection
The quality of the battery governs the starting performance of the engine. Therefore the battery must be routinely inspected to ensure that it functions perfectly at all times.

### 2-3.1 Visual inspection
(1) Inspect the case for cracks, damage and electrolyte leakage.
(2) Inspect the battery holder for tightness, corrosion, and damage.
(3) Inspect the terminals for rusting and corrosion, and check the cables for damage.
(4) Inspect the caps for cracking, electrolyte leakage and clogged vent holes.
Correct any abnormal conditions found. Clean off rusted terminals with a wire brush before reconnecting the battery cable.

## 2-3.2 Checking the electrolyte
(1) Electrolyte level

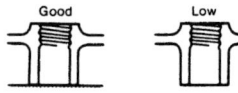
Good  Low

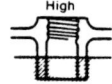
High

Check the electrolyte level every 7 to 10 days. The electrolyte must always be 10 ~ 20mm above the tops of the plates.

NOTES: 1) The "LEVEL" line on a transparent plastic battery case indicates the height of the electrolyte.
2) Always use distilled water to bring up the electrolyte level.
3) When the electrolyte has leaked out, add dilute sulfuric acid with the same specific gravity as the electrolyte.

(2) Measuring the specific gravity of the electrolyte
1) Draw some of the electrolyte up into a hydrometer.

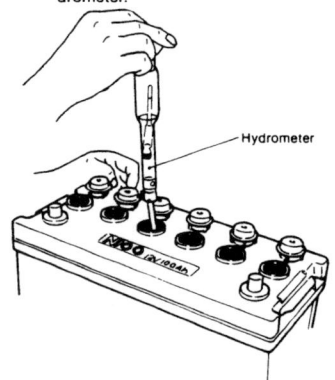
Hydrometer

2) Take the specific gravity reading at the top of the scale of the hydrometer.

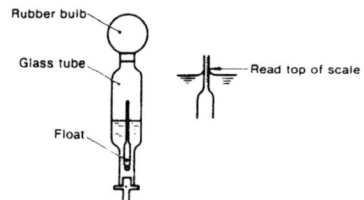
Rubber bulb
Glass tube
Read top of scale
Float

3) The battery is fully charged if the specific gravity is 1.260 at an electrolyte temperature of 20°C. The battery is discharged if the specific gravity is 1.200 (50%). If the specific gravity is below 1.200, recharge the battery.
4) If the difference in the specific gravity among the cells of the battery is ±0.01, the battery is OK.
5) Measure the temperature of the electrolyte. Since the specific gravity changes with the temperature, 20°C is used as the reference temperature.
Reading the specific gravity at 20°C
$S_{20} = St + 0.0007 (t - 20)$
$S_{20}$: Specific gravity at the standard temperature of 20°C
St: Specific gravity of the electrolyte at t°C
0.0007: Specific gravity change per 1°C
t: Temperature of electrolyte

## 2-3.3 Voltage test
Using a battery tester, the amount of discharge can be determined by measuring the voltage drop which occurs while the battery is being discharged with a large current.

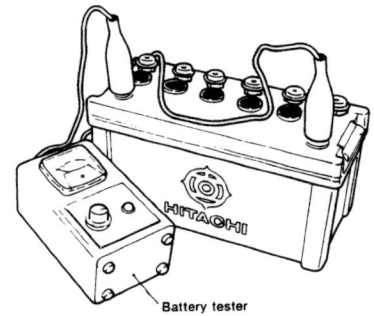
Battery tester

(1) Connect the tester to the battery.
12V battery tester
Adjust the current (A).
(2) Connect the (+) lead of the tester to the (+) battery terminal, and the (−) tester lead to the (−) battery terminal.
(3) Push the TEST button, wait 5 seconds, and then read the meter.
• Repeat the test twice to make sure that the meter indication remains the same.

## 2-3.4 Washing the battery
(1) Wash the outside of the battery with a brush while running cold or warm water over the battery. (Make sure that no water gets into the battery.)
(2) When the terminals or other metal parts are corroded due to exposure to electrolyte leakage, wash off all the acid.
(3) Check the vent holes of the caps and clean if clogged.
(4) After washing the battery, dry it with compressed air, connect the battery cable, and coat the terminals with grease. Since the grease acts as an insulator, do not coat the terminals before connecting the cables.

## 2-4 Charging
### 2-4.1 Charging methods
There are two methods of charging a battery: normal and rapid.
Rapid charging should only be used in emergencies.
- Normal charging...Should be conducted at a current of 1/10 or less of the indicated battery capacity (10A or less for a 100AH battery).
- Rapid charging...Rapid charging is done over a short period of time at a current of 1/5 ~ 1/2 the indicated battery capacity (20A ~ 50A for a 100AH battery). However, since rapid charging causes the electrolyte temperature to rise too high, special care must be exercised.

### 2-4.2 Charging procedure
(1) Check the specific gravity and adjust the electrolyte level.
(2) Disconnect the battery cables.
(3) Connect the red clip of the charger to the (+) battery terminal and connect the black clip to the (−) terminal.

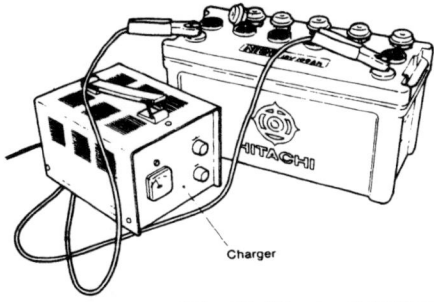
Charger

(4) Set the current to 1/10 ~ 1/5 of the capacity indicated on the outside of the battery.
(5) Periodically measure the specific gravity during charging to make sure that the specific gravity remains at a high fixed value. Also check whether gas is being generated.

### 2-4.3 Charging precautions
(1) Remove the battery caps to vent the gas during charging.
(2) While charging, ventilate the room and prohibit smoking, welding, etc.
(3) The electrolyte temperature should not exceed 45°C during charging.
(4) Since an alternator is used on this engine, when charging with a charger, always disconnect the battery (+) cable to prevent destruction of the diodes.
(Before disconnecting the (+) battery cable, disconnect the (−) battery cable [ground side].)

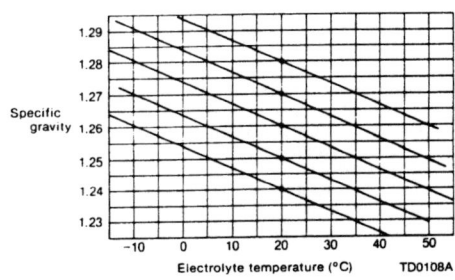
Electrolyte temperature and specific gravity

### 2-5 Battery storage precautions
The life of a battery depends considerably on how it is handled. Generally speaking, however, after about two years its performance will deteriorate, starting will become difficult, and the battery will not fully recover its original charge even after recharging. Then it must be replaced.

(1) Since the battery will self-discharge about 0.5%/day even when not in use, it must be charged 1 or 2 times a month when it is being stored.

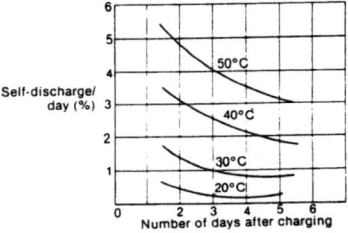

(2) If charging by the engine alternator is insufficient because of frequent starts and stops, the battery will rapidly lose power.
Charge the battery as soon as possible after it is used under these conditions.
(3) An easy-to-use battery charger that permits home charging is available from Yanmar. Take proper care of the battery by using the charger as a set with a hydrometer.
When the specific gravity has dropped to about 1.16 and the engine will not start, charge the battery up to a specific gravity of 1.26 (24 hours).
(4) Before putting the battery in storage for long periods, charge it for about 8 hours to prevent rapid aging.

Simple charger
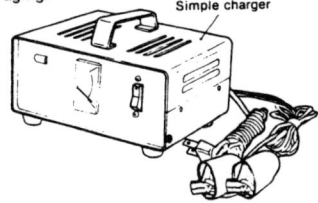

# 3. Starter Motor

The starter motor is installed on the flywheel housing. When the starting button is pushed, the starter motor pinion flies out and engages the ring gear of the flywheel. Then the main contact is closed, current flows, and the engine is started.
After the engine starts, the pinion automatically returns to its initial position when the starting button is released. Once the engine starts, the starting button should be released immediately. Otherwise, the starter motor may be damaged or burned out.

### 3-1 Specifications and Performance.

| Model | | S13 – 90 |
|---|---|---|
| Rating (sec) | | 30 |
| Output (kw) | | 2.21 |
| Clutch system | | Overrunning |
| Engagement system | | Magnetic shift |
| Pinion flyout voltage (V) | | 8 or less |
| No-load | Terminal voltage (V) | 12 |
| | Current (A) | 120 |
| | Speed (rpm) | 4000 or greater |

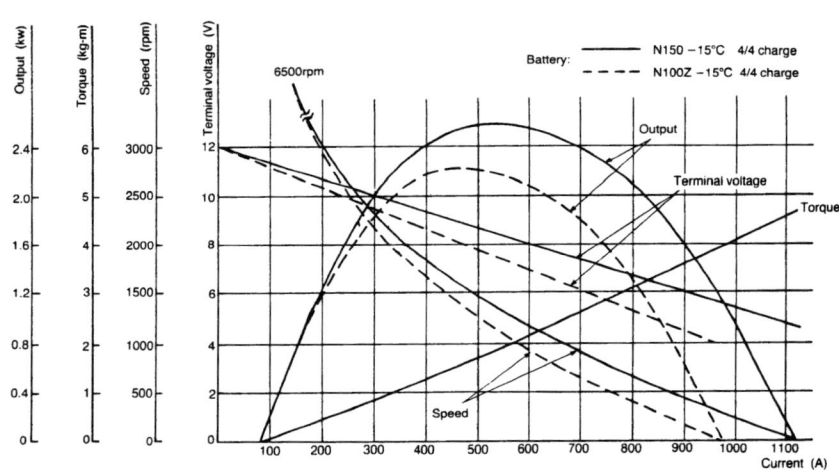

### 3-2 Construction

The starter motor described in this section is a conventional pre-engaged 4-brush 4-pole starter motor with a screw roller drive clutch.
The starter motor is composed of three major parts, as follows:

(1) Magnetic switch
    This moves the plunger to engage and disengage the pinion, and through the engagement lever opens and closes the main contact (moving contact) to stop the starter motor.
(2) Motor
    A continuous current series motor which generates rotational drive power.
(3) Pinion
    This transfers driving power from the motor to the ring gear. An overspeed clutch is employed to prevent damage if the engine should run too fast.

*Chapter 9 Electrical System*
*3. Starter Motor* _____ *TM*

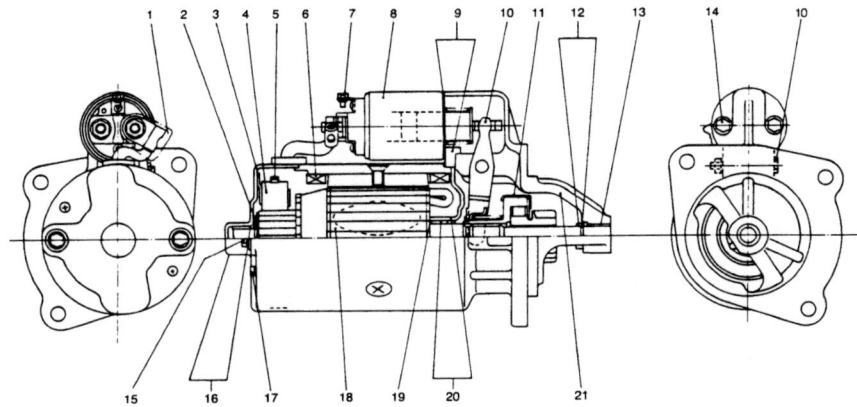

1. Terminal cover
2. Thrust washer
3. Brush holder
4. Brush
5. Spring
6. Field coil
7. Screw
8. Magnetic switch assembly
9. Dust cover
10. Shift lever
11. Pinion Assembly
12. Pinion stopper
13. Bushing
14. Cap screw
15. Through Bolt
16. Rear cover assembly
17. Screw
18. Armature assembly
19. Thrust washer
20. Bushing
21. Gear case

## Chapter 9 Electrical System
### 3. Starter Motor

To prevent the motor receiving a shock when the engine starts and over-runs, this starter motor is installed with an over-running clutch.

Over-running clutch

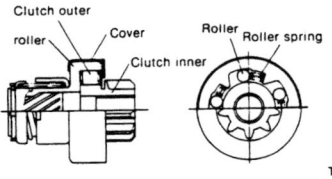

TD0111

### 3-4 Adjustment and performance test

#### 3-4.1 L-size measurement (gap between pinion and pinion stopper)

When the pinion is at the projected position, measure the space between the pinion and pinion stopper. This check should be made with the pinion pressed back lightly to take up any play in the engagement linkage.

| $\ell$ dimension | 0.3 ~ 1.5mm (0.0118 ~ 0.0590 in.) |
|---|---|

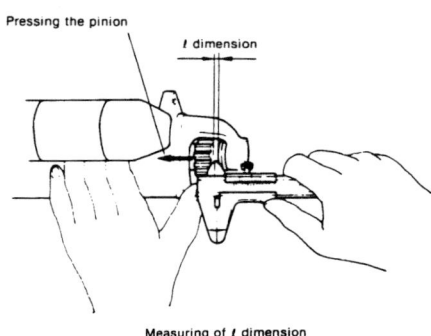

Measuring of $\ell$ dimension

#### 3-4.2 Pinion movement

After complete assembly of the starter motor, connect up the motor as in Fig.

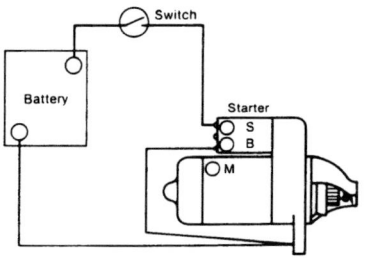

### 3-3 Operation

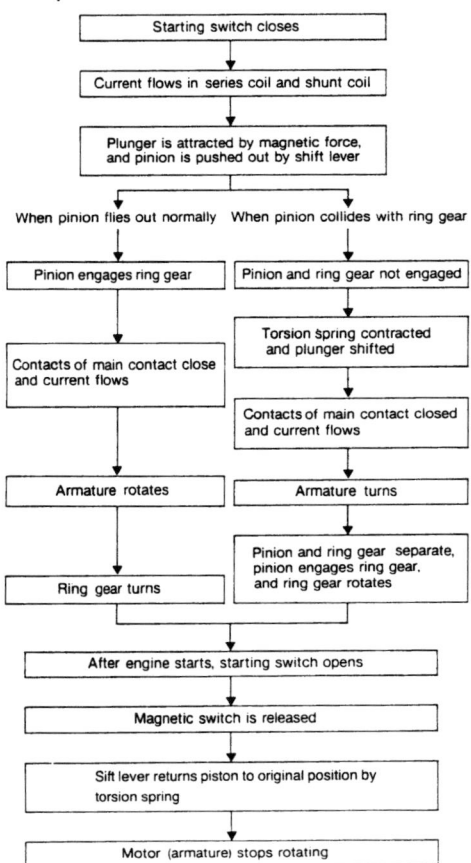

## Chapter 9 Electrical System
## 3. Starter Motor

### 3-4.3 Plunger movement

Adjustment made by adjusting stroke of magnetic plunger to the prescribed value. Adjusting screw type (S12-79). Adjust the -dimension by adjusting the screw and nut.

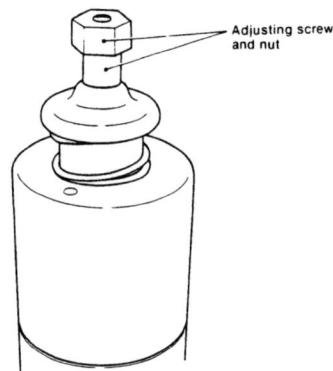

### 3-4.4 Pinion lock torque measurement

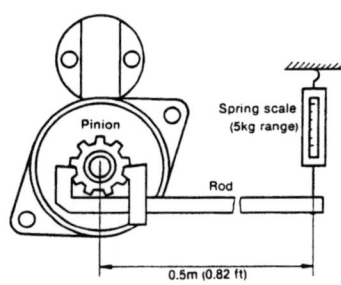

### 3-4.5 Mesh clearance

Mesh clearances is the distance betweeen the flywheel ring gear and starter motor pinion in the rest position. This clearance should be between 3mm (0.1181 in.) and 5mm (0.1969 in.)

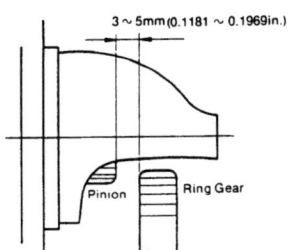

### 3-5 Disassembly

#### 3-5.1 Magnetic switch
(1) Disconnect magnetic switch wiring.
(2) Remove through bolt mounting magnetic switch.
(3) Remove magnetic switch.

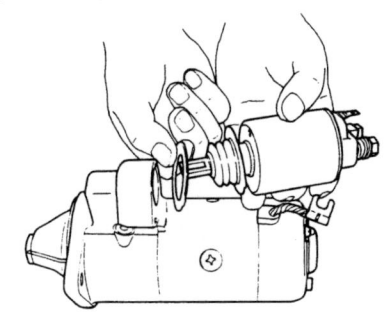

#### 3-5.2 Rear cover
(1) Remove dust cover.

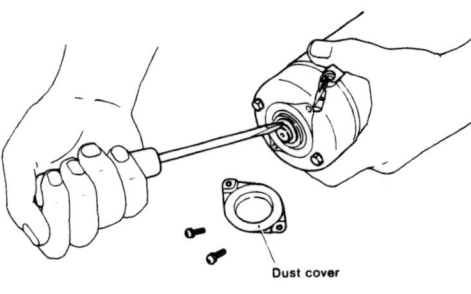

(2) Remove E-ring, and remove thrust washer (be careful not to lose the washer and shim).
(3) Remove the two through bolts holding the rear cover, and the two screws holding the brush holder.
(4) Remove rear cover.

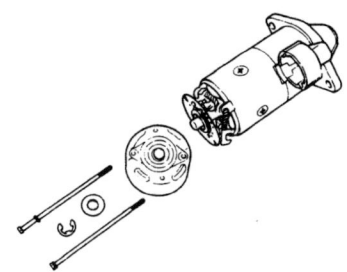

### 3-5.3 Brush holder
(1) Float (−)brush from the commutator.
(2) Remove (+)brush from the brush holder.
(3) Remove brush holder.

### 3-5.6 Pinion
(1) Slide the pinion stopper to the pinion side.
(2) Remove the pinion stopper clip.
(3) Remove the pinion from the armature.

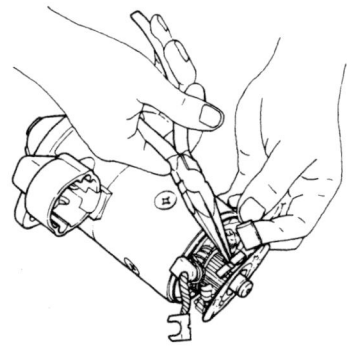

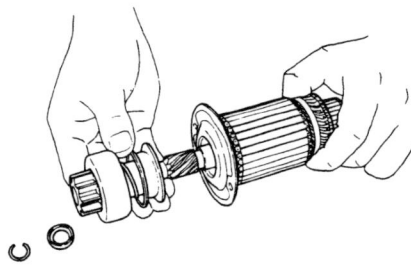

## 3-6 Inspection
### 3-6.1 Armature
(1) Commutator
Inspect the surface of the commutator. If corroded or pitted, sand with #500 ~ #600 sandpaper. If the commutator is severely pitted, grind it to within a surface roughness of at least 0.4 by turning it on a lathe. Replace the commutator if damage is irreparable.

### 3-5.4 Yoke
(1) Remove yoke. Pull it out slowly so that it does not strike against other parts.

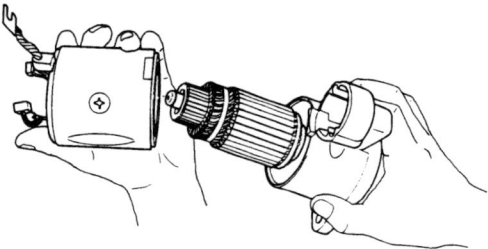

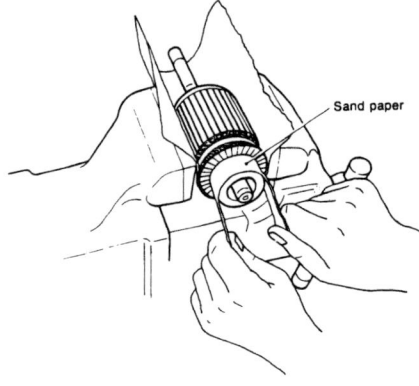

Sand paper

### 3-5.5 Armature
(1) Slide pinion stopper to pinion side.

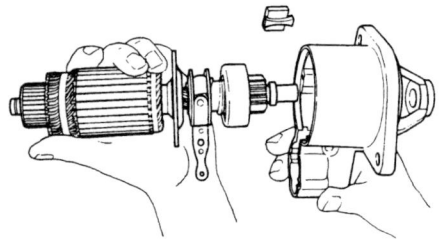

(2) Remove the pinion stopper clip.

|  | Maintenance standard | Wear limit |
|---|---|---|
| Commutator outside diameter | ⌀48 (1.890) | ⌀47 (1.850) |
| Commutator run-out | Within 0.03 (0.0012) | 0.2 (0.0079) |
| Difference between maximum diameter and minimum diameter | Repair limit 0.4 (0.0157) | Repair accuracy 0.05 (0.002) |

## (2) Mica undercut
Check the mica undercut, correct with a hacksaw blade when the undercut is too shallow.

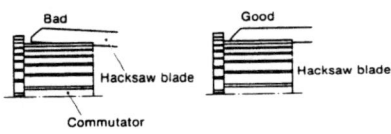

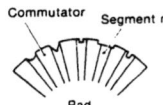

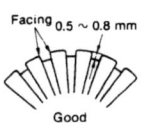

| | Maintenance standard | Repair limit |
|---|---|---|
| Mica undercut | 0.2 (0.0079) | 0.5 ~ 0.8 (0.0197 ~ 0.0315) |

mm (in.)

## (3) Armature coil ground test
Using a tester, check for continuity between the commutator and the shaft (or armature core). Continuity indicates that these points are grounded and that the armature must be replaced.
1) Short test...existence of broken or disconnected coil.
2) Insulation test...between commutator and armature core or distortion shaft.

Checking commutator for insulation defects.

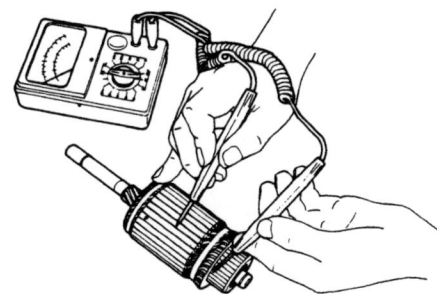

Checking armature windings for insulation defects.

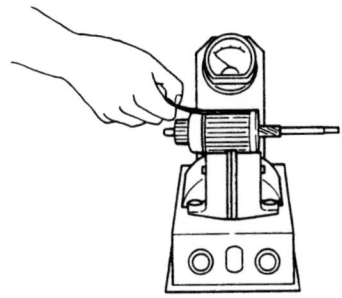

## (4) Armature shaft outside diameter
Measure the outside diameter of the armature shaft at four locations: front, center, end, and pinion. Replace the armature if the shaft is excessively worn.
Check the bend of the shaft; replace the armature if the bend exceeds 0.08mm (0.0031in.)

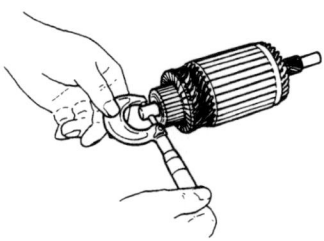

### 3-6.2 Field coil
(1) Open test
Check for continuity between the terminals connecting the field coil brushes. Continuity indicates the coil is open and must be replaced.

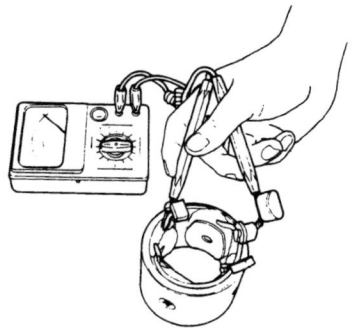

### Chapter 9 Electrical System
### 3. Starter Motor

(2) Short test
Check for continuity between the yoke and any field coil terminal. Continuity indicates that the coil is shorted and it must be replaced.

(3) Cleaning the inside of the yoke
If any carbon powder or rust has collected on the inside of the yoke, blow the yoke out with dry compressed air.
*Do not remove the field coil from the yoke.

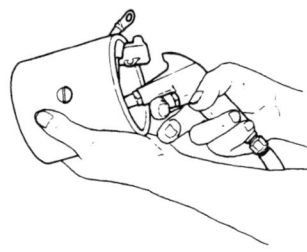

#### 3-6.3 Brush
The brushes are quickly worn down by the motor. When the brushes are defective, the output of the motor will drop.

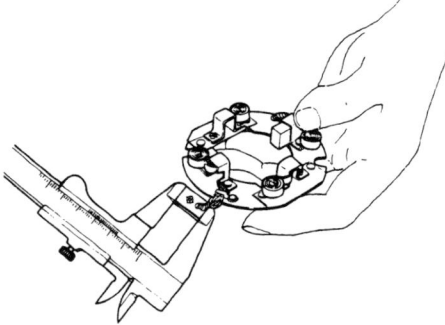

(1) Brush dimensions
Replace brushes which have been worn beyond the specified wear limit.

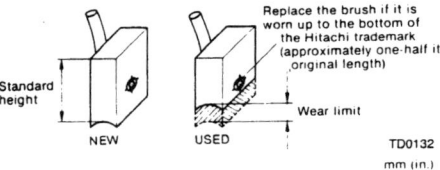

TD0132
mm (in.)

| | |
|---|---|
| Brush standard height | 19.5 (0.7677) |
| Wear limit | 7 (0.2756) |

(2) Brush appearance and movement in brush holder
If the outside of the brush is damaged, replace it. If the movement of the brushes in the brush holder is hampered because the holder is rusted, repair or replace the holder.

(3) Brush spring
Since the brush spring pushes the brush against the commutator while the motor is running, a weak or defective spring will cause excessive brush wear, resulting in sparking between the brush and the commutator during operation. Measure the spring force with a spring balance; replace the spring when the difference between the standard value and the measured value exceeds ±0.2kg.

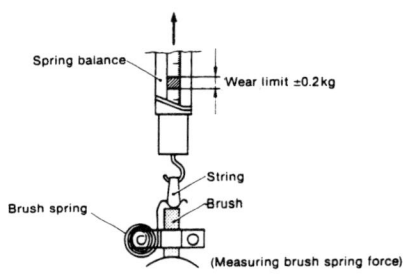

(Measuring brush spring force)

| Standard spring load | 3.1 ~ 3.9kg (6.8335 ~ 8.5970 lb) |
|---|---|

(4) Brush holder ground test
Check for continuity between the insulated brush holder and the base of the brush holder assembly. Continuity indicates that these two points are grounded and that the holder must be replaced.

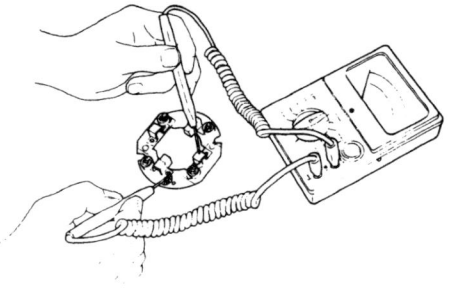

## 3-6.4 Magnetic switch

**(1) Shunt coil continuity test**

Check for continuity between the S terminal and the magnetic switch body (metal part). Continuity indicates that the coil is open and that the switch must be replaced.

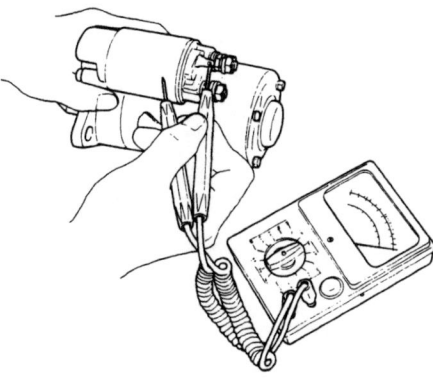

| Coil resistance (at 20°C) | 0.60 Ω |
|---|---|

**(2) Series coil continuity test**

Check for continuity between the S terminal and M terminal. Continuity indicates that the coil is open and that it must be replaced.

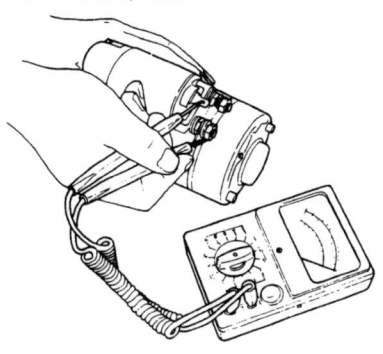

| Resistance value (at 20°C) | 0.22 Ω |
|---|---|

**(3) Contactor contact test**

Push the plunger with your finger and check for continuity between the M terminal and B terminal. Continuity indicates that the contact is faulty and that the contactor must be replaced.

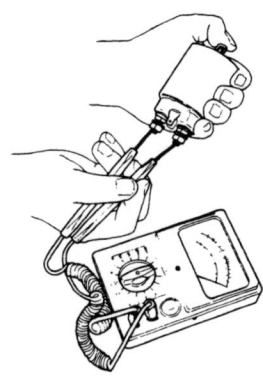

### 3-6.5 Pinion

(1) Inspect the pinion teeth and replace the pinion if the teeth are excessively worn or damaged.
(2) Check if the pinion slides smoothly; replace the pinion if faulty.
(3) Inspect the springs and replace if faulty.
(4) Replace the clutch if it slips or seizes.

### 3-7 Reassembly precautions

Reassemble the starter motor in the reverse order of disassembly, paying particular attention to the following:

**(1) Torsion spring and shift lever**

Hook the torsion spring into the hole in the magnetic switch and insert the shift lever into the notch in the plunger of the magnetic switch (through the torsion spring).

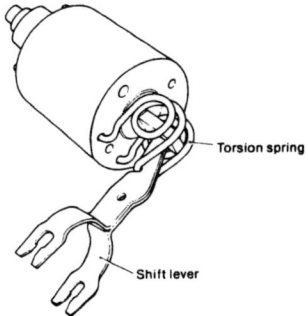

## Chapter 9 Electrical System
## 3. Starter Motor

(2) Mounting the magnetic switch
Attach the shift lever to the pinion; assemble the gear case as shown below.
Do not forget to install the dust cover before assembling the gear case.
After reassembly, check by conducting no-load operation.

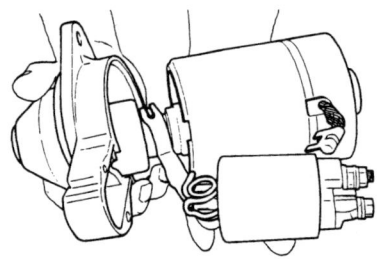

(3) Lubrication
Lubricate each bearing and spline (points indicated in the figure below) with high quality "Hitachi Electrical Equipment Grease A"
The following lubricants may be used in place of Hitachi Electrical Equipment Grease A.

| Magnetic switch plunger | Shell | Aeroshell No. 7 |
|---|---|---|
| Bearing and spline | Shell | Albania Grease No. 2 |

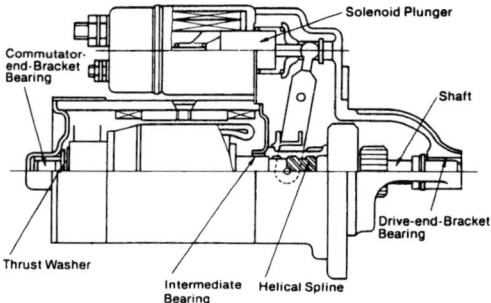

Lubrication chart

### 3-8 Testing
#### 3-8.1 No load test
Test procedure
(1) Connect the positive side of the ammeter (A) to the positive terminal of the battery, and connect the negative side of the ammeter to the B terminal of the starter.

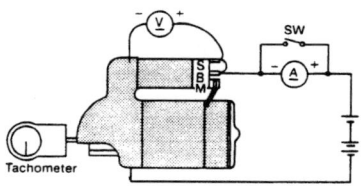

(2) Connect the negative terminal of the battery to the body of the starter.
(3) Connect the positive side of the voltmeter (V) to the B terminal of the starter, and connect the negative side of the voltmeter to the body of the starter.
(4) Attach the tachometer.
(5) Connect the B terminal of the starter to the S terminal of the magnetic switch.
- The magnetic switch should begin operation, and the speed, current, and voltage should be at the prescribed values.
- A fully charged battery must be used.
- Since a large current flows when the starter is operated, close the protection circuit switch before initial operation, then open the switch and measure the current after the starter reaches a constant speed.

## Chapter 9 Electrical System
## 3. Starter Motor

### 3-9 Maintenance standard

| Model | | | | | S13 – 90 |
|---|---|---|---|---|---|
| Brush | Standard spring load | | | kg (lb) | 3.1 ~ 3.9 (6.8335 ~ 8.5970) |
| | Standard height | | | mm (in.) | 19.5 (0.7677) |
| | Wear limit | | | mm (in.) | 7 (0.2756) |
| Magnetic swtich | Series coil resistance | | | Ω | 0.22 |
| | Shunt coil resistance | | | Ω | 0.6 |
| Commutator | Outside diameter | Maintenance standard | | mm (in.) | ⌀48 (⌀1.890) |
| | | Wear limit | | mm (in.) | ⌀47 (⌀1.850) |
| | Difference between maximum diameter and maximum diameter | Repair limit | | mm (in.) | 0.4 (0.0157) |
| | | Repair accuracy | | mm (in.) | 0.05 (0.0020) |
| | Mica undercut | Maintenance standard | | mm (in.) | 0.2 (0.0079) |
| | | Repair limit | | mm (in.) | 0.5 ~ 0.8 (0.0197 ~ 0.0315) |
| Standard dimension | Rear side bearing | Shaft diamter | | mm (in.) | 13.968 ~ 13.950 (0.54992 ~ 0.54921) |
| | | Bearing inside diameter | | mm (in.) | 14.018 ~ 14.000 (0.55189 ~ 0.55118) |
| | Intermediate bearing | Shaft diameter | | mm (in.) | 20.360 ~ 20.349 (0.80157 ~ 0.80114) |
| | | Bearing inside diameter | | mm (in.) | 20.521 ~ 20.500 (0.80791 ~ 0.80709) |
| | Pinion sliding section | Shaft diameter | | mm (in.) | 13.968 ~ 13.950 (0.54992 ~ 0.54921) |
| | | Pinion inside diameter | | mm (in.) | 14.050 ~ 14.030 (0.55315 ~ 0.55236) |
| | Pinion side bearing | Shaft diameter | | mm (in.) | 13.968 ~ 13.950 (0.54992 ~ 0.54921) |
| | | Bearing inside diameter | | mm (in.) | 14.018 ~ 14.000 (0.55189 ~ 0.55118) |

## Chapter 9 Electrical System
## 3. Starter Motor

### 3-10 Various problems and their remedies

**(1) Pinion fails to advance when the starting switch is closed**

| Problem | Cause | Corrective action |
|---|---|---|
| Wiring | Open or loose battery or switch terminal | Repair or retighten |
| Starting switch | Threaded part connected to pinion section of armature shaft is damaged, and the pinion does not move | Repair contacts, or replace switch |
| Starter motor | Threaded part connected to pinion section of armature shaft is damaged, and the pinion does not move | Replace |
| Magnetic switch | Plunger of magnetic switch malfunctioning or coil shorted | Repair or replace |

**(2) Pinion is engaged and motor rotates, but rotation is not transmitted to the engine**

| Problem | Cause | Corrective action |
|---|---|---|
| Starting motor | Overrunning clutch faulty | Replace |

**(3) Motor rotates at full power before pinion engages ring gear**

| Problem | Cause | Corrective action |
|---|---|---|
| Starter motor | Torsion spring permanently strained | Replace |

**(4) Pinion engages ring gear, but starter motor fails to rotate**

| Problem | Cause | Corrective action |
|---|---|---|
| Wiring | Wires connecting battery and magnetic switch open or wire connecting ground, magnetic switch and motor terminals loose | Repair, retighten, or replace wire |
| Starter motor | Pinion and ring gear engagement faulty<br>Motor mounting faulty<br>Brush worn or contacting brush spring faulty<br>Commutator dirty<br>Armature, field coil faulty<br>Field coil and brush connection loose | Replace<br>Remount<br>Replace<br>Repair<br>Repair or replace<br>Retighten |
| Magnetic switch | Contactor contact faulty<br>Contactor contacts pitted | Replace<br>Replace |

**(5) Motor fails to stop when starting switch is opened after engine starts**

| Problem | Cause | Corrective action |
|---|---|---|
| Starting switch | Switch faulty | Replace |
| Magnetic switch | Switch faulty | Replace |

# 4. Alternator, Option

The alternator serves to keep the battery constantly charged. It is installed on the cylinder block by a bracket, and is driven from the V-pulley at the end of the crankshaft by a V-belt.

The type of alternator used in this engine is ideal for high speed engines with a wide range of engine speeds. It contains diodes that convert AC to DC, and an IC regulator that keeps the generated voltage constant even when the engine speed changes:

### 4-1 Features

The alternator contains a regulator using an IC, and has the following features.

(1) The IC regulator, which is self-contained, has no moving part (mechanical contact point). It therefore has superior features such as freedom from vibration, no fluctuation of voltage during use and no need for readjustment.
Also, it is over-heating compensation type and can automatically adjust the voltage to the most suitable level depending on the operating temperature.
(2) The regulator is integrated within the alternator to simplify extermal wiring.
(3) It is an alternator designed for compactness, lightness of weight and high output.
(4) A newly developed U-shaped diode is used to provide increased reliability and easier checking and maintenance.
(5) As the alternator is to be installed onboard, the following countermeasures are taken to provide salt-proofing.
   1) The front and rear covers are salt-proofed.
   2) Salt-proof paint is applied to the diode.
   3) The terminal, (where the harness inboard is connected to the alternator), is nicked plated.

### 4-3. Characteristics

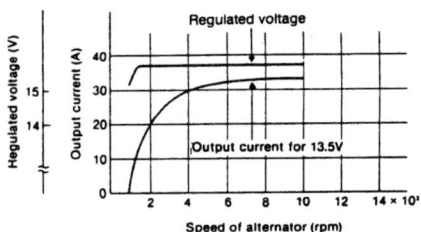

Speed of alternator (rpm)

### 4-2. Specifications

| Model of alternator | LR135-105 (HITACHI) |
|---|---|
| Model of IC regulator | TR1Z-63 (HITACHI) |
| Battery voltage | 12V |
| Nominal output | 12V, 35A |
| Earth polarity | Negative earth |
| Direction of rotation (viewed from pulley end) | Clockwise |
| Weight | 3.5 kg (7.7 lb) |
| Rated speed | 5000 rpm |
| Operating speed | 900 ~ 8000 rpm |
| Speed for 13.5V | 900 rpm or less |
| Output current (when heated) | 5000 rpm 32±2A |
| Regulated voltage | 14.5±0.3V (at 20°C, Full battery) |
| Standard temperature/ voltage gradient | −0.01V/°C |

## Chapter 9 Electrical System
### 4. Alternator, Option

### 4-4. Construction

This is a standard rotating field type three-phase alternator. It consists of six major parts: the pulley, fan, front cover, rotor, stator and rear cover. The IC regulator is an integral part of the alternator.

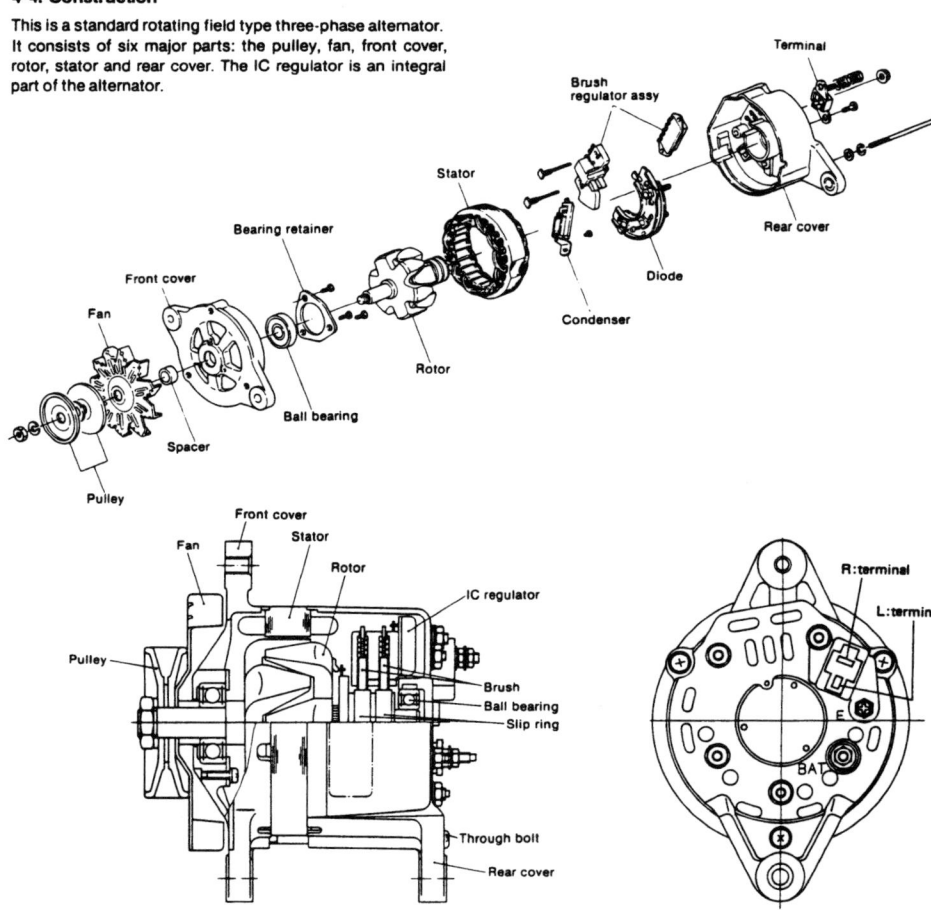

## 4-5. Wiring

(1) Wiring diagram

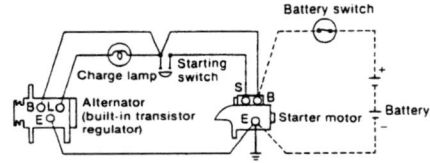

(2) Terminal connections
The alternator has the following terminals. Connect these terminals as indicated below.

| Symbol | Terminal name | Connection to external wiring |
|---|---|---|
| B | Battery terminal | To battery (+) side |
| E | Ground terminal | To battery (−) side |
| L | Lamp (charge) terminal | To charge lamp terminal |

## 4-6. Circuit diagram
### 4-6.1 Circuit diagram

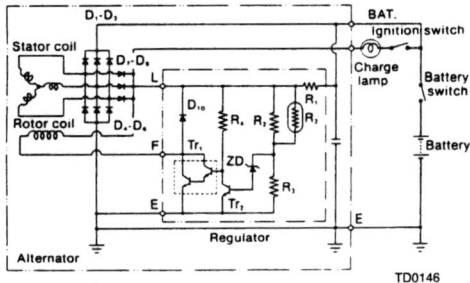

BAT: Battery output terminal
L: Charge lamp terminal
E: Earth
$D_1 \sim D_6$: Diodes for rectifying the output current
$D_7 \sim D_9$: Diodes for switching the charge lamp
$D_{10}$: Diode for protecting the IC
ZD: Zener diode
$Tr_1, Tr_2$: Transistors
$R_1 \sim R_3$: Resistors
F: Rotor current
Rn: Thermistor (resistors with current/temperature gradient)

#### 4-6.2 Principle of IC regulator function

The IC regulator controls the output voltage of the alternator by switching the rotor current (exciting current) on or off by means of the transistor, $Tr_1$ which is connected in series with the rotor coil.
When the output voltage of the alternator is within the regulated values transistor $Tr_1$ is "ON", but when the voltage is outside the regulated value, the Zener diode ZD comes "ON" and regulates the output voltage rise by turning transistor $Tr_1$ "OFF".
The output voltage is kept within the regulated values by repeating the "ONm — "OFF" operation.

### 4-7. Alternator handling precautions

(1) Pay attention to the polarity of the battery; be careful not to connect it in reverse polarity. If the battery is connected in reverse polarity, the battery will be shorted by the diode of the alternator, an overcurrent will result, the diodes and transistor regulator will be destroyed, and the wiring harness will be burned.
(2) Connect the terminals correctly.
(3) When charging the battery from outside, such as during rapid charging, disconnect the alternator B terminal or the battery terminals.
(4) Do not short the terminals.
(5) Never test the alternator with a high voltage meter.

### 4-8 Alternator disassembly

Disassemble the alternator as follows.
The major disassembly point are the removal of the cover, the separation of the front and rear sides, and then detailed disassembly.
(1) Remove the cover attached to the rear cover, remove the through bolts, and disassemble into front and rear sides.

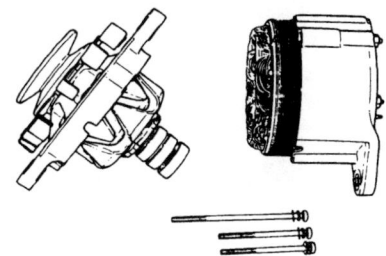

## Chapter 9 Electrical System
### 4. Alternator, Option

(2) When disassembling the front side pulley and fan front cover and rotor, clamp the rotor in copper plates inside a vice and loosen the pulley nut, as shown in the figure.

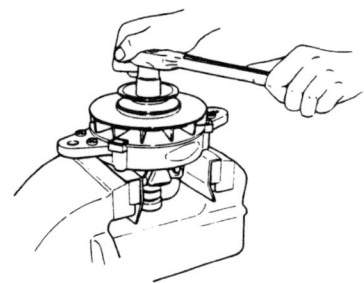

(3) When the fan and pulley have been removed, the rotor can be pulled from the front cover by hand.

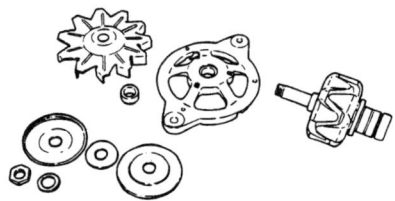

(4) Next, remove the bearing attached to the front cover. Loosen the bearing protector mounting bolts (M4) and pull the bearing by applying pressure to the bearing from the front cover.

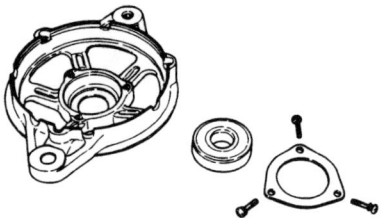

(5) Remove the nut at the threaded part of the BAT terminal on the rear cover, the fixing nut of the diode, and the bolt of E terminal.
After removing the L terminal assembly, separate the alternator into rear cover and stator (with attached diode and brush holder).

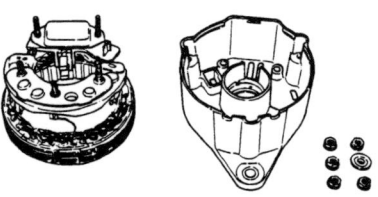

(6) Unsolder the lead wire connection and remove the diode assembly together with the regulator assembly.

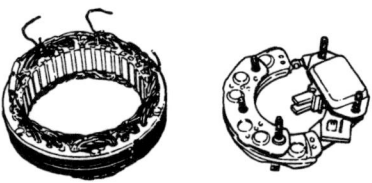

(7) Separate the diode assembly and the brush regulator assembly by removing the 3mm dia rivet which connects these two parts and then unsolder the L terminal connection.

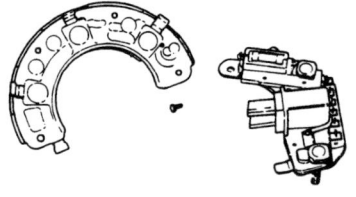

(8) When replacing the IC regulator, it cab be removed by unsoldering the regulator's terminals and removing the two bolts. Never remove these two bolts except when replacing the regulator.

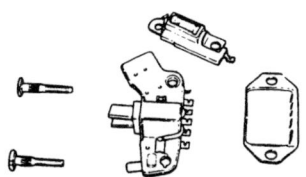

(9) When (1)—(8) above are completed, the alternator is completely disassembled.

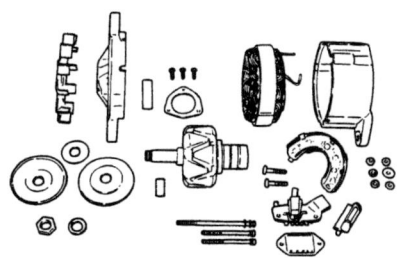

## 4-9. Inspection and adjustment
### 4-9.1 Diodes

| Between terminal | | BAT (+ side diode) | |
|---|---|---|---|
| U.V.W. | Tester in | (+) side | (−) side |
| | (+) side | — | No Continuity |
| | (−) side | Continuity | — |

| Between terminal | | E (−) side diode) | |
|---|---|---|---|
| U.V.W | Tester pin | (+) side | (−) side |
| | (+) side | — | Continuity |
| | (−) side | No Continuity | — |

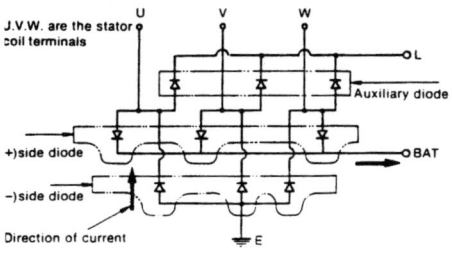

Electric current flows only in one direction in the diode as shown on the previous page. By testing the continuity between terminals (e.g. BAT and U) with the continuity tester, (as shown in the picture), the diode is determined as usable when there is continuity and faulty when there is no continuity. Connect the tester in the reverse way, and then the diode is usable with no continuity but unusable with continuity. If a faulty diode is found in this test, replace it with a complete new diode assembly.
As the auxiliary diode does not have a terminal, check the continuity between its ends.

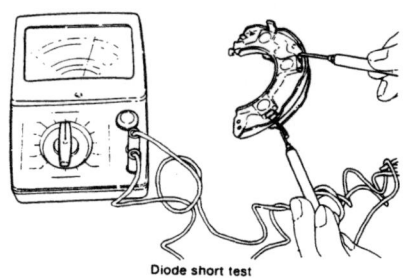

Diode short test

CAUTION: *If a high voltage meter is used, a high voltage will be applied to the diode and the diode will be destroyed. Therefore, never test the diodes with a high voltage meter, etc.*

### 4-9.2 Rotor

(1) Slip ring wear
Because the slip rings wear very little, the diameter of the rings must be measured with a micrometer. Replace the rings (rotor assembly) when wear exceeds the maintenance standard by 1mm. (0.0393in.)

mm (in.)

| | Maintenance standard | Wear limit |
|---|---|---|
| Slip ring outside diameter | ⌀31.6 (1.2441) | ⌀30.6 (1.2047) |

(2) Slip ring roughness
The slip ring should be smooth with no surface oil, etc. If the surface of the rings is rough, polish with #500 ~ #600 sandpaper, and if the surface is soiled, clean with a cloth dipped in alcohol.

(3) Rotor coil short test
Check the continuity between the rotor coil and slip ring with a tester. The resistance should be near the prescribed value.
If the resistance is extremely low, there is a layer short at the rotor coil; if the resistance is infinite, the coil is open. In either case, replace the rotor.

## Chapter 9 Electrical System
## 4. Alternator, Option

| Resistance value | Approx. 3.1Ω (at 20°C) | LR135-105 |
|---|---|---|

(4) Rotor coil ground test
Check the rotor coil for grounding with a tester, or by checking the continuity between one slip ring and the rotor core or shaft.
If there is no continuity it is usable.
If there is continuity, replace it as the rotor coil is grounded.

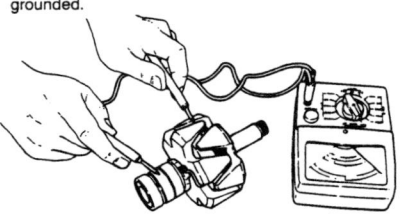

### 4-9.3 Stator coil

(1) Stator coil short test
Check the continuity between the terminals of the stator coil. Measure the resistance between the output terminals with a tester. The resistance should be near the prescribed value.
If the stator coil is open, as indicated by infinite resistance, it must be replaced.

| Resistance value | Approx. 0.16Ω (at 20°C) 1-phase resistance | LR135-105 |
|---|---|---|

(2) Stator coil ground test
Check the continuity between one of the stator coil leads and the stator core.
The stator coil is good if the resistance is infinite. If the stator core is grounded, as indicated by continuity, it must be replaced.

### 4-9.4 Brush

(1) Brush wear
Check the brush length.
The brush wears very little, but replace the brush if worn over the wear limit line printed on the brush.

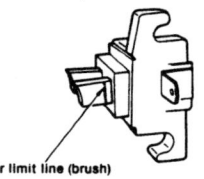

Wear limit line (brush)

mm (in.)

| | Maintenance standard | Wear limit |
|---|---|---|
| Brush length | 16 (0.6299) | 9 (0.3543) |

(2) Brush spring pressure measurement.
Measure the pressure with the brush protruding 2mm from the brush holder, as shown in the figure. The spring is normal if the measured value is over 150 gr.
Confirm that the brush moves smoothly in the holder.

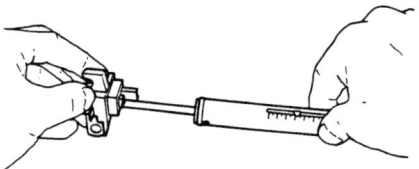

## Chapter 9 Electrical System
### 4. Alternator, Option

### 4-10 Reassembly precautions

After inspection and servicing, reassemble the parts in the reverse order of disassembly, paying careful attention to the following items:

(1) Brush regulator assembly
 1) Soldering the brush
  Solder the brush after setting it as shown in the figure. Take care that solder does not flow onto the pig-tail (lead wire).

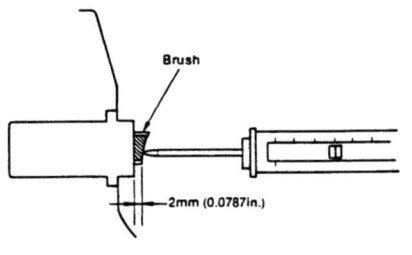

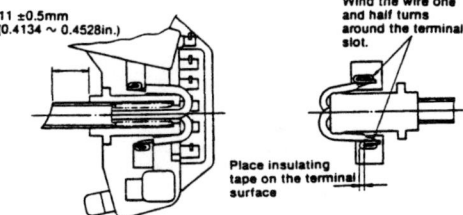

NOTES: 1) Use non-acid flux for soldering.
2) The temperature of the soldering bit should be 300 to 350°C.

| Brush spring strength | 300 ±45g (0.562 ~ 0.761 lb) (New brush) |
|---|---|

### 4-9.5 Checking IC regulator unit

Connect the wiring as shown in the diagram below using a variable register, two 12V batteries, register and ammeter.

(1) Prepare the following measuring devices
 1) Resistor ($R_1$) 100Ω 2W — 1
 2) Variable resistor (Rv) 0-300Ω 12W — 1
 3) Battery ($BAT_1$, $BAT_2$) 12V — 2
 4) DC voltmeter 0 ~ 30V 0.5 class — 1
  (to measure at 3 points)

(2) Check the regulator in the following sequence.
 1) Check $V_2$ (total voltage of $BAT_1$ plus $BAT_2$).
  When the value is between 20V and 26V, $BAT_1$ and $BAT_2$ are normal.
 2) When measuring $V_2$ (Voltage between F — E terminals), shift the variable resistor gradually from the "0" position. Check if the $V_2$ voltage changes sharply from below 2.0V to over 2.0V.
  If there is no sharp voltage change, the regulator is faulty and must be replaced.
  When there is sharp voltage change, stop the variable registor at that point.
 3) Measure $V_1$ (voltage between L — E terminals).
  The $V_1$ voltage is the regulated voltage of the regulator
  ...Confirm that the value is within the standard range.

| Adjusted voltage | 14.3±0.3V (at 20°C, with 2 batteries) |
|---|---|

2) Assembly of IC regulator
 Place the IC regulator on the brush holder as shown in the figure, and insert the M5 bolt.
 After inserting the bolt, solder the brush holder to the IC regulator.

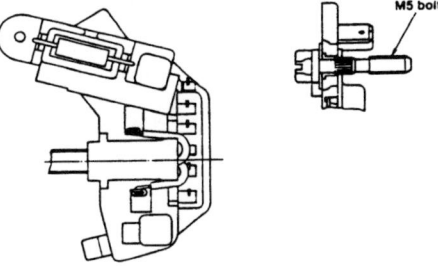

NOTES: 1) Insertion pressure is 100 kg (220.5 lbs)
2) Insert vertically.

(2) Connecting the brush regulator assembly to the diode.
 1) Fixing with rivet
  Insert a 3mm dia. rivet as shown in the figure, and fix it by using the appropriate tool

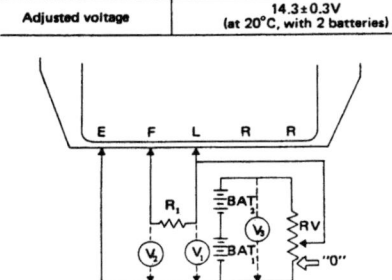

9-22

## Chapter 9 Electrical System
## 4. Alternator, Option

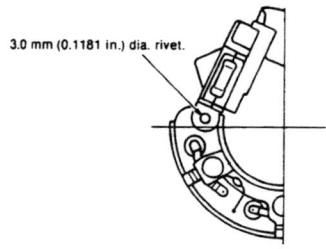

3.0 mm (0.1181 in.) dia. rivet

| Rivetiing pressure | 500 kg (1102 lbs) |
|---|---|

(3) Assembling rear cover
Assemble the rear cover after inserting the pin from outside and fitting the brush into the brush holder.

(4) Tightening torque of each part

|  | kg·cm (ft·lb) |
|---|---|
| Fixing flange holder | 32 ~ 40 (2.31 ~ 2.89) |
| Fixing diode | 32 ~ 40 (2.31 ~ 2.89) |
| Fixing bearing retainer | 16 ~ 20 (1.16 ~ 1.45) |
| Tightening pulley nut | 350 ~ 400 (25.32 ~ 28.93) |
| Tightening through bolt | 32 ~ 40 (2.31 ~ 2.89) |

### 4-11 Alternator performance test
#### 4-11.1 Test equipment

| Test equipment | Quantity | Specifications |
|---|---|---|
| Battery | 1 | 12V |
| DC voltmeter | 1 | 0 ~ 30V Range 0.5 |
| DC ammeter | 1 | 0 ~ 50A Range 1.0 |
| Variable resistor | 1 | 0 ~ 0.25Ω capacity: 1 kW |
| Switch | 2 | Switch capacity: 40A |
| Tachometer | 1 |  |
| 0.25Ω resistor | 1 | 25W |

#### 4-11.2 Performance test circuit
When the circuit is connected the charge lamp will light.

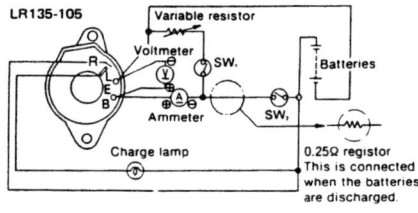

#### 4-11.3 Performance test

(1) Speed measurement at 13.5V.
  1) Run the alternator up to a speed of approx. 1500 rpm with $SW_1$ and $SW_2$ open.
     Then reduce speed gradually and measure the rpm when the voltage reaches 13.5V.
  2) This value is called the "rpm at 13V" and is acceptable if 1000 rpm or below.
     (The alternator speed at which the lamp goes on or off is 1500 rpm, or 1000 rpm or below, respectively, and different conditions apply for each of the two cases.)

(2) Voltage measurement. Acceptable within the range of 14.3±1.3V when the generator rpm is 5000, $SW_1$ is open and $SW_2$ is closed, the temperature is 20°C and two batteries are used.
    (Confirm that the ammeter is 5A or below. If over 5A, connect the 0.25Ω resistor.)

(3) Measurement of output current
  1) In the circuit shown in the figure, set the variable resistor at the minimum value, close $SW_2$ and $SW_1$, and run the alternator.
  2) While keeping the voltage at 13.5V (by adjusting the variable resistor), increase the alternator speed, and measure the current at 2500 rpm and 5000 rpm.

| Acceptable current values | 32A at 5000 rpm | LR135-105 |
|---|---|---|

(4) Remarks on performance tests
  a) For the test leads, use cables with a cross-sectional area of 8mm² or more and with a length not exceeding 2.5m between the alternator B terminal and the positive terminal of the battery, and between the S terminal and the nagative terminal of the battery.
  b) Switches with low contact resistance should be used in the circuit.

### 4-12. Standards of adjustment

|  | LR135-105 |
|---|---|
| Standard height of brush | 16mm (0.6299in.) |
| Limit of height reduction | 9mm (0.3543in.) |
| Strength of brush spring | 255 ~ 345g (0.56 ~ 0.76 lb) |
| Standard dimension of shaft at front end | 15mm (0.5906in.) |
| Part No. of ball bearing | 6302 BM |
| Standard dimension of shaft at rear end | 12mm (0.4724in.) |
| Part No. of ball bearing | 6201 SD |
| Resistance of rotor coil (at 20°C) | 3.1Ω |
| Resistance of stator coil single phase (at 20°C) | 1.6Ω |
| Standard O.D. of slip ring | 31.6mm (1.244in.) |
| Limit of size (diameter) reduction | 1mm (0.0394in.) |
| Limit of swing correction | 0.3mm (0.0118in.) |
| Accuracy of swing correction | 0.05mm (0.0070in.) |

## 4-13. Alternator troubleshooting and repair

### (1) Failure to charge

| Problem | Cause | Corrective action |
|---|---|---|
| Wiring, current | Open, shorted, or disconnected | Repair or replace |
| Alternator | Open, grounded, or shorted coil<br>Terminal insulator missing<br>Diode faulty | Replace<br>Repair<br>Replace |
| Transistor regulator | Transistor regulator faulty | Replace regulator |

### (2) Battery charge insufficient and discharge occurs easily

| Problem | Cause | Corrective action |
|---|---|---|
| Wiring | Wiring shorted or loose, wiring thickness or length unsuitable | Repair or replace<br>Replace |
| Generator | Rotor coil layer short<br>Stator coil layer short; One phase of stator coil open<br>Slip ring dirty<br>V-belt loose<br>Brush contact faulty<br>Diode faulty | Replace<br>Replace<br>Clean or polish<br>Retighten<br>Repair<br>Replace |

### (3) Battery overcharged

| Problem | Cause | Corrective action |
|---|---|---|
| Battery | Electrolyte low or unsuitable | Add distilled water<br>Adjust specific weight<br>Replace |
| Transistor regulator | Regulator transistor shorted | Replace regulator |

### (4) Current charge unstable

| Problem | Cause | Corrective action |
|---|---|---|
| Wiring | Wiring shorted at a break in the covering due to hull vibration or intermittent contact at break | Repair or replace |
| Alternator | Layer short<br>Balance spring damaged<br>Slip ring dirty<br>Coil open | Replace<br>Replace<br>Replace<br>Repair or replace |

# CHAPTER 10
# STERN EQUIPMENT

1. Stern Arrangement (Yanmar Standard) ................................ 10-1
2. Stern Bearings ................................................................... 10-2

*Chapter 10 Stern Equipment*
*1. Arrangement (Yanmar Standard)*
*TM*

# 1. Stern Arrangement (Yanmar Standard)

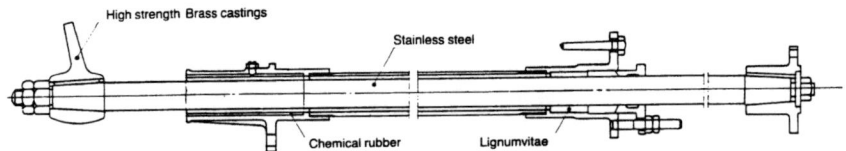

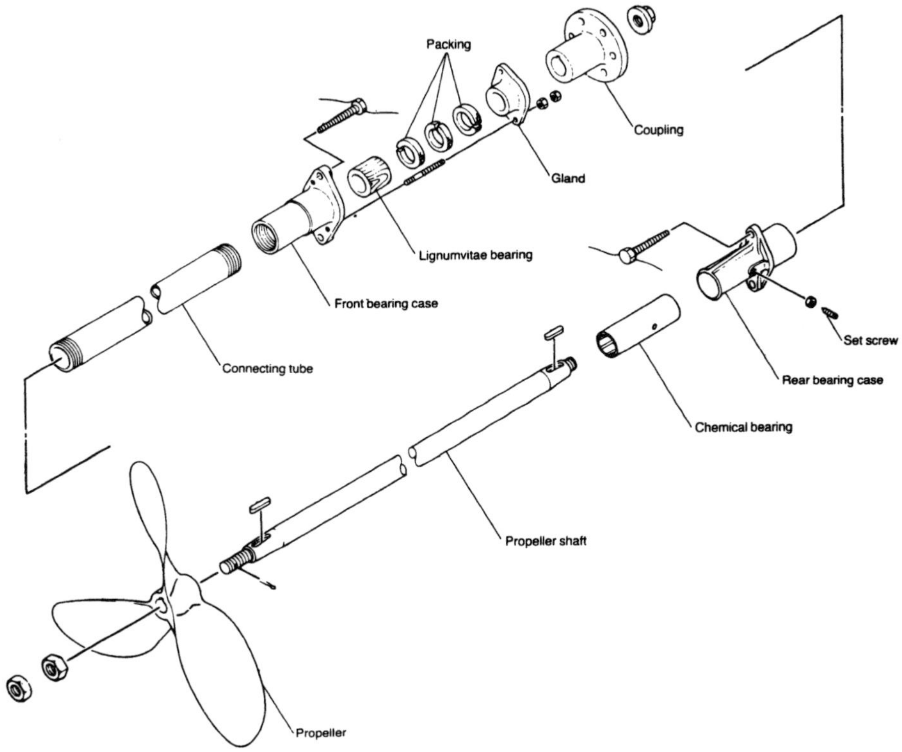

# 2. Stern Bearings

### 2-1 Inspection

After extended use, stern bearing wear may cause centering disalignment of the propeller shaft, excessive water leakage and other troubles.

mm (in.)

| Propeller shaft dia. | Clearance limit |
|---|---|
| Ø34 (Ø1.34) | 0.75 (0.0295) |
| Ø38 (Ø1.50) | 0.75 (0.0295) |
| Ø40 (Ø1.57) | 0.77 (0.0303) |
| Ø42 (Ø1.65) | 0.77 (0.0303) |
| Ø44 (Ø1.73) | 0.77 (0.0303) |
| Ø48 (Ø1.89) | 0.77 (0.0303) |
| Ø50 (Ø1.97) | 0.80 (0.0315) |

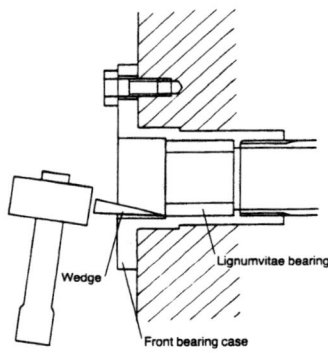

When the clearance between the propeller shaft and the bearings exceeds the allowable limit, replace the bearings according to the following procedures.

### 2-2 Replacement

(1) Extract the propeller shaft.
(2) Loosen the bearing set screw.
(3) Insert the wedges into the joint between the rear bearing case and the bearing (at 4-6 positions), and break the bearing into several pieces to remove.

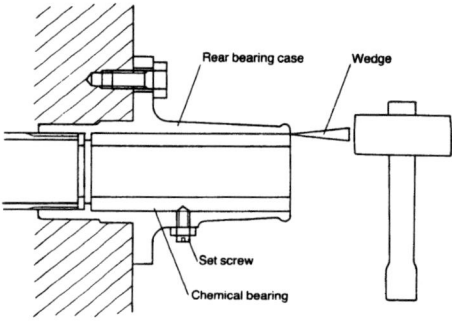

(4) Remove the packing gland from the front bearing case, and extract the packing.
(5) Insert the wedges into the joint between the front bearing case and the bearing, and remove the bearing as at the stern side.
(6) Insert new bearings into the bearing case. To insert, tap the bearing until it makes contact with the stopper in the bearing case.

CHAPTER 11
# TROUBLESHOOTING

1. Troubleshooting .................................................................. 11-1

*Chapter 11 Troubleshooting*
*1. Troubleshooting* _____*TM*

# 1. Troubleshooting

Engine troubles must be detected at an early stage and defective parts be repaired in order to prevent the development of further damages. The symptoms of troubles must be quickly found using all means available: eyes, ears, smell, touch and the report of the operator. Once the location of the engine trouble is found, the method of repair must be decided. To do this properly, it is necessary to carry out a logically correct checking procedure.

In order to readily find and repair the trouble, the operator is required to know each system and the function of each part completely. If a trouble is caused by the misoperation by operator, he must be instructed in the proper use of the equipment so that the same trouble will not occur again. Here, the main engine troubles, their causes and corrective measures are mentioned.

## 1-1 Engine troubles and troubleshooting

| Trouble | Cause | Corrective measure |
|---|---|---|
| Flywheel does not turn correctly (by chain starting). | (1) Incorrect engagement of chain.<br>(2) Roller clutch is defective. | 1) Adjust.<br>2) Replace. |
| Flywheel does not turn correctly (by electric starting) | (1) Battery is not charged.<br>(2) Large voltage drop in the starting circuit.<br>(3) Starter failure.<br>(4) Moving parts stiffened. (Does not turn) | 1) Charge the battery.<br>2) Check for loosened terminals; re-tighten.<br>3) Disassemble the starter, and repair.<br>4) Check and repair. |
| Flywheel turns but engine does not start | (1) Lube oil viscosity too high.<br>(2) Engine is cold. | 1) Exchange the lube oil.<br>   Use a lube oil with proper viscosity<br>   (SAE No.30, 40)<br>2) Warm. |
| | (3) No fuel injection, or insufficient injection | 1) Conduct priming of the fuel system, and vent air.<br>2) Test the fuel injection from the injection valve, and replace the valve needle if necessary.<br>   (Standard injection pressure: 200 – 210 kg/cm$^2$)<br>3) Clean the fuel filter.<br>   (Replace the paper element.)<br>4) Re-supply fuel to the fuel tank.<br>5) Open the fuel tank cock.<br>6) Clean the fuel pipe.<br>7) Remove drain from the fuel tank<br>8) Check the fuel pump, plunger, plunger spring, and delivery valve; replace the defective part<br>9) Check the remote control device, and governor; adjust |
| | (4) Improper fuel injection timing | 1) Adjust the injection timing<br>   (Standard injection timing: b.T.D.C. 18-20 degrees)<br>2) Check for the correct matching of the timing gear alignment marks. |

## Chapter 11 Troubleshooting
### 1. Troubleshooting

| Trouble | Cause | Corrective measure |
|---|---|---|
| | (5) Low compression | 1) In case of insufficient air-tightness of the intake and exhaust valves, conduct valve lapping.<br>2) When gas leaks from the cyl. head, replace the cyl. head gasket; also check for the correct tightening of the cyl. head bolts (Standard tightening torque: 13.5 – 14.5kg-m)<br>3) When piston rings are stiffened, clean the ring grooves and replace the rings.<br>4) When the closing timing of the intake and exhaust valves is too slow: adjust the timing, adjust the valve clearance, and check for the correct matching of the cam gear alignment marks. |
| | (6) Compression drop | 1) If the piston pin, and crank pin bearings are worn, replace the bearings.<br>2) Replace the worn piston ring.<br>3) If the upper part of the cyl. liner is worn, replace. |
| Engine stops suddenly | (1) Fuel supply stopped due to defective governor or governor system<br>(2) Air in the fuel in the fuel tank<br>(3) Air in the fuel system<br>(4) Piston, bearing, or other moving parts are stiffened | 1) Check, repair, or replace.<br>2) Re-supply fuel.<br>3) Vent air.<br>4) Check, and repair. |
| Engine speed drops suddenly | (1) Improper governor adjustment<br>(2) Overloaded<br>(3) Stiffened piston<br>(4) Stiffened bearing<br>(5) Fuel filter clogged<br>(6) Stiffened fuel injection pump (Contamination of the fuel delivery valve; foreign matter caught in the delivery valve)<br>(7) Air in the fuel system<br>(8) Water in the fuel | 1) Adjust<br>2) Decrease the load. (Check the propeller system, and PTO device.)<br>3) Stop the engine for repair, or replace<br>4) Stop the engine for repair, or replace<br>5) Clean the filter (Auto-clean type) Replace the element (Paper element type)<br>6) Stop the engine for repair, or replace<br>7) Vent air<br>8) Drain the fuel tank and the fuel filter; resupply fuel if lacking |
| Abnormal exhaust gas color | (1) Overloaded<br>(2) Improper fuel injection timing<br>(3) Improper fuel<br>(4) Defective injection valve<br>(5) Improper adjustment of intake/exhaust valves<br>(6) Gas leakage from the intake/exhaust valves<br>(7) Uneven cylinder output<br>(8) Fuel injection pressure is too low.<br>(9) Insufficient intake air<br>(10) Large resistance in the exhaust piping. | 1) Adjust the load (check the propeller system and PTO device.)<br>2) Adjust the injection timing. (b.T.D.C. 18-20 degrees)<br>3) Change the fuel.<br>4) Test the injection valve; replace if defective. (Standard: 200 – 210 kg/cm$^2$)<br>5) Adjust the valve head clearance. (Standard clearance: 0.25 mm)<br>6) Provide lapping to the valve.<br>7) Check the fuel injection pump and injection valve; replace if defective.<br>8) Adjust the injection pressure.<br>9) When the engine room temp. exceeds 40°C, install a ventilator.<br>10) Increase the exhaust pipe size by one class; adjust the cooling water flow if the exhaust is discharged together with water. |

*Chapter 11 Troubleshooting*
*1. Troubleshooting*
_____*TM*

| Trouble | Cause | Corrective measure |
|---|---|---|
| Full load operation impossible | (1) Fuel filter clogged<br>(2) Fuel pump plunger worn<br>(3) Injection valve faulty | 1) Check and replace filter element<br>2) Replace plunger and barrel as a set<br>3) Check replace and adjust injection valve |
| Output of cylinders uneven | (1) Air in fuel pump or fuel line<br>(2) Water in fuel<br>(3) Fuel injection volume uneven<br>(4) Fuel injection timing uneven<br>(5) Intake and exhaust valves sticking<br>(6) Injection valve faulty | 1) Prime and bleed air from the fuel pump and fuel lines<br>2) Drain the fuel tank and fuel filter and add fuel<br>3) Check and adjust injection volume<br>4) Check and adjust injection timing<br>5) Disassemble and clean<br>6) If nozzle is clogged, clean; Replace nozzle if necessary<br>If the needle is sticking, inspect and replace |
| Engine knocks | (1) Bearing clearance too large<br>(2) Connecting rod bolt loose<br>(3) Flywheel bolt, coupling bolt loose<br>(4) Injection timing faulty<br>(5) Too much fuel injected because of faulty fuel pump or injection nozzle | 1) Inspect, and repair or replace parts<br>2) Check and retighten<br>3) Check and retighten or replace bolt as required<br>4) Check and adjust<br>5) Check fuel injection pump and injection nozzle and replace if required |
| Engine oil pressure low | (1) Lubricating oil leakage<br>(2) Bearing, crankpin bearing clearance too large<br>(3) Oil filter clogged<br>(4) Oil regulator valve loose.<br>(5) Oil temperature high; cooling water flow insufficient<br>(6) Lubricating oil viscosity low<br>(7) Excessive gas leaking into crankcase | 1) Check engine interior and exterior piping, replenish oil<br>2) Check clearance, and replace bearing if necessary<br>3) Check and replace filter element<br>4) Check and readjust oil pressure<br>5) Check oil pump, and replace if necessary<br>6) Replace with high viscosity index oil<br>7) Check pistons, piston ring and cylinder liners and replace if necessary |
| Lubricating oil temperature too high | (1) Cooling water flow insufficient<br>(2) Excessive gas leaking into crankcase<br>(3) Overload | 1) Check water pump<br>2) Check piston rings and cylinder liners<br>3) Lighten the load |
| Cooling water temperature high | (1) Air sucked in with cooling water<br>(2) Cooling water flow insufficient<br>(3) Cooling system dirty<br>(4) Thermostat faulty | 1) Check water pump inlet side pipe connections<br>2) Check water pump<br>3) Flush cooling system with cleaner<br>4) Replace thermostat |

Chapter 11 Troubleshooting
1. Troubleshooting _____ TM

### 1-2 Reduction reversing gear troubles and troubleshooting

| Trouble | Cause | Corrective action |
|---|---|---|
| Propeller shaft rotates even when clutch is in neutral position | (1) Friction plate seized<br>(2) Steel plate warped | 1) Check and repair<br>2) Repair or replace |
| Clutch slippage (Friction plate slippage) | (1) Clutch lever not fitted in the correct position (Half-clutch)<br>(2) Improper adjustment of the V-lever pressing force | 1) Instruct the user in the correct operation of the clutch<br>2) Check and readjust |
| Lube oil leaks from oil seal. | Improper centering of the propeller shaft | Replace and re-align |
| Ahead, neutral, astern switching faulty | (1) Clutch face seized<br>(2) Moving parts, lever system malfunctioning<br>(3) Remote control system malfunctioning | 1) Replace<br>2) Readjust<br>3) Repair or replace |
| Abnormal heating | (1) Clutch slipping because of overload operation<br>(2) Bearing damaged<br>(3) Excessive oil<br>(4) Oil deteriorated | 1) Reduce load<br>2) Replace<br>3) Check oil level and adjust to prescribed level<br>4) Replace oil |
| Abnormal sound | (1) Gear noise caused by torsional vibration<br>(2) Gear backlash excessive | 1) Avoid high speeds<br>2) Replace |

CHAPTER 12
# INSPECTION AND SERVICING

1. Periodic Inspections and Servicing .................................................. 12-1
2. Specifications .................................................................................. 12-2
3. Tightening Torque ........................................................................... 12-3

*Chapter 12 Inspection and Servicing*
*1. Periodic Inspections and Servicing*
_____TM

# 1. Periodic Inspections and Servicing

The times to carry out periodic inspection and servicing vary according to the application and operating conditions.
The rollowing list shows standard procedures.

●: Consult your nearest Yanmar dealer

| Part | Check | | Daily | Every 50hrs, or 1 week | Every 250hrs, or 1 months | Every 500hrs, or 2-3 months | Every 1000hrs, or 5-6 months | Every 2500hrs, or 1 year |
|---|---|---|---|---|---|---|---|---|
| Fuel oil | Check and add | | ○ | | | | | |
| | Drain fuel tank | | ○ (Before resupplying) | | | | | |
| | Drain filters and oil/water separator | | | ○ | | | | |
| | Clean fuel oil filter | | ○ (Use handle) | | ○ (Clean) | | | |
| | Replace fuel oil filter paper element | | | | | | ○ | |
| Lube oil | Check oil in oil pan and clutch | | ○ | | | | | |
| | Drain lube oil filter | | | ○ | | | | |
| | Clean lube oil filter | | ○ (Remove dirt and dust) | | ○ (Clean) | | | |
| | Check oil pressure | | ○ | | | | | |
| | Replace lube oil | Oil pan | | ○ (First time) | | ○ | | |
| | | Clutch (only for 2,3TM) | | | | | ○ | |
| Cooling water | Check condition of cooling water discharge | | ○ | | | | | |
| | Check tightness of gland packing | | ○ | | | | | |
| Fuel injection pump and injection valve | Lubrication to each linkage | | | ○ | | | | |
| | Check fuel injection timing | | | | | | | ● |
| | Check injection pressure and condition of spray | | | | | | ● | |
| | Replace injection valve | | | | | | | ● |
| Cylinder head | Adjust intake/exhaust valve head clearance | | | ● (First time) | | | ● | |
| | Lapping intake/exhaust valves | | | (Every 2500hrs or 1 year) | | | | |
| Electrical equipment (Electric start | Check alternator V-belt (Tension, breaks) | | | | | ○ | | |
| | Check battery liquid | | | | ○ | | | |
| Check and replace anti-corrosion zinc | | | | | | | ○ | |
| Adjust reduction reversing gear | | | | | | | | ● |

12-1

Chapter 12 Inspection and Servicing
2. Specifications

## 2. Specifications

unit: mm (in.)

| Part | | | Standard size (clearance) | Limit of use |
|---|---|---|---|---|
| Cylinder liner inner dia. | | | Ø100 (Ø3.973) | Ø100.2 (Ø3.945) |
| Piston outer dia. | | | Ø100 (Ø3.973) | Ø99.97 (Ø3.936) |
| Piston ring width | | No. 1 | 2.5 (0.098) | 0.2 (0.008) |
| | | No. 2, 3 | 2.0 (0.079) | 0.15 (0.0059) (Ring/groove clearance) |
| | | Oil ring | 4.0 (0.157) | 0.15 (0.0059) |
| Piston ring end gap | | No. 1, 2, 3 | 0.25 ~ 0.45 (0.0098~0.0177) | 1.50 (0.0591) |
| | | Oil ring | 0.20 ~ 0.40 (0.0079~0.0157) | 1.50 (0.0591) |
| Cylinder head valve seat width | | Intake | 1.44 (0.0567) | 2.00 (0.0787) |
| | | Exhaust | 2.12 (0.0835) | 2.60 (0.1024) |
| Piston-pin outer dia. | | | Ø35 (Ø1.38) | Ø34.95 (Ø1.3760) |
| Crank-in outer dia. | | | Ø62 (Ø2.44) | Ø61.88 (Ø2.4362) |
| Crank-journal outer dia. | | | Ø71 (Ø2.795) | Ø70.88 (Ø2.7906) |
| Crank shaft side gap | | | 0.127 ~ 0.213 (0.00500~0.00839) | 0.33 (0.0130) |
| Deflection | | | 0.0115 (0.000453) | 0.023 (0.00091) |
| Cam shaft outer dia. | | | Ø50 (Ø1.97) | Ø49.8 (Ø1.961) |
| Cam height | | Intake | 42.5 (1.67) | 42.0 (1.654) |
| | | Exhaust | 42.5 (1.67) | 42.0 (1.654) |
| Marine gear | Disk plate thickness | | 2, 3TM 10 ~ 10.2 (0.394~0.402) | 9.0 (0.354) |
| | | | 4TM 10.15 ~ 10.35 (0.3996~0.4075) | 9.45 (0.3720) |
| | Forward (reverse) shaft side gap | | 0.2 ~ 0.4 (0.008~0.016) (2,3TD only) | 0.41 (0.0161) (Adjust the shim plate) |
| | Thrust shaft side gap | | 0.11 ~ 0.40 (0.0043~0.0016) (4TD only) | 0.41 (0.0161) (Adjust the shim plate) |

# 3. Tightening Torque

The bolts and nuts used in this engine employ ISO general metric threads stipulated in JIS (Japanese Industrial Standards). Pay careful attention to the thread dimensions when replacing bolts and nuts.
Tighten the bolts and nuts to the tightening torque given in the table below

### 6-1 Main bolt and nut tightening torque.

| Part | Screw dia. × Pitch (mm) | Bolt head size (side-to-side mm) | Tightening torque kg-m (ft-lb) |
|---|---|---|---|
| Cylinder head fixing nut | M14 × 1.5 | 22 | 13.5~14.5 (98~105) |
| Connecting rod tightening bolt | M12 × 1.25 | 19 | 9.5~10.5 (69~76) |
| Main bearing bolt | M14 × 1.5 | 22 | 19~21 (138~152) |
| Flywheel fixing bolt | M14 × 1.5 | 19 | 19~21 (138~152) |
| Cam gear fixing bolt | M16 × 1.5 | 24 | 14~16 (102~116) |
| Free wheel fixing nut | M16 × 1.5 | 24 | 14~16 (102~116) |
| Bonnet fixing nut | M8 × 1.25 | 24 | 1.3~1.7 (9.4~12.3) |
| Fuel injection valve fixing nut | M8 × 1.75 | 12 | 0.9~1.1 (6.5~8.0) |

### 6-2 General bolt and nut tightening torque

kg-m (ft-lb)

| Diameter of thread | General bolts | | Pipe joint bolts |
|---|---|---|---|
| | 4T | 7T | |
| M6 | 0.5~0.7 (3.63~5.08) | 0.8~1.0 (5.80~7.25) | — |
| M8 | 1.3~1.7 (9.43~12.33) | 2.3~2.7 (16.68~19.58) | 1.2~1.7 (8.7~12.3) |
| M10 | 2.7~3.3 (19.58~23.93) | 4.4~5.0 (31.9~36.25) | — |
| M12 | 4.5~5.5 (32.63~39.88) | 7.5~8.5 (54.38~61.63) | 2.5~3.5 (18.1~25.4) |
| M14 | 7.5~8.5 (54.38~61.63) | 12.5~13.5 (90.63~97.88) | 4.0~5.0 (29~36) |
| M16 | 12.5~13.5 (90.63~97.88) | 20.0~21.0 (145~152.3) | 5.0~6.0 (36~44) |